STOP THE MATCH:
WE'RE GOING TO ARREST THE GOALKEEPER
Scottish Football Referees
and the influence of Scotland
on the Laws of the Game

by Alastair Blair

"There are always two umpires and one referee at each match. The duty of the umpires appears to be arguing with the referee, while he rushes about the field blowing a whistle. Sometimes he forgets to blow it, or else he blows it once too often, and then both teams, dropping their differences for a time, unite in kicking him round the field. I have seen a referee at the close of a match, led off the field delirious. They should be provided with a suit of brick-proof armour, as sometimes the spectators do not agree with them in some decisions, and others show their disapproval by heaving boulders, broken bottles, and slates at his unprotected body…"

Perthshire Advertiser, 4th March, 1889.

Cover by Skep Design, using David Gray's (home-made) flags, shirt and whistle. David was the linesman involved in the incident that gives this book its title.

For Helen

Published by thePotentMix
Newmilns
Ayrshire
July 2022

CONTENTS

Introduction

Only doing it to help out…

Part I

Part II

Part III

Select Bibliography

Appendix: list of SFA proposals to IFAB.

Without Whom

Without the help of the following people, I could not have written this book. John Litster, whose tireless research into Scottish football history will continue to underpin many others' books in the years to come, provided constant encouragement and was a source of wisdom and the other person who went above and beyond is my long-term friend, St Johnstone historian and collaborator, Brian Doyle, who kindly proofed the entire book. More important than either of these august gentlemen, my wife, Helen Green, also proofed the book and provided, as she has done for over 41 years, constant support and encouragement.

Thanks to all the following who in their various ways have contributed to the final, published version:

James Bee, Dick Campbell, Kenny Clark, Willie Conquer, Stuart Cosgrove, Tam Cowan, Tommy Craig, Alan Cunningham, Malcolm Currie, Brian Doyle, Jim Fleming, David Gray, Helen Green, Tony Harding, Steven Harker, Steven Harris, Jim Jeffries, John Litster, Andy Mitchell, Callum McKinnon, Stewart McKinnon, Sean Montgomery, Morag Pirie, Steve Playford, Allan Preston, John Rowbotham, Alfie Smith, Paul Smith, Petra Tabarelli, Louis Thow, Joe Timmons, Stevie Walker, Jim Wallace, Tommy Wright, Doug Yeats and Willie Young (with apologies to anyone I've forgotten).

Normally at this point, there are also copious thanks to the publishers and their editors, however, as the one publisher I approached didn't have the decency to reply to my emails (no wonder Amazon prospers), there are no others to blame for any errors which are, of course, my responsibility.

Introduction

Only doing it to help out…

The only time I tried to referee a football match I was a disaster. It was in Seaton Park in Aberdeen and while I can't quite remember the exact circumstances, I do know I was drafted in because the proper referee hadn't turned up. Although fit enough in those days to do all the necessary running around, I didn't have any linesmen, so every decision was down to me and, to be honest, most of them were wrong.

At least that was the opinion of the players – from both teams – although one kindly soul did suggest politely that the rest cut me some slack, *"because, hey, remember, he's only doing it to help out…"*

Clearly, Aberdeen wasn't the only place with a paucity of referees. My friend, Tony Harding, who was a sufficiently good footballer to have been on Manchester City's books for a short-time as a teenager, told me of playing Under-11 football at Turn Moss in Manchester in the 1980s. The pitches were all small and very close together and on at least one occasion Tony recalled seeing one referee take charge of two games simultaneously.

A football match that has pretensions to seriousness, even at the distinctly unelevated level of a public park in Aberdeen or Manchester, cannot take place without a referee. Why anyone would want to be a referee is a mystery to most normal people, as indeed it was to me when I started to write this book.

However, trying to find out what it is that makes people become referees was only one of the reasons for embarking on this project. I have an interest in football history (and I'd better get this declaration of interest out of the way at the outset – my interest is mainly with God's chosen team from the Fair City of Perth , so there will be some references to St Johnstone throughout this book) and as a result I have come across copious references to the man in the middle, aka today's official, the umpire and ultimate arbiter of everything that takes place on the pitch (until some clown invented VAR), also known by some fans as the bastard in the black, aka the Mason/Fenian in the black if you are from the more demented fringes of the Old Firm support, or, simply the referee.

From poring over more newspaper articles than is good for anyone about games involving St Johnstone, I have read countless stories about referees – good, bad and indifferent. For some reason, and I really am not sure why, it occurred to me that no-one had written a book about refereeing in Scotland and the country's role in the development of the laws of the game. A call to John Litster, the doyen of Scottish football historians, revealed that this was almost certainly the case. A few more chats with other interested parties - among them Andy Mitchell, former Head of PR at the SFA and author of several excellent football history books, and former Grade 3 official David Gray - convinced me that there was a (small) market for just such a book and that, as I suspected, it had not been attempted before.

As a result, I set out to remedy this gap in what is, I know, a specialist market. With my football historian's hat on, I determined to find out about Scotland's part in the key changes to the laws since they were codified and generally agreed in the late nineteenth century, leading up to the most recent changes where technology is increasingly interfering with the decisions previously taken entirely by humans. Concomitant with this was a study of the changes in pitch markings, kit and equipment, the ways the laws have been interpreted in different eras of the game and, of course, the allegations of bias, favouritism or downright corruption that have dogged the game since someone first thought it a good idea to blow up a pig's bladder and kick it about a bit.

For a number of years, I edited the St Johnstone programme and one season, despairing of getting sufficient contributors (that year even the manager – Paul Sturrock - refused to do a 'Manager's Notes'), I came up with the wheeze of running a regular feature looking at different aspects of the Laws of the game. At that time, like most football fans of my (baby boomer) generation, my knowledge of football's rules was based on:

a) the guides that were produced regularly by the boys' comics of the 1960s and the 'You are the Ref' feature which I first saw in Shoot magazine in the late 1960s but which I subsequently discovered began life in the 1950s and was published up to 2016. I also discovered that the illustrations that accompanied 'You are the Ref' were drawn by artist Paul Trevillion, better known as the illustrator of 'Roy of the Rovers.'
b) playing the game (badly) and discovering that telling someone you'd sort them the next time you met them at five-a-sides led to a booking, and
c) shouting at referees and, because I believe in equal opportunities, also at their linesmen and indeed lineswomen, during St Johnstone's matches from the late 1960s up to the present day.

Anyway, that season of explaining the rules in the Saints' programme was a real eye-opener, largely because I discovered that I didn't really know much about them. For example, it was news to me that if a player takes a corner and (for some reason) elects to hoof the ball back towards his own goal and it then goes straight into the net without anyone else touching it then it is *not* a goal. As Law 17 of the game makes clear, a corner can only be scored directly into the *opponents'* goal. Part of me says I'd love to see a player do this, if only to watch the stunned reaction of the crowd (and also to see if the ref actually knows the rules). I noted that over the course of the season, the amount of abuse directed at the officials at McDiarmid Park did not decrease one iota as a result of the supposedly better-informed St Johnstone support.

One other season when I was editing the match programme, we were told who would be officiating from one week to the next and also given their telephone numbers. This seems unbelievable nowadays, given the understandable paranoia of the football authorities about referees' contact information leaking into the cesspit of social media. However, in those pre-social media/mobile phone days everyone was more trusting, so we used to call up the referee for a brief interview which was then published in the programme. The thinking behind this was that by showing that referees are human beings, with normal interests and foibles, we might make the crowds more appreciative of the difficult job they do for us.

Strangely, just like our attempt to explain the rules, this had no effect. Whether the referees liked it or not I don't know, but I got the impression that most of them appreciated the spirt of generosity with which we approached the interviews and welcomed our attempt to engage with them in ways that didn't involve the usual four-letter expletives.

Away from football, my corporate career, like that of many others, required attendance at many black-tie functions, at which I have heard a number of former referees supplementing their income on the after-dinner speaking circuit. Some, it must be said, were/are very funny, but others were dreadful. I particularly recall one unfortunate ref who was the main turn of the evening but was so bad that the entire Dundee United squad, who were in attendance, got up and headed for the bar halfway through his speech. Aware of the lack of tittering, and the overall degree of disquiet that permeated the room, the local comedian who acted as the warm-up was prevailed upon to reprise his act, which, it must be said, he did so well that 30 years later I can still recite one of the (very rude) jokes he told.

That unfortunate official was, I'm glad to say, the exception, and consequently I decided that a section of this book would include a series of interviews with recently-retired referees, finding out how they got into refereeing, learning of their successes (and failures) and exploring some of the more entertaining and outlandish tales they have in abundance and sharing them with you. Also, for (some) balance, I've also spoken to a number of current and retired managers and a couple of well-known radio broadcasters. These interviews form the first part of the book. I'll leave it to the reader to decide whether he or she sympathises more with the refs or the managers.

The second part deals with the evolution of the laws and Scotland's part in this (continuing) process. While containing fewer laughs than the stories of former referees, I found the research involved in compiling this absolutely fascinating. Also, the more I delved into it, the more I went off at tangents, looking at such seemingly obvious (but frequently neglected) subjects such as why referees use whistles, what kit they wore in the past, how much they run about and why the pitch markings are as they are. I discovered that while it's not too hard to find specialist websites that cover subjects such as football kit or just how loud a referee's whistle is, there doesn't seem to be one place that brings all this together. I hope that, in a modest way, this book remedies that.

The third part of the book consists of my personal opinion on the current and likely future state of refereeing as technology takes over more and more of the officials' jobs. As someone who is a technophile, I am generally pretty relaxed about the acceleration of the digital world, but football is a special business and one in which, in my view, we need to tread very carefully. That's not to say that I think technology has no part in the game: on the contrary, it always has (bear in mind that goal-nets were considered a major technological advance at one time), and there are some areas where I'd like to see its use dramatically accelerated. That said, the biggest problem is where technology has changed the nature of the game, specifically when VAR brings a halt to the explosion of joy that I think is, for all of us, the main reason we follow our teams. Consequently, as you'll find, Part III contains a number of occasionally trenchant opinions.

To end this opening section, here is a quote from the article that provides the preface to this book, from the Perthshire Advertiser of 4th March 1889, that, like the preface, serves to illustrate that not much has changed in football since its early days…

"Ministers preach down football on account of the profane language that usually accompanies the game. The spectators are the worst. Some swear when a goal is scored, some when a goal is missed, and some, who have no other chance of swearing all week, take this opportunity, and shutting their eyes, swear all the time."

Be warned, this book does contain quite a bit of swearing. It is the natural language of football. This is why many footballers (and even some managers), when interviewed by the media, don't sound very bright: it's simply because they are speaking slowly, wondering if they can get to the end of the next sentence without dropping in an 'f-bomb' - or worse. Also, the referees' stories related below are much funnier with the swear words in…

Part I

Chapter 1
Tales of officialdom

"You don't know what you're doing," is a chant that most senior referees hear on a fairly regular basis. It's ironic, because invariably the referee is the only person in the ground, other than the Assistants/Fourth Official, who actually *does* know what he or she is doing. Even retired referees and linesmen in the crowd may be a bit confused as to the latest interpretations of the laws, so what chance have the players – who really should know the rules – got of getting it right? Yet, as everyone is well aware, without the person in the middle and their intimate knowledge of the Laws of the Game then we have no match…

This book contains quite a lot that might put people off refereeing. This section will, I hope, redress the balance (I'm getting my retaliation in early). It consists of a number of interviews with former referees and linesmen. In each case, I asked them to explain how they got into refereeing, what they most enjoyed and, because it is probably the main reason you bought this book, I also asked them to relate some of the amusing stories they have from their time as a ref.

While there is no doubt that it's a hard road to the top in refereeing, for those who do make it there are many rewards, not least of which is the chance to be on the same football pitch as some of the world's great players. It wasn't that long ago that this applied as much in Scotland as in European matches, with the likes of Willie Miller, Gordon Strachan, Paul Sturrock, David Narey, Terry Butcher, Henrik Larsson, Paul Gascoigne, Paolo Di Canio, Sergei Baltacha, John McGinn and Andy Robertson (amongst many others) plying their trade in the Scottish Premier League. However, just because they were great players didn't necessarily mean they were the easiest guys to handle on the pitch, as we'll discover in the interviews that follow.

It should come as no surprise that current officials would not talk to me for this book. That is, of course, up to them and the SFA, but it is a shame that they would not do so. I spoke to one up-and-coming female referee who will become a fabulous role-model for others to follow, but she was told by her local Association that they could not let the interview be used. It contained nothing other than a description of her career to date, plus some very brief stories about matches that she has officiated in, both here and in Europe. It would, in my opinion, have encouraged other girls (and some boys) to take up refereeing. While I understand that current referees do not want to be hung out to dry in the press, if they wish to address the current shortage of officials in parts of the country then a more proactive strategy of engagement with the football world at large is, in my view, not just necessary but essential. I was saddened to find what seemed to be a wee bit of a bunker mentality amongst current day referees and some of their admin support. It's not unlike the omerta that underpins football journalists and pundits, where an attack on one is an attack on all, although arguably some football journalists have much thinner skins than referees. For the officials though, the biggest barrier is everyone else's lack of understanding of the laws, as expressed in that chant referred to at the start of this chapter. I don't kid myself that this book will change that, but I hope that it might make at least some readers more sympathetic to referees and the job they do for us. To that end, these interviews with former referees will, I trust, reveal both their deep love for football and the fact that they really *do* know what they are doing.

It is important to point out that the different levels for referees have been referred to as Grades, Categories and Classes at different times. Moreover, the number of Categories/Grades/Classes through which referees move up (and sometimes down) as their career develops has also changed over time. However, for the avoidance of doubt, these words are effectively synonyms in the chapters that follow.

I sent Lubo off. Kenny said, 'that's fine, I'll bring on a sub.'
Willie Young

"I was a football fanatic when I was a boy and really proud to be captain of Ayrshire Schools. I played for the Under-18s when I was 15 and played in the annual match against Manchester Schools several times, twice in Manchester and once at Rugby Park in Kilmarnock. I signed up for Junior side Craigmark Burtonians when I was 17 but I got a dislocated knee in my second season. I'd also sustained ligament damage so my knee was never stable and I was finished as a player at the age of 18."

Like many referees, Willie Young was – and is – a football fan. He comes from a similarly addicted family: his uncle, Lewis Thow, was chairman of Ayr United and his two brothers both played Junior football and one played with Clyde. Once he'd finished playing, he would go and see Ayr United although he didn't particularly enjoy watching football. Then, in 1980, his cousin, Louis Thow (son of Lewis), suggested he take up refereeing. Like Willie, Louis would be one of the many first-class referees to come out of Ayrshire at this time but at the time Willie was aghast. *"I was the world's worst towards referees when I was a player,"* he told me, but Louis' advice was *"you will enjoy the training and after getting through the first six months of abuse you'll find you either like it or hate it."*

In the event, Willie liked it, for a variety of reasons…

"It kept me reasonably fit but it was just a serious hobby, even when I got to run the line for Senior games. Then, one day in 1986 I got a call from Drew Herbertson, the SFA's Head of Refereeing Admin. He asked if I was available for a game the following midweek. I thought it would be a League Cup tie in Dingwall or Stranraer Reserves – Drew would never tell you straight away what the game was, he always just asked 'are you available?'. Then he said, 'we've had a call off from a linesman for the Nantes vs Torino game. Davie Syme is going to be the referee, can you go? It took me about half a second to say 'yes, I certainly can!'"

Willie had hardly ever been abroad before, but he went and enjoyed it so much that when he got home he told his wife that he was going to start to take refereeing much more seriously and that he needed to get much fitter. She changed his diet and he increased his training. Both those things helped…

"I was refereeing Juniors and running the line at Seniors, then I started getting the better Junior games, including the 1990 Junior Cup final at Rugby Park. That was a great honour; having played it I loved Junior football and if refereeing the final was as far as I got, I'd have been delighted. However, I knew that if I did well enough in the final it could be a gateway to Category One. It was and I became a Grade 1 referee in 1990 and was fortunate enough to stay at that level till I retired in 2005."

One thing I didn't know, until Willie told me, was that FIFA cocked-up the officiating in the 1990 World Cup in Italy. They only took the best referees from the countries chosen to provide officials and not any currently acting as linesmen. Once refs get to a high standard, many of them, understandably, don't want to run the line and in 1990 there were quite a few at the World Cup who hadn't performed a linesman's duties for many years. Unsurprisingly, they weren't very good at times and thereafter FIFA decided they wanted specialist linesmen and so they created a list. Willie was one of three Scots on that list, as were Kenny Clark and Hugh Dallas. However, the SFA was pulling a bit of a flanker by putting these three forward as they were Grade 1 referees and not linesmen. As Willie recalled, *"They saw it a means of getting us experience in international football so we'd go on to become FIFA referees. FIFA then changed the rules in 1993, realising that lots of countries had done this. After that, you could not be nominated as FIFA ref if you were on the linesmen's list, so the SFA took me off that list in 1994 and I then became a FIFA referee, eligible to referee any fixture anywhere in the world.*

"I never got to a World Cup finals, but I refereed in 71 matches in Europe and elsewhere in the world and was the fourth official as part of the Scottish contingent of officials for the 1999 UEFA Cup final between Parma and Marseille in Moscow on the 12th May. Hugh Dallas was the referee and Robert Gunn and John McElhinney were the linesmen. I did a few World Cup qualifiers and European Championship and Champions League matches but I was never quite good enough to get onto UEFA's elite list."

I wondered if this diverse experience helped Willie referee in Scotland but, as might be expected, the difference between our game and the European one was as pronounced for the officials as it is for the teams.

"I found the European game totally different from Scotland," Willie said. *"The laws are the same but the approach of the players is different. In southern Europe they have a different attitude. What they regard as an acceptable tackle is very different from what we are used to here. Towards the end of my time as a referee we wore heart monitors and my heart-rate was much higher in Scottish Premier games than in any European match. It's nothing to do with the crowds, it's simply that the pace is much faster in Scotland, hence the higher reading. In my era, you didn't get a second on the ball in Scotland, whereas in Europe it was all a bit more measured."*

Interestingly, a scientific study of referees' running referred to later in this book, confirms Willie's thesis. This study's results showed that in 2005, *"although European competition football may be considered to be more intense, the referees actually cover the least distance."*

Next, I asked, does anything prepare you for refereeing at the top level? I assumed that it would be totally different refereeing the Premier Division as opposed to the Junior ranks, but Willie was adamant that it's the time a young referee spends in the lower levels that sets him (or her) up for the senior game…

"Refereeing the Juniors was a real education. There was nothing I encountered in the top level that I hadn't seen in the Juniors - and more! This was especially so for the Ayrshire Juniors. In my time they were still mining communities, with local rivalries that are as intense

as the Old Firm. Kilbirnie vs Beith, Beith vs Dalry, Glenafton vs Cumnock and, of course, Auchinleck vs Cumnock – you really learned your trade at the Juniors.

"These games are more physical than the Old Firm, but the Old Firm game has a different set of problems attached to it, mostly off the pitch. Referees are all aware of the potential for violence after the match and are very conscious of how a wrong decision might pour fuel on the flames. Consequently, I hardly slept the night before a Rangers vs Celtic game and I didn't enjoy them because I was always worried something would happen. I lived and worked in Glasgow and was virtually housebound in the week before and the week after the match. People knew you were going to be the referee and it could get quite bitter. I never had any windows broken, but I did have one genuine death threat, although that was after an Edinburgh rather than a Glasgow derby.

"In that match, I'd given Hearts a penalty in the last minute and they scored and won the game. On Monday, the Head of Security at the SFA called me to say someone had emailed to threaten to bomb me out of existence. The email had been passed to Special Branch and they took it seriously. However, the would-be bomber wasn't very bright as he'd sent the email from his personal account on his home computer, so they got him – and he got six months."

"Tynecastle has a great atmosphere with its small pitch with the fans right on top of you. But the Old Firm is the noisiest game to do; it's unrelenting and I invariably had a headache after the match. I've refereed Celtic vs Rangers at all three big Glasgow grounds and I'd say Hampden is the best (and fairest) because you have 50-50 split, not the 95% you get at Parkhead and Ibrox.

"Part of the problem – a major part – is that the players are psyched up and do things in an Old Firm game that they wouldn't do in any other game. In my experience, referees take this into account and players often get more leeway in an Old Firm match because refs are acutely conscious that drama on the pitch can be multiplied tenfold off it.

"One of the added complications of Old Firm games in my time was Paul Gascoigne. Gazza was difficult to referee. I have a record of every one of the 1,297 games I officiated and there isn't much that I haven't encountered, but he was hyper all the time. He'd do things no one else would do. He tripped me up one day at Raith when I was running backwards: he thought it was hilarious. Another time, I was lecturing a Motherwell player who had brought Gazza down and he was standing behind me while I did my spiel. He started bouncing the ball off my head: the fans loved it. On another occasion, I recall telling Gazza, 'don't react to players who are trying to foul you,' and he said, 'Aye-aye Willie, that will be fine,' then he put his hands up to his ears gave me a huge raspberry. He was a child on the park but a fantastic talent and it was a privilege to watch him play football at close quarters.

"The other mercurial player from that era was Paolo Di Canio. Like Gazza, he was difficult to referee as he was on the edge all the time, but like Gazza he was unbelievably talented and fantastic to watch. That said, we did fall out a few times, especially when he accused me of 'wanting to be Rangers' manager'.

"One Rangers' match I especially remember was the 1998-99 League Cup final against St Johnstone at Parkhead. I was fourth official and at one point the Rangers' manager Dick Advocaat and his assistant Bert Van Lingen wanted me to stop the game. What happened was that St Johnstone had got a corner early on and when the Rangers players went to mark their opponents they discovered Saints didn't have their squad numbers on their shirts, but instead were numbered one to 11. Consequently, the Rangers players didn't know who to mark. Dick shouted to me that they wanted the game halted, but I pointed out that in the League Cup the teams were allowed to be numbered one to 11. He wasn't happy...

"Dick was always shouting about something. We'd fall out from time to time but when the game was over we respected each other. Once, at Ibrox, I was checking the boots before the game and then approached Dick. I took my wee black book out of my pocket and said, 'Mr Advocaat, if you'll give me an approximate time when you will be shouting and bawling at me, I'll make a note to come across then.' 'Ah,' said Dick, 'you do realise the shouting is not for you? It's for the spectators so they can see I'm committed.'

"Some players were more problematic than others: some had too much to say while others tried to con you on occasions, which I hated. Sometimes you have to make a statement, make a stand as it were. I recall once booking four players for simulation in a Hibs vs Dundee match. Probably every decision wasn't 100% correct, but I was putting down a marker and the players and managers responded as I hoped and the nonsense stopped.

"Not many managers confront you after a match, most calm down and realise that it's all done and dusted during the heat of the game. Few would nurse their grievances for weeks; instead, you usually got an apology when they next saw you. One manager called me for everything during a game in which there was a penalty - and then again afterwards during the press conference. A day later, I was driving my car and he called up to say he'd seen the penalty and he wanted to apologise. That was fine, because for me it was just water under the bridge. Referees can't carry their feelings from one game to the next and neither should managers and players."

There is, of course, a tremendous focus (largely driven by the media) on the Old Firm derby, but Willie reminded me that many other local clashes are just as feisty.

"The Edinburgh derby is, I'd say, physically tougher than the Old Firm, but without all the pseudo-religious baggage. Dundee vs Dundee United isn't as tough as Hearts vs Hibs, but when you go down the leagues you find some really competitive local games. Most fans wouldn't think of Stranraer vs Queen of the South as being a derby, but once you start refereeing it you realise just how seriously they take it. It's the same with Montrose vs Arbroath while, being from Ayrshire, I am well aware of the importance of Ayr United vs Kilmarnock games. Ayr had a good record against Killie in most of the games I refereed.

"However, for real intimidation you have to go abroad. I was involved in some international games between countries that didn't like each other and I've been to games in the Balkans with very high security, but the most passionate/lunatic fans in the world are in Buenos Aires.

I once attended the 'Superclasico' – the Boca Juniors vs River Plate game, not in an official capacity, just as a neutral (probably the only one) and it was just off-the-scale. There were six security checks before you got to the ground. These weren't just to make sure you had a ticket; they were proper searches for weapons. Once we got to the Bombonera (the Boca ground) we saw that River had a small section behind the left-hand goal. The Boca Ultras were in the right-hand end, behind a 40-foot high metal fence with barbed wire on the top and a Perspex screen in front so nothing can get thrown through. I was astonished to see fans sitting on top of the fence! Then when River got a corner, no-one came to take it. I asked' what's happening?' and was told they needed to wait for the riot police. A policeman came with a shield and held it over the River player while he took the corner. Once it was cleared, a man came and took about five minutes to remove all the debris that had been thrown at the corner-taker. We may think we're daft about football in Scotland, but the Argentinians are in a league of their own."

Of course, it's not just players and fans that cause problems for referees. Willie recounted a few of the well-known Scottish managers with whom he had crossed swords over the years, starting with the one who had perhaps the shortest fuse of all … Jim McLean.

"The first time I recall meeting Jim McLean was in one of my earliest games as a referee. It was Dundee United vs St Johnstone and I sent off Davie Narey. He'd already been booked for a poor foul, then he got a second yellow when his arm stopped the ball in the box. I awarded a penalty and sent him off for deliberate handball. Wee Jim went ballistic. He had been watching from the corner stand but appeared on the track as if by magic, shouting and gesticulating. I went over, intending to tell him off, and ended up getting a barnstorming lecture from him. After the game, the referee's dressing room door was kicked in, nearly coming off its hinges, followed by wee Jim who started to give me dogs' abuse. Bear in mind, he's never seen me before as I've only just arrived on the scene as a referee. I said, 'you're going to have a heart attack, you've turned purple, you need to calm down.' I then told him 'I can't go back and change the decision. I'll have a look at it on the TV and if it's wrong I'll tell you the next time I see you.' As he was leaving, I said, 'were you not a joiner? Perhaps you could put that door back on?' That didn't go down well! However, by the time I finished my 15 years at Grade 1 we had a great mutual respect.

"One of the problems with Jim was that when I started refereeing, you got marks every week for your performance. The SFA observer gave 50% of the marks and the club gave the other 50%. Jim gave every referee zero. I don't know if he realised that this meant the very savvy, top-level referees, some FIFA ones, would often say they weren't available for a United game because they knew it would affect their marks and if these fell then they would no longer be on the FIFA list. I think Jim just thought he was being fair (and expressing his contempt), but it meant that he actually missed out on having some of the best referees for United's matches.

"Savvy managers know they need to keep in with the referee. Some guys would gut you after a game, but they wouldn't go to the press. The ones who go to the press are the ones referees don't like. I didn't mind any manager giving me grief because I would happily give it back. I'd say things like, 'you put that turkey up front, he's not had a goal in 15 games, so don't

blame me for you getting beat.' If the manager went over the top I'd report them, but in my latter days I stopped reporting managers. A one-to-one in their dressing room was usually more effective. I once followed Jim Jeffries after he'd confronted me at half time in the tunnel at Tynecastle. He knew the cameras were on the tunnel at half time and that he'd be seen laying down the law as he saw it. I wasn't having this and said, 'Jim that's not acceptable,' and as he went to go into his dressing room I said, 'Jim, I need a word.' The Hearts dressing room, has a separate area for showers, so we went in there and I said, 'do you think I'm going to give a decision I don't think is correct?' I made my point, and while we still had a few fall outs, eventually we got on really well.

"It's odd what changes their view of you. Often, it's small things. Jim Jeffries said he hated me when he was at Berwick and Falkirk, but our relationship improved after a semi-final when Hearts beat Aberdeen 2-1. After that game, I said 'good luck in the final,' which I said to every team that won a semi-final, but Jim told me that after that he changed his attitude towards me.

"You need to be able to stand up to managers. There was a game between Hamilton and Morton when Sandy Clark was the Accies' manager. I'd given Morton a penalty and after the match there was a chap on my door. 'That will be Sandy to complain about the penalty,' I said to one of the linesmen. Sure enough, in he came: "Aye, you had a good game, but what about that fucking penalty, it was the softest I've ever seen.' I retorted, 'Sandy, it's like a boiled egg: it can be soft or hard-boiled, but it's still a fucking boiled egg. Soft or hard it's still a penalty.'

"For me, the most important thing was that any dispute didn't appear in the papers. As long as it's kept between themselves, referees and managers will get on. Sometimes, managers will phone you up and apologise. Other times, they reveal a slight lack of knowledge about the realities of the laws.

"For example, there was a game between Celtic and St Johnstone at McDiarmid Park when Kenny Dalglish was the Celtic manager. While leaving the field at half-time, Lubo Moravčík, who had been getting a lot of abuse from some Saints' fans, swore at a spectator. Tayside's finest, then well-known to be the Scottish police force most likely to interfere in a game, decided they would take action. I saw two policemen follow Lubo up the tunnel into the Celtic dressing room, so I quickly followed them in before they did something stupid. I told them, 'I've got this under control, I can deal with this, you'll not need to worry about it. I'm going to deal with it.' Fortunately, the two officers then left, so I turned to the dressing room and said, 'Mr Moravčík and Mr Dalglish, please come to my dressing room.' Once there, I sent Lubo off. Kenny said, 'that's fine, I'll bring on a sub.' 'Kenny,' I replied, 'you don't understand; he's been ordered off for foul and abusive language,' to which Kenny replied, 'Fuck's sake!' To make matters worse, Saints had to make an announcement about Moravčík so the fans knew why he wasn't out for the second half. I did it to save him from the police, but he never forgave me."

Willie Young has a fund of really funny stories. Unsurprisingly, Ally McCoist features in one of the best…

"I refereed a game at Ibrox when Motherwell were the visitors. They, Motherwell, had had a really good season and it was a vital game for Rangers. I was in the dressing room before the match to check the players' boots. I knew McCoist was a sub that day as he had a track-suit on and as I checked his footwear he said, 'Willie, can I ask you a question?' 'Yes,' I said, and he replied, 'Can you believe I'm no in this fucking team the day?' Walter Smith ran the length of the dressing room – 'what did he say, what did he say?' – but I was laughing too much to answer."

On the other side of the great sectarian divide, Willie reckons that Neil Lennon is much misunderstood.

"I never had a problem with Neil Lennon. He's a lot brighter than the average footballer. On the park, we could relate to each other and if I told him, after, say, a foul or an injudicious remark, 'that's the last of it,' he would toe the line thereafter. He's well-read and his intellect, breadth of knowledge and sense of humour set him apart from many others in football."

On the other hand, another Celtic player did cause Willie some real pain…

"Peter Grant once kicked me during a game but only admitted it 20 years later. It was a game at Hampden and Celtic were playing Partick Thistle (who won 3-2). During the match, I awarded a free kick to Thistle and then I felt a toe-end into my calf. It wasn't a slight dunt, it was a real kick and quite painful. I turned round and there were Paul McStay and Peter Grant. I knew fine who it would be, but as I hadn't seen it and neither had the linesman, I couldn't do anything. Years later, Peter was the assistant manager at Birmingham and I was in the hospitality at a match there. He came into the room and I took the opportunity to ask if it was indeed him who had kicked me all those years ago. He admitted it was, so I, not unnaturally, asked him why. It transpired it was because I had booked him earlier and that would have put him out of the final of the League Cup.

"At the other end of the scale there were some players who were real gentlemen. St Johnstone's Jim Weir was one of them, although, much to my shame, I did once send him off at Dumbarton for coming on as a sub without my permission. At his testimonial, against Newcastle, I gave Saints a penalty at the end of the game, so he could score. Unfortunately, he missed it. Sandy Stewart did much the same when I refereed the official opening of the new Airdrie stadium. It was a friendly match so again I gave a penalty, hoping to allow Sandy to have the chance to be the first to score at the new ground, but he too missed it...

"Another gentleman was John Collins. He was very fair, never a dirty player. I remember he once committed a clear-cut yellow card foul. I walked over and said, 'I can't believe you did that and I don't think you'll do it again, so I'm just talking to you instead of cautioning you.'"

I've been told by St Johnstone players that referees will occasionally 'even-things-up' during a match, although this only applies to minor incidents. Willie concurred, saying that this most definitely does *not* apply to major things like goals and penalties, but that good game management means that sometimes you make a decision that nullifies a minor error. For example…

"There was a game between Celtic and Aberdeen at Celtic Park and the first throw in of second half was to Aberdeen. I pointed the wrong way. Celtic captain, Paul McStay said, 'Mr Young, that's our throw in,' and I replied, 'I know but I can't take my hand down or I'll look a dickhead, just get close to him and I'll give you a free kick - the crowd will never know.'"

After 25 full-on years of refereeing, with games, travel, training, seminars and the like, Willie wanted a complete break, so when he was offered the chance to appear on BBC radio and TV he told them that he would be happy to do so. He'd explain decisions but wasn't going to criticise any fellow-referees. He also wrote for the Daily Mail for three years, but, at his insistence, on sport in general and not refereeing specifically. Then the SFA asked him to become involved in helping the next generation of referees by becoming an observer and going on the Referee Committee. As a result, while he may have hung up his whistle, he's been pretty busy since 2008 and is now Chairman of the Scottish FA Referee Committee. He watches games as a Referee Observer at all levels, both in Scotland and for UEFA in Europe. It has afforded him some interesting roles. He was part of the IFAB (the game's lawmakers) group that looked at goalkeepers' positioning on the goal-line at penalty kicks. There was a desire amongst the referees for the keeper to have both feet on the line, but they asked a number of goalkeepers for their views. Former Newcastle keeper, Shaka Hislop gave advice, pointing out that it is physically impossible for a goalie to save a penalty if he has to have both feet on the line when the ball is kicked. At his insistence, the group watched a lot of footage of penalties and discovered he was right!

Over his lengthy career, Willie has experienced the game at close-up, at levels most fans can only dream of, but his love for football has never dimmed. He finished by saying, *"I've been very lucky as I've been able to see everything from Paris Saint Germain to Pollok Juniors. I've been an observer for officials who have refereed World Cup finals and others whose ambition stretches to Junior Cup finals. I feel welcome when I go to any ground in Scotland and, for a referee, that's a real accolade. There is a respect for my generation of referees that makes it all worthwhile. I really, really enjoyed it and would do it again without a moment's hesitation."*

Stop the game linesman! We're going to arrest the Hearts' goalkeeper David Gray

David Gray spent 25 years as a referee and linesman, reaching Grade 3 Level and running the line in numerous Premier and lower league games, from the final rounds of the Cup competitions to Old Firm and Edinburgh derbies. His refereeing career goes back to the late 1960s, but he never set out to be a referee...

David was working in Glenfield and Kennedy, a very-long established engineering foundry in Kilmarnock, when one of his friends from work started refereeing. One day, his friend said that he was double-booked and asked if David could do one of his matches. It should be stressed that this wasn't remotely top-flight football. The double booking was for schools (teenage) football and for a Boys Brigade match. David did the BB match, which was at Howard Park in Kilmarnock and, as he told me, *"Given that the BB officers were there, I was never likely to get much stick. I'd just stopped playing myself ('cos I wasn't very good), but I enjoyed the experience and started going to refereeing classes run by the local (Ayrshire) Association at the YMCA in Kilmarnock. Bill Quinn was the coach and he used to say, 'I'm going to help you pass the exam but I can't make you a referee.' When I asked to explain what he meant, he said it was like passing your driving test: you were then, in theory, technically competent enough to drive a car, but you didn't have the experience and know-how to react in real-life situations."*

Bill's other advice was that refereeing a game is a bit like riding a new horse. You start a match on a tight rein and then relax after about 10 minutes, but after a goal you have to rein the players in a bit as the losing side are all fired up to try to get back into it, while the team that has scored is all pumped up and excited. One of Bill's other maxims was, *"there will be some games you have to referee and others you will just referee,"* by which he meant that some games were easy and some require all your skill and experience.

After David passed the exam, he refereed schools (Under-18) and amateur football. The latter was important if a referee wanted to progress. However, although the local match secretary for the Ayrshire Amateur Association handled appointments to games, the club committees influenced the choice of referee: if they didn't like you then you didn't get many games. They preferred referees they thought they could influence or were somehow malleable and wouldn't cause their teams any grief. One day, the Association brought in a new match secretary and everything changed. The new secretary was Tom Kirkland, whose grandson is now a Grade 1 ref, and he had an old-school approach to the club committees, namely, *"I'll pick the refs, not you lot."*

David recalled that at amateur level in those days you were supervised by old boys, some of whom were refereeing back in the Second World War days. However, they were very keen and gave a lot of encouragement to those who were up-and-coming. One supervisor, Bill Gemmell, was particularly helpful to David, off-the-pitch rather than on it. One of his match reports commented, *"if there is a better turned-out referee than Mr. Gray I've yet to see him."* Given the work that David's wife, May, put into keeping his kit pristine, she (and he) was, understandably very proud!

Referees' kit in those days was black. In fact, it was all black and more black, apart from the white tops or stripes on the socks and the (somewhat bizarre) requirement for white bootlaces. May used to wash David's bootlaces and even ironed them, as she did for his linesman's flag, which was home-made, using old golf club shafts. Few clubs provided linesman's flags (some of the bigger ones did), so the officials used to make them themselves.

The all-black theme included the boots. Most refs and linesmen, like most players in those days, bought Adidas or Puma, both of which have white facings/stripes. David used to apply black shoe-polish to the white stripes, but this, inevitably, wore off. Then he discovered Bukta produced all-black boots and, even better, the 'All Sports' shop in Kilmarnock was able to procure him a pair. As a result, he was the first referee in the Ayrshire Referees Association to have all-black boots.

When it came to the shirts, socks and shorts, many of the referees in Scotland availed themselves of the services of John Workman. John travelled around Scotland on public transport to the different, regional Referees Associations. He first appeared on the scene in 1973 and continued in business until the year 2000. He would arrive as the refs were heading into their Association meeting and when they came out, there, displayed for them to see and buy, was all the kit they ever needed. As David said, *"we had to buy it off him. You couldn't get it anywhere else."*

SFA list referees were entitled to wear the SFA badge, however, as they had to have a change strip, this badge was usually sown onto Velcro so it could be transferred from one jersey to another.

There were then, and still are now, a lot of young referees who dropped out of the game. Grade 1 was (and is) the ultimate goal, but there was a problem for David and some of his compatriots. As he explained: there are only c. 30 Grade 1 referees in Scotland, but you have to realise that they are not necessarily the best 30 referees in the country. This is because the SFA needs referees in every region - for pitch inspections and also so that all refs don't come from the west coast (a major source of anger for the more paranoid supporters of east coast teams). When David was coming through the ranks in Ayrshire, there were a lot of good referees – Louis Thow, Willie Young and Joe Timmons amongst them - which made it difficult for those just below their standard, even if they were arguably better than some others from elsewhere in Scotland.

The other thing that helps with being a referee is the type of job you have. If you are self-employed, or in the professions, it's often easier to get time off work. If you work in a factory, there is not usually much chance of getting time off. However, David found that one of the advantages of working at Glenfield and Kennedy was that the Secretary of the Ayrshire Juniors worked there as well. Another thing that helped was that, as everyone in Scotland knows, Ayrshire Junior football is a hard battleground. Moreover, for the aspiring referee, when you do Junior matches, you get assessed by SFA supervisors (as opposed to local Association supervisors). David had high quality, former referees like Jack Mowat supervising him, which was very encouraging for a young ref who wanted to progress.

He must have impressed Mr Mowat and the other supervisors, because he was doing well in the Juniors and in due course became a Grade 3A linesman. This meant he refereed Junior games and ran the line in the senior game. As well as Grade 3A, there was also Grade 3B. In the diagonal system (which will be explained later in this book) that referees and their assistants (linesmen) use to control a game, the Grade 3A official runs the far-side touchline and the Grade 3B is on the stand-side (almost invariably, the side with the dug-outs). Before the days of the Fourth Official this meant that the Grade 3B used to have to handle the managers.

In 1977, David was appointed to the senior list and, as he recalls…

"The first league match I did was at Shawfield, where Clyde were entertaining Stenhousemuir. The referee was John Paterson of Bothwell and I was nervous, but he nursed me through the game. Before that, I had done a pre-season game at Dam Park in Ayr, where Ayr United played Celtic. Jim Brogan was the left-back for Celtic and I remember he was standing next to me during a break in play. 'Your first game, eh?' he said, and when I said it was, he told me that Jock Stein knew that too and had told his players to claim for everything 'because he'll be nervous and give us the decision.'

"Other big-name managers made big impressions on me too. John Greig was always very calm, even though he was Rangers' manager at a time when the club was struggling. One of his successors was Graeme Souness, whom I got chatting to after a pre-season game at Kilmarnock. We talked about players' discipline and he told me that the best thing that happened to him was going to Italy. There, Graeme explained, the players take everything very seriously, eating carefully, living like monks before the game (although not always after it!) and generally being ultra-sensible about their fitness and health."

Another famous manager who David came across during his career was Ally McLeod. During a reserve match at Ayr, David disallowed a goal because the ball had not crossed the line. When he was next near to the dug-out, McLeod berated him, saying, *"linesman, that was a goal, you could see from here it was over the line."* David quickly slipped into the dug-out beside Ally, looked down at the goal-line (miles away) and said, perhaps with a hint of sarcasm, *"aye, you get a great view from here,"* before resuming his beat along the touchline. Ally wasn't exactly happy, but as David said, *"he was the kind of man you couldn't really get angry with."*

Most club officials were OK, David said, but some were not. Let him take up the story again…

"One Assistant Manager, whom I'd better not name, came bursting into the referee's changing room after a semi-final, kicking the door off the hinges in the process. He was

shouting and swearing that his team never got anything. The referee was Hugh Alexander, a Kilmarnock man, who wasn't having any of this. Hugh got him by the throat and physically threw him out. Years later, the same man was a manager in a game I was officiating at and he was giving me dogs' abuse. The referee that day was Jim McCluskey, but I took matters into my own hands, telling the manager that if he didn't go to the dugout and sit on his arse, I would report him to the SFA, despite never having done that before to anyone. Grudgingly, he went, but a few minutes later he was shouting again. He was so mad, he jumped to his feet, bashed his head on the concrete roof of the dugout and knocked himself out.

"A famous Scottish manager once did something similar, battering down the door at half-time to tell Brian McGinlay that 'you're not protecting my players,' and such was his rage Brian told him he would be reporting him to the SFA. At the end of the game, the enraged manager had calmed down and came to apologise, saying he was out of order and bringing a bottle of champagne by way of compensation. When he was told that he was still going to be reported, he stomped off in a huff ... only to return a bit later to remove the champagne."

Jim McLean's propensity to outbursts was well-known and even though referees are virtually immune to any amount of swearing and name-calling he could go off the scale at times. However, David recalls that wee Jim was quite cute in many respects, usually getting animated while the linesman was down near the goal-line and then calming his language down when the lino got back near the dug-outs. The officials usually got a break at half-time, but at Love Street (the old St Mirren ground) the away dressing room was right next to the officials' changing room and every curse and blaspheme was clearly audible.

Of course, it wasn't just the managers who were big personalities in those days (far more so than nowadays, arguably). Many of the referees also fitted the description 'big personality,' none more so than Tom (Tiny) Wharton. Tiny, for those who are not old enough, was anything but: a huge man who eschewed the modern ref's black tunic for the old-school blazer over a white shirt. One of his famous sayings, David told us, was made for the benefit of young referees who were struggling to control a game. *"If you're finding it difficult to control 22 players,"* Tiny said, *"try 20!"*

Grades 1 and 2 referees and Grade 3 (both Grade 3A and Grade 3B) linesmen were dependent for their games on Maureen Cooper, the admin lady for referees at the Scottish League and latterly the SFA – who sadly died while this book was being written. Maureen used to do all the allocation of referees and linesmen to games by means of a ballot every six weeks, which she organised by memory, with no computer, just a big list of all the games down one side of a big piece of paper and another list of the officials' names down the other side. By all accounts, she was brilliant: *"you never got the same team twice in the ballot,"* David said, adding, *"When the ballot came out, you'd find who you were officiating with. If it was Kenny Hope* (who also died during the writing of this book), *he'd call you before the game and say, "what pub are we going to after the match?"*

Then there was Jim Renton – *"what a man,"* David recalled. Refs used to get comps – two complimentary tickets – for family or friends. However, Jim had five brothers and they'd often all be found in the referee's dressing room after games. Partly as a result of this, the SFA put a stop to anyone going to the ref's room other than the officials or players and officials from the clubs.

Dougie Smith was the referee who, much to his misfortune, made headlines after his first Rangers vs Hibs game. These were always regarded by the refereeing fraternity as hard games. Dougie, who was one of the Ayrshire Referees Association, had inadvertently dropped his yellow card on the pitch and, unfortunately for him, the player who found it was Paul Gascoigne. Gazza trotted up to the ref and brandished the yellow card, as if booking him. Dougie Smith took the card and brandished it back at Gazza, booking him for real. The press, naturally, filled their boots, using the opportunity to castigate the referee for his lack of nous and humour. Yes, it was a poor decision, but the Ayrshire refs rallied round one of their own, all aware that 'there, but for the grace of God go I.' At their next training session, in Irvine, when Dougie came out of the changing room he found the pitch strewn with yellow cards. However, as well as taking the piss, his Ayrshire colleagues made the time to support their colleague. This support was, I am assured, much appreciated.

In David's time, there were no specialist teams of referees and linesmen who act together for international and European games. Rather, as he related, *"Back then, we all got a shot and my turn came in 1978. It was at a club almost no-one at that time had heard of, called Bodo Glimt, who play about 80 miles inside the Arctic Circle. They were playing Inter-Milan, who were five up after the first leg in Italy. It was -14C and the game should never have been played. Then the Inter centre-half booted one of the Norwegians off the ball. I flagged to Ian Foote, the referee and told him, "you've got to send off the No. 5. He deliberately kicked the opposing player." Ian sent him off and that was that, or so I thought. About three weeks later I got a call from a representative at the SFA, who told me the Inter player was appealing and Ian and I had to go to Zurich for the hearing. I was incredulous. 'How on earth can he appeal, it was as plain a sending-off as it's possible to be,' I said, only to be told he wasn't appealing against the sending-off, but against the length of his suspension.*

"When we got to Zurich we were put up in the Hilton. There were other referees there for hearings, including the Frenchman, Robert Wurtz, who had refereed the (in)famous Wales v Scotland game when Joe Jordan had performed his tartan version of the hand of God. We thought, 'we've got to ask him,' so we said to Robert, 'as ref to ref, it was Joe that handled the ball, wasn't it?' ... only to be told, 'no, no way, it was a Welsh player.' So that's fine then and the Welsh have been complaining for decades incorrectly..."

Sometimes, the polis get a bit carried away and try to intervene in football, much to the chagrin of the officials. One such incident involved Henry Smith, goalkeeper to many clubs and the cause of one of David Gray's most memorable moments. With half-time only minutes away in the Edinburgh derby, David felt a tap on his shoulder and turned round to see a very high-ranking policeman standing immediately behind him. *"Stop the game linesman!"* was the command from this imposing figure, *"we're going to arrest the Hearts' goalkeeper."*

As David says, there is nothing in the referee training book that prepares you for this sort of thing, so he pointed out that there were only a few minutes till half-time and wouldn't it be better to wait till then, not to mention why did they want to arrest Henry anyway? *"Because he's been making V-signs behind his back to the Hibs fans and they are going nuts,"* was the answer, but David's argument that they wait till half-time prevailed and the policeman went with him to the referee's changing room. The referee was the very experienced Bob Valentine, who wasn't easily intimidated. While he didn't exactly say, *"to what are we the indebted for the privilege of this visit?"* he did interrupt the policeman's spiel by pointing out that he didn't know who he was, and therefore would he give him his name and rank, which he did. Bob, not unreasonably, then pointed out that if they had arrested Smith there might well have been a riot and said he would deal with the situation. David was sent to the Hearts' dressing room to fetch Smith and the Hearts manager. He knocked on the door, went in and told them both they were required by the referee. The Hearts' manager had no idea what was going on and wasn't best pleased to have his half-time talk interrupted but he had no choice. On the way there, he made his own enquiries, along the lines of, *"Henry, what the fuck have you been doing?"* and when he arrived and saw the seniority of the policeman, he realised it was something serious. However, Bob Valentine took charge, telling Smith he was receiving a yellow card and that if he did the same in the second half then he would be in trouble. *"No problem,"* said Henry, *"I won't do it in the second half, because I've got the Hearts' fans behind me."*

David, well-retired now, has a season ticket for Rugby Park. The vast majority of referees love to carry on watching football, even if they aren't actively involved any more but they tend to watch the game through a different lens from the average football fan. For a start, they tend not to barrack the referee and linesmen…

The average fan has no such inhibitions. As David recounted, *"I remember doing a game at Brockville when Celtic were visiting. It was very cold, so before kick-off I tucked my flag under my arm and rubbed my hands together to warm them so I wouldn't drop the flag when the game started. Behind me, a Celtic fan asked politely, 'is that you taking your masonic ring off, you wee bastard?'"*

Fortunately, it's very rare to get seriously unpleasant abuse (you do get lots of abuse, but most of it just washes over you once you get used to it). However, once, when David was doing a match involving Ayr Reserves at Somerset Park, with a crowd that you could just about count on the fingers of both hands, he disallowed a goal and this guy ran down the terracing to tell him, *"I hope your wife and weans get killed in a car crash tonight."* Sadly, there is no accounting for such nutters.

One of David's claims to fame was running the line for the first match that was televised live in Scotland. It was Hearts vs Aberdeen and although you might think that most of those watching it would have concentrated on the players, David was somewhat surprised to find strangers accosting him in the street to tell him they'd seen him on the telly. However, one of the disadvantages of being a referee is that not only do people recognise you from the television, they also see your picture in the papers. David has kept a copy of one such photo, from a Celtic vs Rangers game. At that time, he was working for Scottish and Newcastle Breweries, who just happened to sponsor both halves of the Old Firm. Consequently, David's wife May was a guest in the Rangers directors' box, sitting next to the Ibrox chairman, David Murray. During the game, David disallowed a Rangers' goal for offside. The press photo has several Rangers' players – notably Ian Ferguson – 'remonstrating with him.' May, who at her own admission knows almost nothing about football, turned to David Murray to ask what had happened. *"I think your husband has just ruined the game!"* replied the chairman.

Finally, David gave me some insights into how referees bring important games to an end. He was running the line for referee Alistair Hewitt in the final game of the season at Parkhead: a match that Celtic needed to win to become champions. David was on the stand-side line: over on the far side was another linesman, who will remain anonymous but who had three brothers who were all die-hard Celtic fans. Before the match, the officials discussed how they would escape the hordes who would undoubtedly invade the pitch if Celtic won the League. Alistair told his colleagues that he would make sure he was near the tunnel and would pick up the ball before he blew the final whistle, to signal to his linesmen that the game was about to end. *"Davie and I will make a run for it. You* (indicating the other linesman) – *well, you can, er, good luck!"*

In the event, all went to plan. David and Alistair made it safely to the referee's dressing room but after a few minutes the other linesman hadn't turned up. They waited a few minutes longer, but still no sign. A full eight minutes passed before their colleague appeared. *"What happened?"* he was asked. *"I was dashing across the pitch when my brothers appeared, grabbed me and took me back to the terracing where the fans were celebrating like crazy. It took me some time to escape…"*

Five minutes later they were interviewing mum and the dog
Morag Pirie

Morag Pirie, as described in more detail later in this book, holds a special place in the history of Scottish refereeing. The first woman in Scotland to officiate at a semi-professional match and then at a major, national final, she was subsequently the first woman to be on the FIFA list. Consequently, she was someone I very much wanted to include in this book and, fortunately, she was willing to chat about her career. Like the men featured here, Morag began her journey to becoming a referee by playing football as a child…

"I played football in the garden in Aberdeen with my twin sister and also at primary school in the playground with the boys, but girls weren't allowed to play in the school team. However, when we were in Primary 6, we were both allowed to play in a girls' team at the annual Dyce Gala.

"When I went to secondary school, there were no opportunities for girls to play football, but when I went to Aberdeen University I was delighted to discover they had a women's team, which I promptly joined. Around the same time, the SFA had just established a Women's Development Officer for the north-east, as a sign of the increasing interest in women playing the game. A year or so later, a new women's team started up in the city and placed an advert in the P&J (Press and Journal) looking for players. This was Aberdeen Accies, and I and my twin sister and also the development officer turned up and became players in this team.

"Whilst I was playing football, I also did some coaching courses, which I quite enjoyed. Then, the person who is responsible for my refereeing career came on the scene, or rather up the path to our house. It was the postie, who had seen an advert in the P&J for the refereeing course. He gave the paper to my mum and explained that he had seen me coaching at Bridge of Don and suggested, 'perhaps Morag would like to do the refereeing course?'

"At much the same time, the Women's Development Officer was looking for girls to help out by refereeing games, so I said I would and she gave me a whistle and away I went. I really enjoyed it, although in truth I didn't actually know all the laws of the game. Then I thought that if I went and learned them, it would help me with my coaching. I didn't do anything about it until I was in third year at university, but then I had a bash and scraped through the refereeing exam. My excuse was that I was studying very hard for my university exams at the same time, but anyway, having made the effort and passed, I thought I'd give it a go and see whether I liked it or not.

"The following summer, once I'd finished university, I started refereeing at Category 6, the level for those starting out. I did Juvenile football and some girls' league games - Under-13s, 14s and 15s - and then on Sundays I did Under-11s and 12s. After a while, I was given some adult ladies' football. It was all quite tiring, but I was young and very fit, plus I was enjoying it.

"In the first two years that I did Juvenile games no-one came along to assess me. In truth, I didn't really know a lot about refereeing at that time and it looked as if my career was going to be just doing youngsters' matches, but then I got a big break. For many years, Aberdeen used to host an annual International Football Festival, which brought youngsters to the city from all over the world. I put my name forward for the Festival and was given some games as an Assistant Referee, running the line and, crucially, having other referees helping me, talking me through games and teaching me a lot more than I'd learned in the previous two years. To give you an idea of how little I knew, I hadn't even heard of the diagonal system at that point, but the advice and encouragement I received really buoyed me up and I began to go to referee training and then my games started being assessed. Sandy Roy, who ran the Aberdeen Association at that time, and Carol Baxter, who ran the Juvenile league, had a sort-of unwritten agreement with me that if I stuck in, I'd get games with the oldest age group. I did that for another year or so and was then told that I'd need to do adults to 'toughen you up.' Another key figure in the Association for me was Brian Christie. He played a big part in my development. He's a large guy with a big heart and a big personality who is not slow in coming forward. One of the first things he did was to get me into doing Sunday Welfare League games. I'd never heard of the Welfare League before. Anyway, I soon discovered it is similar to amateurs, with the games played at Hazelhead Park where there are lots of football pitches. I was told that the refs doing the other games would help if there were any problems, but my first game was a Cup tie which went to extra-time. The rest of them, the ones I was relying on to sort out any grief, all shoved off! That certainly did toughen me up.

"Looking back, I did a _lot_ of matches. I didn't realise just how many different levels and leagues there were in the area. For example, when I was doing Juvenile games on Saturday, I was also running the line for midweek Highland League Under-19s. That was voluntary; there was no pay, but the ref would get you chips on the way home. I had six months of that, then progressed to Highland League Under-21s. All this time as an Assistant helped me a lot. As an Assistant you get the chance to watch the refs and see what they are doing well (and badly!).

"In total, I did four years in Juvenile/Welfare football, then I was assessed and promoted to Category 4, which meant I started to referee Junior football (as opposed to being an Assistant). Today, there is a shortage of referees, but back then there were lots of us. Initially, I did First Division Junior games one week, which meant that I was on my own without any Assistants, and the next week I was an Assistant in the Juniors. Once I started to referee Premier Division Juniors I had Assistants, but the experience of trying to manage games without a linesman or woman helped develop me and toughen me up even further.

"After two years doing the Juniors, I got an email telling me I was being promoted to Category 3 (Assistant Referee level). This meant that not only did I referee Highland League games, but I also ran the line in Scottish Football League Divisions 1, 2 and 3. What happened was that I did Highland League matches most Saturdays but then once a month I'd get to run the line in an SFL match.

"On 2nd August 2003 I became the first woman to referee a Highland League game. It was between Huntly and Wick and a few weeks after that, on 16th Aug 2003, I did my first SFL match, running the line for Peterhead vs Gretna with John Underhill as the referee and Jim Lyons as the other Assistant.

Being the first woman to officiate at this level did, as Morag recalls, lead to some excitement in the media…

"Doing those games at Huntly and Peterhead introduced me to something that I had to get used to over the next few weeks, months and indeed years; namely a huge degree of media interest in a woman officiating in what had traditionally been regarded as a male domain. I had TV, the press and radio all following me during the matches and although they were mostly positive and reasonable, some were less so. The Sun, in particular, published photos that left a lot to be desired and a few journalists were inclined to twist quotes. Fortunately, I didn't have a lot of bad games, so there wasn't much controversy, apart from the Peter Hetherston incident (described in Part II below).

"The local Referees' Association were supportive in that they gave me some advice, mainly to be sensible and keep it positive, but also a reminder not to talk about incidents during a match. That apart, when I got promoted to handle bigger games, I was basically given carte blanche to talk to anyone, but the phone would go all the time, or they would call my work, and it actually got to be a bit of a nuisance, with frequent calls from journalists and photographers. Having to deal with that by yourself was sometimes very hard.

"I wasn't really conscious of being a trail-blazer, certainly not in the early stages of my refereeing career. One thing did happen regularly though when I was doing Juvenile matches. You used to get a courtesy call before the game, to make sure you knew where the pitch was, the team colours etc. and because I was listed as 'M. Pirie' the secretaries of the clubs would call the house and ask for Mr Pirie. My mum invariably answered the phone and would say, 'oh, that will be my daughter you're looking for…' followed by a short silence until they realised she was being serious. Then, when I turned up at games, I was aware that there were some perplexed glances and, 'oh it's a woman here.'"

For some men, perhaps especially the older generation, there is a tendency not to swear if women are present, but in today's society there are generally no such qualms and Morag quickly got used to the language used by the players…

"Three years into my refereeing career, I was in Blackpool for a youth tournament. There were teams from Ireland and they swore more than anyone I'd ever heard. Every second word seemed to be a swear word, but being Irish they said, 'feck' instead of our Anglo-Saxon version. Eventually, I had had enough and told one of the lads, 'you need to stop swearing or I'll send you off.' He didn't seem to get this, but one of his team-mates came to his rescue, telling him, 'you'll need to stop fecking swearing or she'll fecking well send you off.'"

As her career progressed, did Morag notice a marked improvement in the quality of the football she was refereeing, I wondered…?

"You really do notice the difference as you move up in the game. At Juvenile male games, there are a lot of adolescent teenagers bursting with testosterone, but the speed and quality is obviously limited. Generally, the testosterone goes down as the quality of the football goes up. I remember Gary Cheyne, from the Aberdeen Referees' Association, telling me that I'd notice a big change when I started doing Junior football. He wasn't wrong. I contacted him after my first Junior match and said, 'Wow! How fast was that?' Then, when I began to do Highland League games, I noticed a step change again. It's faster, sharper, fitter and, you might find it hard to believe, more polite. You get far less crappy abuse the higher you go as a referee – and the football is better."

Sometimes, though, the players don't really understand the rules…

"I remember a game in Huntly where they had a tactic they adopted at goal-kicks. They would position a forward at the edge of the opposition box and hope that the ball would come through to him. It worked and they scored, after which the opposition went nuts. I had to explain patiently that you can't be offside from a goal-kick…"

It was clear that Morag had the ability and temperament to advance further in the game. In 2005, she became the first Scottish woman on the FIFA Assistant Referees' list, however, there was a problem…

"There were no other women from Scotland – no refs or other Assistants to go with – so I got no games! While I was obviously delighted to be on the FIFA list, it obviously hadn't been very well thought out. However, in July 2005, I was an Assistant in the men's Champions League game in Cyprus, between Famagusta and Dinamo Minsk. It was 40C and I just about died in the heat. However, it was the biggest game I'd done to that date and it was a memorable occasion; the crowd and the atmosphere were amazing and I remember there were lots of toilet rolls thrown on the pitch for some reason.

"Subsequently, I did a few men's European and international games – in the Champions League, the UEFA men's Under-19 championships in Spain, where I got some great marks from the assessor, then my first ever women's match at the Women's Under-19 championships in Switzerland, where I ran the line in the final. Then I had a few chats with Hugh Dallas and we decided that I'd stop doing matches as an Assistant and I took a year out from international football. In 2009, I was nominated as a FIFA referee and then did a lot of international games. It also helped the other girls coming through the system as it meant that they had a female referee to work with. Lorraine Clark became my Assistant and in time she too became a FIFA ref and paved the way for other girls to rise up the ranks. After that, Kylie McMullen replaced Lorraine as my main assistant, and now, only a few years later, Kylie's the only female FIFA Assistant Referee in the Scottish Premier League. I was gutted to go to the World Cup finals but not get an appointment at them, but I did do several qualifying matches and FIFA courses and other tournaments, including the Women's

Under-19 World Cup in Azerbaijan, where I did the semi-final and was the fourth official for the third-fourth place play-off. I've had many Women's Champions League matches, including a quarter final with 10,000 spectators. Also, I have seen countries and cultures that I could never have imagined I'd see, some of which were a real eye-opener. You see people whose main means of getting around is a horse and cart and then somewhere else you see goats living under people's houses. It's humbling and certainly puts materialism into perspective, making you realise that you actually don't need the latest mobile phone and every modern gadget."

Without the postman suggesting to Morag's mum that her daughter that she might like to become a referee, none of this might have happened. Morag's parents have encouraged her at every step of the way…

"My parents are proud of what I've achieved, but they don't say a lot about it. My mum will tell people, 'my daughter is a referee,' and my dad, although he is a man of few words, did come to every game I did in the Highland League and the SFL. He's a Dons' fan and I think he got frustrated with them and he quite liked watching a different type of game where he said the players were more committed. When he came to games, he always made sure he stood away from the other fans. If my games are on the TV, the family watch the start of the match to see me, then, when whistle goes, they change the channel because they don't like to hear the fans shouting at me. Mum has come to watch a game but she only saw the first half because there was Chris Harvey and a TV camera crew there filming for 'The People Show.' She had brought our dog with her and they stood in the far corner, which was where the camera was located. Mid-way through the first half, I noticed they were interviewing my mum - and the dog! It's hard to referee when you're laughing…"

The next thing I know, McCoist is chasing me to the halfway line
Kenny Clark

As a boy, Kenny Clark was obsessed by football. He loved Subbuteo, loved the Rothmans' Yearbooks, loved football cards, but was, as he admitted to me, not actually very good at playing the game. A broken leg in his youth didn't help, but, in hindsight, he thinks this was probably a sign that any ambitions he had to become a footballer were misplaced at best. Anyway, in the autumn of 1978 he was heading to university, to study law and begin a different kind of professional career. Moreover, not only had he become a student, but he had a Saturday job, in an outdoor clothing shop, so that also made it a bit difficult to play football.

"I didn't like, no, I loathed, my Saturday job," Kenny told me, "and when my Dad saw an advert in the Evening Times for refereeing classes and suggested I gave it a go I thought anything was better than the job, so I went along, out of curiosity as much as anything. By chance, Alan Nairn, the father of a girl I knew from school, was a linesman in the senior game and he took me under his wing.

"His influence was critical: he got me to go to the monthly Referees Association of Glasgow meeting as well as the weekly training. The training was what really got me interested, because as well as the fitness work you were mixing with top referees every week. I wasn't put into a group with junior referees, instead I'd be rubbing shoulders with the likes of Brian McGinlay and Davie Syme and I got to hear all the stories from the top games - what was said, who said it, what was going on and all about the true nature of the players. I jacked in the Saturday job (which was a great relief), and I did two games on Saturdays and at least one on Sunday. Sometimes I'd be doing up to five games in a weekend. To help keep fit, I also played football at university for four years during the week, but that stopped when I started to referee Junior football as I didn't want to take the chance of getting injured and not being able to referee."

Junior football presents unique challenges to aspiring referees. Kenny's first game at this level was at Cumbernauld. He was still a fresh-faced young man, so to welcome him to the match, one local supporter shouted, *"when did they start selling refereeing kits in fucking Mothercare?"*

Kenny also recalls Jim Farry asking him how intimidating it is refereeing an Old Firm match. He put Mr Farry right, telling him*, "I'm not being funny, but in deepest, darkest Ayrshire everyone knows where the referee parks his car, sometimes the linesmen are club committee men and instead of spectators there are what appears to be a thousand dervishes watching you, waiting for the slightest mistake. If you can referee there you can referee anywhere. In the senior game you are very safe, but in Junior or amateur football there is, sadly, more risk of assault. Without proper assistants, you had to develop a sixth sense, being aware of what was going on behind you. In the absence of eyes in the back of your head you missed stuff, but you built up strength of character and resolve. At its best, say Scottish Junior Cup days or the Auchinleck Talbot vs Cumnock Juniors derby, virtually the whole village comes to see the* *match and the atmosphere is fabulous. It's hard, tough football, but there are some funny moments. I remember being on the line at Auchinleck in a game they were winning comfortably, when I heard a voice behind me…*

'Nee'bor what size are your boots? I'm playing football tomorrow and I fancy them.' Thinking that as a fit young man I'd be smart enough to avoid any grief, I retorted, 'you'll need to catch me first.' A hand the size of a JCB shovel appeared as he leaned over the perimeter fence and grabbed me, literally holding me off the ground, and adding, 'Aye, you're no so fucking smart now, eh?' Then he let me go…"

Getting to senior level was the next step on Kenny's journey to the top of refereeing. All referees have to pass a written exam to begin with, followed two years later by a refresher course with a further exam to make sure they are keeping up-to-date. As Kenny explained to me, at this stage in a ref's career, it's all about the feedback you get from the clubs and league secretaries. If that's satisfactory, you get given better games, then supervisors come and watch you, putting in written reports after the match, hopefully giving you good reviews. Referees get to see these reports and during the Covid pandemic Kenny told me that he and his younger son, who is refereeing Junior football just now, were looking at some of them… *"my son was laughing, because these were so different from the reports they have nowadays. My old reports were only a couple of paragraphs long, plus a mark out of 10, whereas his go into far more detail about aptitude, management and match control, fitness etc."*

For referees wanting to make the top level of Grade 1, once they had reached the Junior level the next step was Grade 3, where they run the line at Senior level and continue to referee Junior matches. Having reached this, the next step for Kenny was Grade 2, which involved refereeing Reserve games at Senior level while continuing to referee Junior games. This was full-on stuff, as Kenny recounted, telling me, *"You could be refereeing a hammer and tongs Junior game and then go to a Reserve match where you'd have first-team players coming back from injury up against youngsters out to prove themselves. In addition, you'd have senior pros who had been dropped from the first team squad. This made for a volatile mix, because the senior pros who were coming back to fitness didn't want to risk being injured again, while those who were out of the first-team were not happy about it and the younger lads were not holding back. The dynamic of these matches was awkward at times: the refereeing became much more technical but you still had to pick out the incidents and potential flashpoints. And, of course, you were being watched and assessed. I remember Jack Mowat saw me as a Grade 2 ref at Celtic Park and gave me eight out of 10. Given that Jack refereed the famous 1960 European Cup final at Hampden between Eintracht Frankfurt and Real Madrid, that made me really proud. Incidentally, to show how things have changed, Jack travelled to that game on the tram - and the apocryphal story has it that he submitted a claim for travelling expenses of only 6d: how times have changed! His endorsement was encouraging, as was that of the older guys in our Association who told me that I was doing well and as a result I was hopeful that I'd make it to Grade 1."*

Kenny was indeed Grade 1 material. However, even at the top level, there were still challenges, especially in getting the top clubs to take their responsibilities to the referee seriously. After every match, both clubs had to submit a mark our of 10 for the referee and in theory it was the manager who did this. However, as Kenny recounted, *"I remember once returning to a ground a few days after the game because I'd left some kit there and I was told the groundsmen had it. We got chatting and he confided that the manager had asked him score my performance that day."*

There was one manager who was consistent in his marks for referees. This was Jim McLean, who gave every referee the same mark – zero. Wee Jim's stupendous temper was another problem for referees and Kenny told me of the time when, as a relatively new Grade 1 referee, he crossed swords with the Dundee United manager.

"It was in my first or second season at Grade 1 and after the game was over, Jim came into the referee's changing room. I was in the shower at the time, but he was shouting something about a goal that he had a problem with. I shouted back from the shower, 'try to keep calm and come back in again in about ten minutes and we'll have a proper conversation. Of course, when he returned, he hadn't calmed down and just kept shaking his head and swearing, but he finished off by giving me a backhanded compliment, along the lines of, 'at least you spoke to me - those other bastards won't speak to me.' I do wonder if he ever realised why that might be…"

Some referees apologise to managers when they have made an obvious error, but Kenny wasn't usually one of them. When I asked why, he said, *"I wasn't in the habit of apologising because they wouldn't apologise to me. If questioned on the park about, say, a disputed free kick I'd tell the truth. For example, if someone blocked my view then I'd tell the players that I couldn't see what had happened. Some managers were fine about errors. I remember when Jim Duffy was manager at Dundee and they were playing Hibs at Dens. I stupidly allowed Hibs' Derek Riordan to retake a free kick after he'd put his first attempt over the bar, on the grounds that I wasn't ready for him to take it. I should have given a goal kick. Inevitably, Riordan put the re-take right in the top corner. After the game I admitted the error to Jim Duffy. I was (pleasantly) surprised when he said, it was fine and that he realised it was an honest mistake.*

"On the other hand, when Jim Jeffries and Billy Brown were at Hearts, they were like one of those Swiss clocks where one little man comes out and then when he goes back in the other one comes out. Jim and Billy were like that: you'd calm one down and he'd go back in to the dug-out, then the other would pop out and take up where his colleague had left off.

"Jim Jeffries was the only manager who regularly brought you the team-lines. All clubs have to give the referee the team line-ups 30 minutes before kick-off and most managers just delegate it to someone else. But Jim used to like bringing you his team, because it gave him the opportunity to dig you out about some perceived injustice from an earlier game. It became a standing joke amongst referees."

There were other managers who were good fun at times. Kenny described Jimmy Calderwood as *"funny and likeable,"* while Gordon Strachan at Celtic was *"sharp and kept you on your toes, although he liked to play the good cop to his Assistant Manager Gary Pendrey's bad cop."*

Another big character that Kenny regularly did battle with was John (Yogi) Hughes, both as a player and manager. *"Everything you've heard about Yogi is true,"* Kenny told me, *"He always seems a bit mad but he always has time for a bit of chat and banter. When he was manager at Falkirk, I was doing a game at the new stadium. After the final whistle, as I came off the park with my linesmen, Yogi came up to me and shook my hand. However, he didn't let go of it and instead held on so I couldn't escape. 'Is your wife from Falkirk?' he asked me. I had no idea where this was going, so I said she isn't. 'No, well, I just wondered if she was and that's why you fucking hate us so much,' was John's pithy reply."*

Kenny is more fortunate than most football fans, because his work meant that not only did he get into games that he'd have happily paid to watch as a punter, he also got really close to the action and saw at first hand some of the amazing talent that Scottish football had in its ranks in the 1990s. The two men who gave him most difficulty on the park were also two of the most skilful players we've been privileged to see in the last three decades.

"Gazza and Di'Canio were amongst the most difficult to control. Both were incredibly volatile: they might have scored a hat-trick and be coasting to an easy win, but then they'd go and do something crazy or reckless. But they could still be very funny. I remember a Cup tie at Clyde when Gazza was moaning about the ball, telling me it was like a pub ball. I thought, let's have some sensible man-management here and I'll get a new ball at the first available opportunity. When this came, I took the ball, gave it to Stuart McCall and said, 'put it off please.' Stuart kicked it like an arrow, some 60 yards to the stand touchline. 'See,' said Gazza, 'I told you that ball was fucked, he can't normally kick it ten yards straight.'"

On another occasion, Kenny's pre-match snack disappeared from his dressing room before a midweek game at Rugby Park. At Kilmarnock, the home team dressing room is at the top of the tunnel, then there is a long passage and at the end of that there are the referee's and the away team dressing rooms. Kilmarnock provide the officials with a tray of sandwiches, fruit and a pot of tea, which is much appreciated by all concerned. On this particular evening, Kenny and his colleagues had gone to check the pitch markings and nets, but when they returned, they found the sandwiches had gone. The Fourth Official went off in search of some more while Kenny went to check the players' boots and kit. To cut a long story short, Gazza was found stuffing sandwiches into his mouth (*"it was like one of those American eating contests"* said Kenny). To add insult to injury, Gascoigne asked, *"Hey, ref, are you hungry?"* just before Walter Smith came along. *"What's up?"* asked Walter, to be met with the (justifiable) complaint, *"that bugger stole our sandwiches!"*

While he was a bit put out that evening, Kenny did say just how great Gazza was and how much he enjoyed watching him play. *"His peripheral vision was incredible,"* he told me, *"he was like a fly, you know, when you're trying to swat it and it just sees your rolled-up newspaper coming and flies away. Paul just seemed to know when players were coming. His sense of space was incredible."*

Many people hearing Paul Lambert speak in his strong, Glaswegian accent think he's not very bright. Kenny is happy to put them right, telling me, *"Paul is actually razor-sharp. I remember doing the Celtic vs Hibs Cup final in 2001. At that time, we were getting an extension built to our house and the builder told us that his roofer's son played for Celtic. It was Paul's dad. Anyway, 20 minutes into the game I went to give Paul a warning for a bad foul. He wasn't having any of it, telling me, 'Any more of that pish and I'm getting my dad to take your fucking roof down.' I just burst out laughing."*

Another huge personality of that time (who still fits that description today) was Ally McCoist. Everyone assumes that Ally is a permanently happy-chappie, but one of the reasons he has been so successful is that he has a phenomenal will-to-win. Kenny was refereeing a testimonial match for John Lambie at Firhill, between Old Firm legends and Thistle legends. With a few minutes to go and the Thistle legends losing, Lambie put a few extra players on the park, without taking any others off. Then the Thistle legends got an equaliser. *"There may have been a hand-ball,"* Kenny said, *"but given it was a friendly testimonial I didn't' see it. The next thing I know is that McCoist is chasing me back to the halfway line, protesting about the goal. That's how focused he is on winning. I told him that if I sent him off, he wouldn't be able to sit in the dug-out the next Saturday so he calmed down. He was the Rangers assistant manager at that time and that next Saturday was the Old Firm game…which I was going to referee."*

Perhaps one of the funniest one-liners Kenny remembers came from Owen Coyle, when he was player-manager at St Johnstone. Coyle was playing in a reserve game against Kilmarnock and the Killie keeper was hurt and had to go off. The substitute keeper came on and the first thing he had to do was take a goal-kick. Unfortunately, he sclaffed it straight to Coyle, came running out, brought the Saints' manager down and was promptly sent off. As he was leaving the pitch, Owen said politely, *"Mind and do your warm-down son."*

Another game involving St Johnstone was the only time that Kenny had to get someone from the crowd to replace an injured official. Saints were playing Hibs in midweek and the far-side assistant referee had been involved in quite a lot of controversy which didn't endear him to the Perth fans in the East Stand. At half-time, he said, *"Sorry, my calf's gone, I can't continue."* Kenny found Stewart Duff, Saints' Secretary and got an announcement over the Tannoy asking for any qualified referees to make themselves known.

He wasn't too impressed by the first candidate. Not only did he look like Private Lawrie from Dad's Army, he also looked as if he might have had a drink. Luckily, there was one volunteer who was actually attending the game as a scout for Millwall, but who also was a member of the Edinburgh Referees Association and had run the line at Junior matches. Unluckily, he was of a similar build and appearance to the injured linesman and when he went out in the second half the fans didn't appreciate that the change had been made, so, as Kenny told me, *"he still got the 'you fat bastard' chants."* However, he did fine and all seemed to have ended well, until full-time and the officials returned to their dressing room. Kenny takes up the story… *"The last thing you want to see after a game is a senior policeman. On this occasion, it was the Match Commander for Tayside Police, who was none too happy with the replacement linesman. 'We've had a complaint,' he told me, 'that your linesman has been giving the 'Vs' to the St Johnstone fans.' I was not best pleased, telling the policeman, 'talk sense, did you hear the abuse he got? Not only that, but he saved you from having to deal with an abandoned match, with all the fans complaining like mad and giving your officers grief as they tried to herd them out of the ground.' He grudgingly agreed that I had a point and nothing more was said..."*

I asked Kenny if he wished that football could be more like rugby, with the players showing the referee more respect. *"In short, yes,"* he said, *"but since rugby went professional there is more criticism now than there was before, although it is still miles better than football. One of the main differences is that when you take up rugby, you learn how to behave, but in football, from the word go it's the other way. When I do after-dinner speaking at a golf club, I make the point that the vast majority of golfers would never dream of cheating, so why in football do you actively encourage your own kids to lie?*

"Another difference between rugby and football is that in rugby the players generally know the rules. Football has a real problem here: not many people, whether it's the fans, the players or the club officials, know the laws of the game. I used to do a column for The Sun newspaper and every week I'd send a quiz to the sports journalist who helped organise it. Apart from one, who knew his stuff, hardly any of the other journalists ever got a single question right and if they did then they'd do a lap of honour around the newsroom!"

As well as the fabulous players Kenny was privileged to see in Scotland, his international refereeing career allowed him to see some of the world's greatest footballers. You might think that after years of officiating in top matches Kenny was inured to brushing shoulders with famous names, but as he said, *"there were times when I went abroad to do these games and was just star-struck. I refereed in one of Scottish football's golden eras, when we had a stack of world-class players. I remember I did a game at Windsor Park to celebrate the 20th anniversary of Northern Ireland's amazing game against Spain in the 1982 World Cup in that country. Afterwards, I went to the Boardroom and two of my all-time heroes were there, Pat Jennings and George Best. When I tried to play football, I was a keeper and Jennings was my hero. I thought, wow, I started my career in Clydebank's public parks and this is where I end up. Later, George Best spoke to me, saying he thought it was straight-forward enough for me that night but that he knew I was doing the Old Firm game that weekend. At that, he turned to his wife and said, 'if this guy can referee that (Old Firm) game, he can do any game.' I felt ten feet tall. Going overseas, whether to officiate or simply as a UEFA observer, it was just the icing on the cake for my refereeing career. When you get to shake hands with people like Paolo Maldini you just become a fan again. Every referee I know is a massive football fan. I'll watch football anywhere. I love going to wee grounds and if I'm driving and see a match on a local park I want to stop and watch. That's why I became a referee: I just wanted to be part of the game I love."*

It all kicked off, with punches thrown and players kicking each other
Callum McKinnon

At time of writing in 2021, Callum McKinnon was 22 years old and training to become an accountant. He's part of a football-mad family: his older brother, Sean, appeared on the front cover of the Daily Record's football supplement, aged just six months, after a Cup tie at Cliftonhill in sunny Coatbridge. Admittedly, Sean was none the wiser, being cocooned in a sling by his dad, who was there as part of the visiting St Johnstone support, but there was no chance of either boy, or the youngest brother, Jamie, not growing up with an interest in football. Unsurprisingly, as a teenager, Callum played locally in Dunfermline but, in his own words, "*I knew I probably wasn't going to make it at amateur level.*"

That helped crystalise his thinking, but he had actually begun to think about a different role in football from an early age. In fact, it was when he started High School that Callum had first thought about becoming a referee. It's not something that most young lads consider at that age, so the most obvious first question to ask him was, why on earth he wanted to become a ref when he was still a teenager?

"*I'll be honest, it was mainly because I heard the money was good. You were paid £40 per game and so it was more or less equivalent to £20 an hour. Not many young teenagers are able to earn that kind of money. I'd more or less lost interest in playing at the team I was at and I didn't see myself moving up to Under-19 level.*

"*One thing that helped me get into refereeing is that we went to matches with the father of a boy called Kyle Hall. My brother Jamie is friends with Kyle's brother and Kyle's dad is now the President of the Fife Referees Association. Consequently, I had a point of reference and also someone who would take an interest in how I was getting on. I started the refereeing course with about 30 others, although some of them dropped out towards the end. Three guys from my school went, but they're all now footballers rather than referees; one is very good and now plays for Cowdenbeath.*

"*There were four tutors for the course, with classes involving learning from PowerPoint presentations, one for each rule. IFAB's guide is in two parts: one covers the actual laws, the second how referees should interpret them in game situations. We were taught both together – what the actual law is and then how to interpret it - before going on to the next law, and so on. We also had to review video clips, often from the preceding weekend's matches, and we would discuss the referees' decisions.*

"*You learn so much about the game that you don't know from playing it. I did my exam on paper, but I think it's all online now because of the pandemic. The exam is pretty much just to show you know the laws. There were two parts to it: we got shown five clips of Scottish games, at Senior and Junior level. I remember Albion Rovers featured a lot for some reason. There were three marks available from each video: for example, for the first mark you had to say what the foul was, then for the second one you had to say what you'd give – a direct free kick, an indirect free kick and the sanction for the player. The final mark was for how you justified the sanction. I remember the only one I got wrong featured Scott Brown, playing for Celtic against Aberdeen. I was going to send him off, but apparently that was the wrong decision.*

"Once you've passed the exam, you get let out to learn by refereeing games and being supervised. Younger referees are supervised more than the older ones, mainly to see what level they can safely put you at. I did a lot of youth football from the word go and at the end of my first season did one of the local finals. I was told if you are assessed a lot, it's because you are someone with the potential to go further.

"Youth football starts at Under-13 and goes up to U-19 and I did all the various age groups apart from Under-18s, because, for some reason, there is no Under-18 League in Fife. Occasionally, you come up against a famous name: once, I booked Rudi Vata's son, who was playing for Celtic's youth team.

"One problem I had was that I qualified in 2014, just before I was 16. Officially, you are not allowed to do this. The local Association knew I wasn't 16, but part of the test to qualify is to attend a referees' training session. I had gone along and they told me, 'that's you ticked that box, but you can't come back until your birthday as our insurance won't cover it.'"

I presumed that being only 16 carried many challenges when you have to referee older boys. Callum had an advantage here: his dad was the Disciplinary Secretary for the local league in which he was refereeing. His dad's role was to receive the match reports and discipline forms and then to dish out sanctions and chair disciplinary committee hearings when clubs appealed or were called before the committee.

"That meant he could forewarn me if one of the teams I was going to referee had had any issues in recent matches. Once, he told me about a player who had attempted to headbutt the referee in his last game. I was to referee this boy's team the next Saturday and it turned out to be a real experience.

This particular lad was clearly a problem because when I called him offside he told me I was a 'fucking specky mongo.' That was the first time I gave someone a red card. However, that wasn't the end of the matter. My mum used to give me a lift to and from games (I was still too young to drive) and she told me that this guy was waiting outside my changing room. Fortunately, his coach got rid of him prior to me even noticing him.

"Although nothing happened that particular time, I have heard of others receiving death threats, albeit most threats of violence towards referees are usually just that – threats rather than action. That said, I've been punched during a match, although I actually think it was meant for a player and not me.

"Swearing at the referee is very common. I did a pro-youth game at Stark's Park, Fife vs Glasgow, and some of the players' behaviour was ridiculous. A lot of officials put up with

bad language and give it back, especially the older ones. I remember taking the stance early on by telling the teams that if they swore at me then it was going to result in an immediate red card. In that game at Kennoway I sent someone off in the first half an hour.

"I remember doing a youth game between Blue Brazil and Letham. One of the people I'd been doing my training with was the son of a coach and was at the side of the pitch. I sent a guy off for giving the finger and telling a spectator to fuck off. If it wasn't for him, I would have got a lot more abuse than I actually got, because at least he was able to tell his dad - the coach - that my decision was correct. I have done Cup finals at Central Park in Kelty where you are there for five hours and if you make one dodgy call then it might have rather serious consequences.

"Since the game when I was punched, I haven't been able to do many matches, not because of the threat but because I'm working to gain my accountancy qualifications and I need time off for the exams - and also games were suspended due to Covid on the few occasions when I would have had time to do them.

"I know that the thing about abuse is it's taken with a pinch of salt, but I also think that it feeds into a belief about a lot of referees – people, that is football fans and, to be honest, some referees, think that they (referees) are not prepared to take any crap and feel they are above everyone else on the park. I found this to be true to a degree, which I think smacks of arrogance and puts off a lot of young referees. Players and teams appreciate it if you make the attempt to explain why you'd done something, even if they don't agree with you. I think that helps everyone.

"In one game where I was being assessed, a lad turned up with a plaster-cast on his arm and I wouldn't let him play. I told his manager I was happy to explain my decision after the game, but my assessor said that I shouldn't have to answer those types of questions. That might be true of some questions, but during the game it's important to communicate with the players, especially in development football. For example, if someone kicks the ball back to the goalkeeper, I'll always tell him if it's deemed a pass-back and whether he can pick it up or not. I've only once had a coach say after the game that he didn't agree with me, but he did concede that I had certainly warned the keeper who should have listened to what I told him! If we communicate during the game to clear up decisions, surely, we should do the same afterwards?

"There are Youth Co-ordinators who help young referees like me and they do make an effort to reach out and encourage us to come along to meetings and training. Unfortunately, some of the ones higher up don't have much to do with you and won't go out of their way to speak to you. I think it would help immensely if all the referees in a local Association made an effort to encourage young referees making their way up.

"To be fair, this doesn't apply to every older referee. I ran the line in a charity match when my older brother was playing, and I was with two experienced refs, guys 20 years older than me, and it made for a much more relaxed environment. They had a bit of banter while I was

doing the line and really helped me.

"I enjoy refereeing. You have to be smart in how you manage a game. Sometimes, it does go all wrong. In my first and, to date, only amateur match, between a team from Kirkcaldy and a team from Dunfermline, I felt I could have handled the contest better if I'd been stricter. You know within the first ten minutes how the game is going to go. Once you learn that, it becomes easier. However, on this particular occasion, with about ten minutes remaining the team that was losing (it was 5-1 so they weren't very happy), lost the plot. When one of the opposing forwards was clean through, their keeper didn't let the fact that he had already been yellow-carded stop him from wiping out the attacker.

"I gave the penalty but the other team (the one that was winning) said, 'don't send him off, there's only ten minutes to go'. I was in the process of calling the captain over when it all kicked off, with punches thrown and players kicking each other. I tried to re-start the game but it all flared up again so I abandoned the match. I later found out that the keeper was given a three-match ban and the captain and another player of the Kirkcaldy team got a five-match game. After the match, one of the players messaged me to apologise and to say that their team would be taking it to the League and would fine a few players as a result.

"It's really hard to prepare yourself for this sort of thing. I did that game when I was 19. In retrospect, even though I put myself forward for it, I think I should have had someone watching me."

With all this grief from the players, I did wonder if this had put Callum off trying to make his way up the Grades with a view to becoming a top-flight ref…

"Not really. I have got to Grade 5, then for Grade 4 there are more tests: I found from speaking to Kyle that there was a little tutor sub-group, with a fitness test plus a test on advanced interpretations of the laws of the game, with a scenario and essay type answers. However, at present my accountancy exams have to come first and with Covid there wasn't much football for a period of time anyway. The next stage for me is going back to youth level, rebuild my confidence and fitness, with a view to doing amateurs and hopefully Juniors. And we'll just see how it goes after that…"

I was thinking about becoming a referee. It was either that or the shopping. John Rowbotham

For many years John Rowbotham was, arguably, the most recognisable referee in Scotland. A combination of being (well) above average height and having a bald head meant that you couldn't miss him and as such he was the butt of many a ribald comment from the stands, frequently involving the words, *'you baldie bastard,'* usually prefaced by, *"Hey, big man."* In fact, my favourite piece of referee abuse of all time was directed at John and it was unusual in that it not only was genuinely funny but also didn't include (perhaps uniquely) any swear words.

St Johnstone were away to Partick Thistle and as the second half got underway, John gave a decision which did not go down well with the visiting fans. *"Hey, Rowbotham!"* shouted one, *"you're supposed to drink the tea at half-time, not smoke it."*

When I recounted this to John, he said he hadn't heard it, which just goes to show how much of a waste of time and effort it is shouting at referees when there is a halfway-decent crowd - even though it did amuse me and a couple of hundred other St Johnstone fans. However, he did immediately concede that it was funny. Being on the receiving end of allegedly humorous remarks from spectators is something he got used to early in his career…

"In my first match, refereeing Under-18 football, there were two players who went on to make it in the senior game: Shaun Dennis, who played mainly for Raith Rovers, and David Bingham, who went first to St Johnstone and then to a number of clubs, but is best known for his time at Livingston. Anyway, Bingham was the first player I ever booked and after I'd done the necessary a voice shouted 'Ref, you've dropped something.'"

Slightly panicking, John cast an eye back over the pitch in case he'd lost his whistle or something else. It was only when he lifted his gaze to where the voice had come from that he saw his interlocutor waving a pair of glasses…

Like virtually every senior referee, John was a keen player in his youth, playing amateur football in his native Kirkcaldy up to the age of 29. *"I played for the Railway Club and we went from Division 3 to Division 1 of the Kirkcaldy District and then at the end of the season I scored a 'Tam Forsyth goal' in the last minute of a Cup final – that, for those too young to remember the Rangers' defender's legendary Cup final goal, is a touch over the line from about three inches where you only just manage to make contact with the ball. After the game, I went home and said to my wife, 'I think I'll stop playing now; it's best to go out at the top.' She thought this was great and suggested that we'd be able to spend our Saturday afternoon's shopping. That wasn't actually in my plans, so, without really thinking, I said, 'I was thinking about becoming a referee.' It was that or go shopping, so I had to go through with it.*

"I was quite old to be starting refereeing and I didn't want to hang about, although at that time I had no intention of trying to go up the ranks. I tried to learn by watching senior referees, especially Jim McCluskey. However, although I wasn't especially ambitious, the Fife Association were happy to get me into refereeing amateur games quickly, which is why I ended up booking David Bingham in my first game."

After cutting his refereeing teeth on the Kirkcaldy and District amateurs, John progressed to Junior level. Ron Ross, the Secretary of the local Junior association approached him and said they had had good reports about his refereeing. The Fife Referees Association asked John to do three trial games. The first one was between Lochgelly and Hill of Beath and it led to an unfortunate misunderstanding, as John recalled…

"Hill of Beath had just won the (1990) Scottish Junior Cup, but for some reason this hadn't registered with me. When I came out of the dressing room the Lochgelly team were lined up, applauding me and Hill of Beath as we went onto the pitch. I was a bit embarrassed, thinking, 'I didn't realise I was this good.' They soon put me straight!

"At this time, I was Grade 3 and I was doing well. I was given the Scottish Junior Cup final, between Tayport and Glenafton. Tom Brown, who went on to play for Kilmarnock, scored the winner for the Ayrshire side. The supervisor for that match was the legendary Tiny Wharton and I was well aware that if you did the Junior Cup final it usually meant that you would go on to Category 1 level."

By this time John was 35; old for someone who wanted (as he then did) to become a top-flight ref. He needed a break and, fortunately, got one because with a set number of referees at Grade 1 in Scotland, if he was to be promoted then someone had to leave the list. That someone was Jim Renton, who had recently had the misfortune to forget to take his notebook on to the field: a fact that he discovered when he went to book a player. While this might not seem too serious, it is in fact in contravention of Law 5, which stipulates that a referee must have (amongst other things) a notebook when he takes the field. As one door shut, another opened and John was elevated to the top level…

"My first senior game was Berwick Rangers vs Arbroath. Danny McGrain was the Arbroath manager – a nice man. I was nervous, but the game zoomed past. Even up to my last game in charge, I always had a touch of nervous tension beforehand. As a referee, you know that it is as important for Berwick and Arbroath to get the correct decisions as much as it is for Celtic and Rangers. It was strange to be the man in the middle though. When I was a linesman, I used to look to the ref for inspiration. The very first time I was on the line, Hugh Dallas was on the other touchline and Eric Martindale was in the middle. Eric was a good referee and when I became a referee, I wanted to inspire my assistants as he had done for me that day.

"As I progressed to bigger games, I became aware that you usually don't pick up what's shouted from the crowd. It's really just a wave of noise, or on a bad day a wave of groans. However, sometimes you do pick up a few comments. I remember coming off the park at

Ibrox and I heard, 'Hey, big man, we know where you stay.' Somewhat concerned, I looked up and saw my mates from Kirkcaldy – Rangers' fans to a man.

"There is always someone who tries to be funny in front of their mates. Occasionally it backfires on them. I remember a game at Aberdeen, with a crowd of about 8,000, when I didn't give the Dons a penalty. This boy shouted, 'Rowbotham, you're just chicken, Quack Quack!' I just thought, 'he obviously hasn't realised that chickens don't quack. His mates were shaking their heads in embarrassment…'"

It is fairly well known (and if it isn't then it is now), that John Rowbotham, as befits a Kirkcaldy boy, is a Raith Rovers fan. Referees are not supposed to be given games in which 'their' team is taking part, but once, when the six-weekly ballot of matches came out, John was surprised to find that he was down for Raith's trip to Falkirk…

"I got in touch with Maureen, who organised the ballot, and it transpired that Stuart Dougal was supposed to be doing the Raith game but he had been given another instead. 'Just go with it – it will be fine,' she said.

"Before the match, the first line in the Daily Record's match preview began, 'Kirkcaldy Whistler John Rowbotham…'. To make matters worse, my cousin, who is a Raith fan, asked if he could get my referee's complementary tickets. I said of course, but told him 'to make sure you don't broadcast that you're related to me. Keep it low key.'

"Obviously, when I went out with my assistants to do our warm-up, we got some stick. 'Hey, big man, did you drive the Raith bus today?' was one of the more printable comments. I told my colleagues that we would go to the far side to avoid getting any more grief, then I heard a well-known voice, 'John, thanks for the tickets.' There was my idiot cousin, in his Rovers shirt, tammy and scarf.

"Six minutes into the match I gave Raith a penalty, right in front of the Falkirk home support. To say they were not pleased was an understatement."

Complementary tickets were also involved in another incident, this time at Firhill. This time, it wasn't a relative, but a player…

"Chic Charnley was much-loved by the fans of each team for which he played. He very much fell into the category of loveable rogue though. That day, he was injured, but that didn't stop him knocking on my door and asking, 'Big man, are you using your comps?' I assured him I wasn't so he asked if he could have them. I gave him six tickets.

Before the match started, I was chatting to one of the Thistle backroom staff and told him what I'd done. 'Big man, you do realise he'll be outside selling them right now?' It wouldn't have surprised me if he had been: he was a great character in the Scottish game and on his day a match-winning footballer.

Football, in John's opinion, has changed since his days as the "Kirkcaldy Whistler," however, not perhaps in the ways you might think. Scottish football has always had a reputation for being blood and snotters, with no quarter asked or given...

"I liked all the derbies, even the lower divisions; there is always that needle and it means as much to them as it does to Edinburgh or Glasgow. Even in my days of reffing the Juniors, Hill of Beath and Kelty was just like Rangers and Celtic. The tackling was off-the-scale. In normal Scottish games it's 100%, but in these matches the dial goes up to 110%.

"Today, though the level of power and skill is immense, the game is played more side to side, rather than back to front as it was in my day. That makes it slightly easier for the referee. In my time, the pace of some games was just incredible and your fitness, as a referee, was really important.

"Mind you, no matter how fit you are, sometimes other things get in the way of the smooth running of a game. I remember big John Hughes, when he was playing for Falkirk, had a tackle over by the touchline. Anyway, Yogi took out not just the ball and the man but the linesman as well. The linesman got up and discovered his flag was broken. At this time, the linesmen's flags had buzzers, which linked to the referee for offside decisions and other infringements. I asked if he could still use his flag, which he said he could, so we got on with the game.

"A bit later, there was this 'beep, beep.' I thought, 'it can't be the one that's broken, so I looked across at the other linesman and he's going, 'it's no me.' Then I realised that a bairn had picked up the broken handle and was pressing the buzzer, which was still working. I had to go over and relieve the child of his new toy, which, as you can imagine, didn't go down well with the fans nearby."

Like all referees of his generation, John has many stories of the famous players he was fortunate enough to see close up on the pitch. Some were easier to referee than others…

"Gazza was a bit of handful. There was an infamous Rangers vs Aberdeen game in which all my worst nightmares seemed to come true. I missed almost every one of Gazza's misdemeanours on the pitch, and there were many that day. Unfortunately, it was as if I'd piled all my bad games into just that one. A bit later in the season I had Hibs against Rangers in Edinburgh. It was the first time I had seen Gazza since the match at Aberdeen. I was outside the ground when the Rangers' bus pulled up. Of course, the first man off the bus was Gazza. He came across and said, 'I'd like to apologise for my conduct in the Aberdeen game.' He was a decent man, and some player."

Then there was a Celtic vs Rangers game, after which The Herald reported John's performance as follows, *"...in last week's Old Firm match at Parkhead, which ended in a 1-1 draw, Mr. Rowbotham booked eight players in an erratic performance in the first half, and sent off Paul Gascoigne when he appeared to raise his hands to Morten Wieghorst in the second. Whether or not each of Mr. Rowbotham's decisions were right or wrong has been well discussed in various parts of the media."*

Another famous Rangers' player features regularly in one of the stories John relays when he's on the after-dinner speaking circuit.

"Ally McCoist was, in my view, underrated as a player. He was far more than a goalscorer and a joker. I remember once being in the Rangers' dressing room before a match to check the boots. Some of those present obviously didn't realise I was there, because I heard Ally's voice asking Walter Smith (the Rangers' manager at that time) 'Who's the ref today?' – to which Walter replied, 'it's that tit from Kirkcaldy.' McCoist seemed to think that was good news, because he then replied, 'that's good, I'll get a hat-trick today.' He was then slightly surprised to hear that tit from Kirkcaldy's voice tell him, 'no you'll fucking no...' To be fair, Ally was as amused as I was and was always gracious and welcoming to me afterwards. When I retired, I was in the hospitality at Dunfermline and he was Rangers' assistant manager, but he made a point of giving me the thumbs-up and then coming across and asking 'how are you doing big man?'"

Other managers provided entertainment too. Dick Campbell for instance…

"Dick was assistant manager at Dunfermline and even though he knew I was a Raith Rovers' fan we got on great away from the pitch. However, on this particular day he wasn't very happy with my performance in a game at East End Park. He was giving me dogs' abuse and I thought I'll have to have a word. He was shouting, 'you are having a nightmare, in fact it's a disaster.' I stopped the game, said, 'Dick, a train going off the Forth Bridge, leaving no survivors, that's a disaster.' He wasn't convinced. In the second half, one of the Dunfermline boys went down. Dick shouted over, "Hey you, in the black, hey, that'll be another fucking train off the rail bridge then…'"

Then there were Billy Brown and Jim Jeffries at Hearts, who feature in many referees' stories…

"Billy Brown was an ex-Raith player so he should have known better, but one day he and Jim Jeffries were giving me the proverbial dogs' abuse in a game at Tynecastle. I gave a free kick right in front of dugout, then heard Jim shouting, 'That's it, I've had enough, get out there Billy and fucking tell him!' So Billy got out of the dug-out but then turned to Jim and said, 'what have I to fucking tell him…?'"

John also has fond memories of St Johnstone…

"When wee Paul Sturrock was the manager at Perth, I was refereeing a pre-season friendly in which the teams were allowed seven substitutes. Big Ian Ferguson was coming back from injury and before the game Paul approached me, 'Can I get a word, Fergie's been out for ages with this injury, can I put him on the bench? I told him, 'sorry, you've already got seven subs Paul, you can't do that. 'Oh, go on,' he pleaded,' I'll no say anything and I'll no put

him on – it's just to build up his confidence.' Reluctantly I agreed. Suffice to say, with 10 minutes to go a board was held up for another sub. It was No.18, so it's Fergie... and to cut a long story short, we 'agreed' that Fergie would disappear up the tunnel rather than make an appearance on the pitch.

"On another occasion, even the groundsman at McDiarmid was at it. He had put a cross on the penalty spot rather than a conventional circle. The law just says it has to be a mark, but this cross consisted of a three-foot line with a foot long line running across it. In answer to my query, 'What the fuck's that?' the groundsman replied, 'It's the penalty spot.' I said, 'I'll tell you what I'll do, if you get a pen today, I'll put the ball at the back of the long line. Amazingly, it was changed before the match started.

"Still with Saints, one of the biggest pains in the arse but also one of the nicest guys I refereed was Roddy Grant, who used to like to tell me if my decisions were right or wrong. Roddy always gave 125% - 100% for the team and an extra 25% which he expended on telling me how to referee the game. Dick Campbell has a great story about Roddy, when he – Dick - was manager at Brechin. Roddy was with Partick Thistle at that time, a Division above Brechin, and Dick thought Roddy would help their promotion push. So Dick called up John Lambie, the Thistle manager and asked, 'how much for Roddy?' He was slightly surprised when John told him he could have Roddy for nothing. Not unnaturally, he asked John why he was being so generous. "Because I've got £100 on Brechin to win your league,' was Mr Lambie's eminently reasonable answer...

"Despite everything I've just said, I also must say that St Johnstone was my favourite place to referee. That was because of Aggie. Other clubs had their own version of Aggie, but there was no-one like her. She was always there to bring us tea and sandwiches in our dressing room and always asked how we were getting on. All clubs should have someone like Aggie."

And like all referees, he has a story about Jim McLean...

"My first ever reserve game was at Gussie Park in Dundee on an artificial surface that was used for other sports and therefore had basketball and hockey pitch markings as well as football ones. One of my linesmen was Graham Cowper from Perth. Unfortunately, Graham got mixed up and was standing on the basketball court line when he flagged the ball out of play. Wee Jim just gave him a caustic look, accompanied by a typically pithy remark, to wit, 'you fucking idiot.' Then some wee laddies who were watching threw a half brick and it nearly hit a United player. The last I saw of Jim that night was him chasing the wee boys. In truth, I never had a problem with wee Jim, possibly because he was leaving the game as I was coming in. The respect that man has at Dundee United to this day is remarkable and testament to what he did for the club."

Sometimes, managers would turn to the referee for advice...

"I was the fourth official for a match at Pittodrie when Ebbe Skovdahl was the manager there. Aberdeen were getting humped – the score was about 3-0 I think and Ebbe jumped out

of the dug-out, telling me he was going to put on a sub. I needed to know who it was so I could hold up the correct board (this was before the days of electronic boards), but Ebbe couldn't make his mind up. Eventually, he turned to me and said, 'you fucking choose one!' so I replied, 'OK, I'll take Winters off then.' At this point, Ebbe realised that asking me to pick a sub wasn't such a good idea after all…"

One thing that John is sure of though is that he was fortunate to be an official at a time when Scotland had so many quality players in the Premier League – and also lucky enough to referee some of the world's greatest on the international stage…

"The Old Firm were buying in players like Larsson, Amoruso, Van Bronckhorst, Moravčik and Laudrup – to add to Scots' lads like McCoist, Lambert, Barry Ferguson and Tom Boyd. Aberdeen had Hans Gilhaus, who was a fantastic wee player. Laudrup and Larsson were amongst the best players I refereed.

"On top of all these great players I was also able to see some fabulous footballers in the European games I did – people like Paolo Maldini and Franco Baresi, Jean-Pierre Papin, Ruud Gullit and Jurgen Klinsmann. I just stood back and was gobsmacked that I was involved with that quality of player.

"European football was different in those days - more like the game we see in Scotland and England today – side to side and possession-based. It was also different for referees. I know Scottish fans may find this hard to believe, but countries abroad rated the Scottish referees of my day. Continentals could be just as hard – but were usually more skilled footballers and they were (sometimes) less argumentative. It was much easier to give a foul abroad. There, if a player gets touched and goes down everyone expects you to give a foul. If a player goes down in Scotland it's, 'get up you fucking cheating bastard.'"

For anyone too young to remember John, his height and bald pate were something he had in common with one other, and with the greatest respect, slightly more famous referee…

"I met Pierluigi Collina when I went on the FIFA international list. Not for nothing was he considered the greatest football referee ever. Once, I was doing a match in Salonika, in Greece. The home team were playing Atletico Madrid so it was big game with a lot of attention on it locally. Anyway, I went to check the nets and Kenny Clark, who was the fourth official, was checking the substitute boards. The ball-boys were all out on the pitch, mucking around. This wee Greek ball-boy came across to me, holding out a bit of paper - 'autograph, autograph please?' I felt pretty flattered so I signed it, 'Best Wishes, John Rowbotham' and handed it back. The wee boy looked at it, then turned to his mates and in much better English than I was expecting announced, 'huh, it's not fucking Collina.'

"To make matters worse, Kenny Clark then re-appeared, hurpling badly. 'Are you OK?' I asked, and Kenny replied, 'Aye, I'm OK, but see that boy in the wheel-chair, he's just aimed his wheelchair and crashed right into me, shouting 'Spanish bastardo!'. He obviously thought Kenny was a player…"

Finally, I asked John if, looking back, he had enjoyed it?

"I loved it: if I could, I'd do it again tomorrow. It's hard to describe what it's like to have a role inside football. It's not like other jobs. You don't become a traffic warden because you love parked cars, but you know that, like a referee, you'll get abused publicly. For me, refereeing was all about the love of the game. Despite the times when things went wrong, I wouldn't change a second of my time as a referee, especially as it got me out of the shopping on Saturdays!"

For me, there is nothing like the Edinburgh derby
Willie Conquer

Back in the day there were linesmen. Then they became Assistant Referees. Then the best of them became Specialist Assistant Referees (SARs). According to the SFA website, *"A SAR should also have demonstrated an exceptional potential and ability to perform to a high and consistent standard within the FIFA International List of Referees."* Willie Conquer, the boy from Bingham in Edinburgh, was one of the very best SARs and, arguably, one of the biggest personalities in the refereeing profession during his 20 years in the game. Like many other officials, his path to the FIFA list began with his love of playing football. However, the reason he then progressed to become a referee was as a result of a drunken bet…

"I was a left back, playing amateur football in Edinburgh at decent level and I was even invited for trials with Bonnyrigg Rose. I went to training with them, but I could see that, in all honesty, I wasn't good enough. I was working at John Lewis at that time and we had a Sunday team. Unfortunately, I got a bad injury – I did my ligaments - and was out for two years. Then, one evening in 1996 I was at a Race Night at the Maybury Hotel in Edinburgh with two of my mates. As usual, the last race was an auction and we got horse No. 4 for £20. To cut a long story short, it won and we got £220 between the three of us, so we went on the town. Later, we met a couple of referees who did amateur games and they were asking after me, wondering why they hadn't seen me playing. After I explained, one of them said, 'why don't you take up refereeing?' My mates were pissing themselves laughing at the prospect of me becoming a referee as I was never the most generous towards the officials when I was playing. We were due to go to Ibiza that summer on a lads' holiday and they said 'if you take this seriously, and pass the course we'll buy all the drinks in Ibiza.' That struck me as a decent bet…

"Anyway, I got 97% in the mock exam and 98% in the actual exam, so I had a good time in Ibiza! However, because of my work I didn't do many Saturday games. I was a flooring estimator at John Lewis and worked Tuesday to Saturday, but then my role changed and I got my first lucky break, refereeing an Under-19 Cup quarter final between Hutchie Vale and Buckhind (from Buckhaven). There was an incident where the centre half and centre forward both challenged for the ball but knocked each other out cold. I wanted to abandon the match, but an ambulance came for the lads and the clubs said they wanted to continue. Buckhind eventually went on to win on penalties and after the game I asked the clubs' secretaries to let me know how the boys were. I was doing an Under-14 game the next day and the Secretary of the Fife Association said they were impressed by how I'd handled the previous game and asked if I'd like to do some league matches. I was quite old for a referee for this level (Under-16) as I was nearly 30, but that meant that I wasn't so easily intimidated as some of the younger refs who tend to do these matches. Also, being older – and essentially not giving a flying fuck if someone swore at me – I got more respect. Then I got a call from Don McVicar, who was the Head of Referee Development at the SFA. Don told me that a number of people had been in touch with him about how I'd handled the Hutchie Vale vs Buckhind game and two weeks later I was doing Under-21 games in Fife with two Observers. My first one was a

bit traumatic: I abandoned it after seven minutes because there was a 22-man battle going on in the middle of the pitch.

"The grades for referees were different then, but I was a Category 4 ref at this point and wanted to get on the Senior list. In the event, I only did a few games at Under-21 level before I was offered the first of the three Junior games that referees in Fife were usually given to see if they could take a step up. I did one only - it was between Tulliallan and Newburgh - and then I became a Category 3. I thought I'd get promoted again but when Douglas Downie (who was Association Manager of the Fife Referees' Association) offered me a move up to Category 2, I sat down with him and said, because of my age, I'd only get a couple of seasons at Category 1 and that by the time I'd done the lower leagues in the Senior game I would be lucky to get many, if any, Premier matches. They were introducing Specialist Assistant Referees at this time and I thought I'd have a better chance of making it to the top flight in that role. Douglas wasn't happy and the SFA referee supervisor George Smith called and gave me a dressing down, telling me that although he understood what I was doing he was really disappointed and thought I had a cracking career ahead of me. His view was that you should always try and referee at the highest level. Although he wasn't very pleased then, subsequently, I got on really well with George, even being on first-name terms, which didn't apply to everyone in the refereeing world, so it was a real compliment."

Having decided to go down the Specialist Assistant Route, Willie then partnered with his namesake, Willie Collum and, on the other touchline, Martin Cryans. It was a smart move. Being part of a high-profile group meant that Willie got to do the big matches that he wanted, not just in Scotland but all over the world. It also meant that he was introduced to some of the big characters in Scottish football…

"I remember the 2013 Scottish Cup final between Celtic and Hibs when we met with the team captains beforehand to discuss at what end penalties would be taken in the event of the game being drawn. In reality, the police usually decide this, but you have to go through the formality of consulting the teams. Willie Collum was going through the protocol but Broony (Scott Brown) stomped off, saying 'this is a fucking waste of time.' Willie wasn't having this and called Broony back, telling him he was being disrespectful. 'No, it's you that's being disrespectful,' said Scott, 'telling us that the game might go to penalties. There's no way it's going to fucking penalties: we're going to pump them.' They did too…

"There were some big personalities in those days. Probably my favourites were Billy Brown and Jim Jeffries at Hearts. It's fairly well known (of which more below) that I'm a Jambo, and I remember during one match at Tynecastle I gave an offside decision against Hearts and Jim shouted to me, 'you're fucking meant to be one of us.'

"Dick Campbell was another. One of the first times I met him was when he was manager of Dunfermline. "Rowbotham has warned me about you,' was his opening line, followed by 'are you a Pars' man?' I replied, 'get back in your fucking hutch,' and that was us off to a good start. He's a great man.

"When it comes to the players there were some right nutcases. Some are right animals on the park, but real gents off it. Of course, none of those mentioned here fall into those categories. Marius Žaliūkas was a man mountain on the pitch but the complete opposite once the game was over. Broony never used to speak to you in the tunnel, although he did once try to pull my shorts down there when he knew there were TV cameras about. Fortunately, I was ready for him and had tied them up tight! These were the kind of players who, if they told you to fuck off were not put out when you replied, 'and who the fuck are you talking to?'

"Yogi (John Hughes) was always entertaining. If I didn't give him a decision he thought he was due he'd invariably shout, 'get that flag up you Hearts' bastard.' Tommy Wright is another very nice man. I only fell out with him once, but he came into the dressing room straight away afterwards and apologised. Neil Lennon is another really good man. I've had a couple of fall-outs with him, but he was always honest. When he became Hibs manager, he had criticised me in the media, but then the next time I was at Easter Road he pulled me into his office and said he was sorry and he shouldn't have done it. I went to a golf charity day recently and Neil was there. He made a beeline to speak to me, to the amazement of my friends. I pointed out that having officiated in nearly 1,000 games it was always possible there were some managers I got on with…"

There were, naturally, some with whom Willie didn't have such a good relationship…

"There was one Assistant Manager who, after an Under-21 game I'd refereed, was not pleased when one of my Assistants gave a late goal against his team. He came into our dressing room, shouting and swearing, so I reported him and he got (a ban for) four games.

"Then there was a Celtic player… who had probably better remain nameless, who threatened to ram my flag up my hole. Stuart Dougal was the referee the next time I was on duty at Parkhead and after the match, which Celtic had won easily, we had a 'discussion' in the tunnel. Gordon Strachan was the Celtic manager at that time, and he came running up to see what was happening. We ended up in the referee's dressing room and the player said, 'where's your flag?' to which Stuart retorted, 'I'd pay good money to see you try to ram that up Willie's arse; I don't think you'd win. Now fuck off or we'll report you.' He fucked off, his tail between his legs…

"Sometimes it really kicks off. There was a quarter final where the losing fans were outside protesting against their team and, especially, their manager. One of their players had been sent off and he came into our dressing room, trying to get at Willie (Collum). Let's just say I got involved and although Willie wanted to report the player, we decided that it was better not to. We were then advised to wait until the protest had petered out but when we eventually left the ground there were still about 100 fans milling around. One guy was giving me pelters but he said one thing too often and I suggested he came and said it to my face, rather than when he was surrounded by his mates. The polis had to intervene, but his mates were taking the piss and calling him a shitebag. I was laughing all the way to the car!"

Sadly, there are some even more stupid people than that out there…

"After an Old Firm game, our phone in the house rang and my daughter, who was about eight at the time, picked it up. A voice said, 'can I speak to your dad?' but she said, 'he's not come home yet.' Then the voice said, 'you'll be lucky if he does come home...'"

And of course, not every game was played at the top level...

"I did a lot of games down the leagues, but to be honest, I didn't actually know most of the players' names. As a referee, I used to ask the Assistant to read the numbers out from the team-lines so I could write them down in my wee book in case I needed to take action against them. Even in the Premier League, I never looked at the team-sheet and didn't always know the players' names. The big personalities you know, but if there is someone making only his second appearance then it's unlikely that you'll know who it is. The fact is that you need to divorce your decisions from the personalities. One thing I will say is that in the lower leagues there was generally a bit more respect from the players. Often, they had seen you on TV at the weekend and therefore they would come and chat to you during the warm-up and discuss the game they'd watched and in which I'd taken part."

" All the clubs in the lower league tend to look after you better than the bigger clubs. That's not to say that the bigger clubs are bad. Strangely for a Hearts' fan, I always felt Hibs were the best in the top flight. They have two dressing rooms for the officials, plus a lounge for us with nice food and a telly: they can't do enough for you."

As well as refereeing and running the line at every ground in Scotland, Willie has been fortunate to officiate all over the world...

"I've done all the big games in Scotland. I was officiating at the Old Firm game at Parkhead in 2011 when Ally McCoist and Neil Lennon had to be separated. For a boy from a council estate in Edinburgh that was really something. However, and I know many will find this controversial, Old Firm games are overrated for atmosphere. They are not a patch on places like Bucharest, Budapest or Rome. We did one game in Hungary when the away fans were all brought in on trains. After they had wrecked the trains, they started on the ground. It was the only time I've seen tear gas used at a football match. We had to stop the game after about eight minutes. This seat flew over my head and I could hear Willie (Collum) over the headphones, 'what the fuck's happening?!' Seats were raining down and the crowd were kicking the shit out of each other.

"We do have trouble-makers in Scotland, but they're nothing compared to some of the so-called fans you get abroad. We were regularly told not to go out after a game, but we went out anyway. We'd ask the club representative looking after us where was safe to go and we were never met with anything but warmth and genuine hospitality. There was a qualifying match for the Champions League in Europe – I'll be honest, I've no idea where it was, apart from being in Romania - when, after the game, we found this party of about 30 men. One had just become a dad and they were wetting the baby's head. They had all been to the game and so they invited us in for a drink. You always get a goodie-bag from the home team on these

jaunts so I went and got mine and gave it to the father of the new baby. We were there to three in the morning…

"The vast majority of supporters just want to talk to you about the game and are no bother. Willie Collum is a quiet, religious, man, so we'd wait till he went to bed and then sneak out. He knew fine well we were doing it. In my two and a half seasons working with him and Martin Cryans we had some great nights out. Willie doesn't drink, but he'd bring a bottle of red wine for us. Unfortunately, UEFA and Covid have put an end to officials going out socialising.

"There are a lot of other things that have changed. I'm still involved in refereeing, as an Observer, but today's refs can't get away with what we used to. Nowadays, if a ref swears at a player he'll be reported and demoted off the ballot (the six-week schedule that allocates officials to games).

"The best atmosphere I've experienced was in Turkey, at Galatasaray and Fenerbahçe. It took us 45 minutes to drive the two kilometres to the ground, then when we got out of the car the local fans were shouting, 'Scottish bastardos, we're going to kill your mother.' Bobby Madden was the ref on that occasion and we were just laughing at them all the way to the ground. We never felt in any danger.

"I've done games in Madrid, in the San Siro, at Bayern Munich and Dortmund. The best game I've seen was probably a friendly between Germany and Uruguay. This was around the time that Suarez was hitting the headlines for biting opponents, but I have to say that you could not meet a nicer guy. Another real gent is Didier Drogba, but he's a bit of a unit. In a Champions League game, he rattled someone, cleanly though, right in front of me. Willie gave the foul and said over the earpiece, 'do I book him?' I replied, 'no, don't caution,' and Drogba heard me. He came over and said, 'you're a great ref.' The UEFA Observer told me it was 'brilliant man management,' but in reality it was just applying Law 18 – use your common sense!"

Europe may be great, but for Willie there is only one place that is home.

"It's almost certainly just my native bias, but for me, there is nothing like the Edinburgh derby. I was born in the council estate that is Bingham. It's famously Hibs territory and my family was split between the Hibs and the Hearts. I was due to be taken to a Hibs vs St Mirren game, but it was called off, so we went to Tynecastle instead. That was the start of my love affair with the Jambos. I've been known to wear a maroon top underneath by referee's strip, but it would never influence me in making decisions. Strangely, quite a lot of fans still don't know who I support. When I go to Easter Road, there are lots of guys in the crowd that I was at school with, so they all give me the 'you Jambo bastard' stuff. But when I'm at Tynecastle, there are Hearts fans who call me a 'Bingham bastard,' assuming I'm a Hibee. How wrong they are!"

The ref booked 14 players and sent off four. It was a highly competitive match. Alfie Smith

Unlike some referees, Alfie Smith had a more than decent career as a footballer, in his case in the semi-professional game that is the Highland League. Starting as a teenager with Deeside, he then played for Junior side Buchanhaven Hearts in Peterhead, then had two seasons at Deveronvale, two at Peterhead, two more at Fraserburgh and one final season at Forres Mechanics. In his own words, Alfie was *"a tough-tackling left back, good enough to have a trial for Dundee United but not good enough to get signed!*

"The standard was very good in my day. What we lacked was the fitness and pace that the players have nowadays, but we were just as skilful, if not more so. The biggest change is in the approach to diet and fitness. It was more of a boozers' league in my day. We got paid a basic of £6 a game, with £2 for a draw, £4 for a win, plus a signing-on fee of £200 or £300, which was decent money in the 1970s."

Towards the end of his career, Alfie went along to watch a local Sunday Welfare League match in Peterhead and the referee didn't turn up so he was asked to step in. The thinking behind this was that because he was still playing, they thought he could do it. The teams knew him so he said he'd give it a go…

"I quite enjoyed it and decided to go through the classes and get my badge. I did this while I was still playing, so I'd be a footballer on Saturday and then on Sunday I'd referee the Sunday Welfare in Peterhead.

"I then moved on to refereeing the amateurs. The deal was that you did them for a season or two and if you show promise you got recommended for Juniors. The latter were not at a great standard in Aberdeen in my time although Banks o' Dee are good nowadays. Although I live in the north-east, I have family in Troon, so I watch a lot of Juniors in Dundee and Ayrshire. I'd say the standard is comparable with the top six in the Highland League and Junior sides are now putting Highland League clubs out of the Scottish Cup.

"Of course, everyone thinks of Ayrshire as the real home of Scottish Junior football, but it could still be quite a battlefield in the north-east. Sunnybank vs Banks o' Dee was the top match and I remember one game between them at Spain Park which I refereed. It was weird, because I expected blood and thunder, but it ended up a damp squib, with lots of the players just passing it about … very strange. I don't think I had a caution in that game, which was practically unheard of given its reputation. Of course, like all aspiring referees, I was supervised throughout these early years and if you showed promise then more, different Supervisors watched you to see if you really were any good. It was a great learning curve and I must have been doing something right because I was promoted up to Grade 3, so I could run the line at Premier games. Decisions on promotions were often made at the annual Referees' Conference in St Andrews. It's a bit of a piss-up to be honest: we'd arrive on Friday and go straight to the pub. Then there was a putting competition on Saturday and

more drink on Saturday and Sunday. There was also the serious business of the conference as well as the drink, but it was in the pub that you were sometimes tipped the wink that you'd be moving up a Grade. Obviously, a lot depended on the reports from your local Referees' Association.

"There were some very helpful people in the Aberdeen Referees' Association. Sandy Roy was the main man in my time and he always encouraged me. George Simpson was another. I've been on the line with Sandy a few times, including one game at Tannadice when United were playing Aberdeen: that one stuck with me because it was unusual to have an Aberdeen ref for an Aberdeen game.

"In my view, Sandy Roy didn't get the credit he deserved. Games that he refereed generally had very little controversy. There was a bit of a feeling in the north-east that the power-base of the refereeing world was central Scotland, with some of the promotions down to politics as much as an individual's ability."

The biggest problem for referees is…

"Part of the problem, if not the biggest problem, for officials is that very few players know the rules properly. Over the years, on three occasions when an offside decision has been given, I've seen the defending team take the free kick from inside their own half. I've seen players taking throw-ins from off the field. I don't know the answer, unless it is that they all have to referee a proper game at some stage. I think a lot of senior refs would pay good money to see that!

"I liked to think that because I played at a decent level, I knew what a bad foul was and although I did send a few players off, I think they respected me because they knew I'd played the game."

As well as the prestige of the Premier League, Alfie reminded me that referees and linesmen also do the rather less glamorous midweek Reserve (or Under-21 today) fixtures…

"It's something else to be running the line at a Reserve match at an almost empty Gayfield. However, I took the view that this was a level I'd never expected to be at, so I gave it 100% and enjoyed it. My experience of these types of fixtures was that they generally didn't give the officials many problems, although I didn't like Arbroath because they made egg sandwiches in the Boardroom and I don't like eggs!

"I remember one game at Arbroath when Ally McLeod was managing Queen of the South. They were losing by a couple of goals but turned it around and won and Ally was cock-a-hoop. After matches at Gayfield, the ref and linesmen usually went to Tutties Neuk, the pub across from the ground. As everyone knows, Baltic is an understatement for the weather at Arbroath's ground, but you had a chance to warm up in the pub before you headed home. On this occasion, Ally McLeod came in with some of the Queens' players. He was holding court with them when he suddenly turned to our table and asked what we'd like to drink.

Fair play, he bought not just us but everyone else in the pub a drink. Then the Queens' coach driver came in and told them all the needed to go, otherwise it looked as if they were there for the rest of the night."

On the other hand, some players could be a bit of a pain…

"I was at Dens for a match which Dundee won 4-0 against Clydebank. Dundee were three up with only five minutes to go and one of their players burst through and was brought down. It was a definite penalty, so I put my flag up and ran to the corner flag. Sean Sweeney, the centre back, led the charge of the Clydebank players, all shouting and berating me. The referee, whom I'd better not name, just left them to it rather than come and help. Anyway, Dundee, inevitably, scored and the game was soon over. As we were coming off the park, Sweeney made a move to come over to me, looked me right in the eyes and said, 'well done, great game,' then put his hand out to shake mine. He had an iron grip, and, in my view, was deliberately trying to crush my hand. By my definition, it was deliberate, violent conduct, but in the circumstances I couldn't really ask the ref to send him off. I just had to grin and bear it!"

And as well as the lows, there were some highs … including some rather honking kit.

"I had quite a few highs, including refereeing some Cup finals in the Juniors and being linesman in some Cup finals in the Highland League (the Scottish Cup Qualifying Cup North and Aberdeenshire Cups). Also, in my last game on the Senior list, I was linesman in the Reserve Cup Final between Dundee Utd and Celtic at Tannadice.

"A couple of friendly matches also ranked pretty highly. I ran the line at Pittodrie in two such matches: firstly, Aberdeen vs Man Utd to commemorate the Tall Ships Race, which finished 1-1 (the Dons won on penalties); and secondly Aberdeen vs Hamburg for the opening of the Dick Donald stand at the ground.

"However, the absolute highlight of my career was a game in the old European Cup between PSV Eindhoven and Žalgiris of Lithuania. The referee was Jim McCluskey – a great ref and a great guy, with Mike Pocock on the other line and Alistair Hewitt as the Fourth Official. PSV is one of the richest clubs in Holland but they were very friendly and we got very well treated. Their Phillips stadium is heated, so you can wear shorts and T-shirt inside it and it has five restaurants, in one of which we had a sumptuous meal.

"As we were changing for the match, I noticed that Alistair Mike and Jim were all putting on Adidas kit. I only had Umbro kit, but we knew we all had to wear the same so the others were going to change into their Umbro kit. However, we were told we had to wear Adidas, so they found me a spare jersey and socks. But, of course, these didn't have an SFA badge, so one of my colleagues had a rummage around and found a spare one. As four, how shall we say, domestically-challenged males, we were a bit stuck, but fortunately the PSV President's wife came into our dressing room and sowed on my badge.

"When we were in the tunnel with both the teams, there was this smell: it was the Žalgiris players, whose personal hygiene seemed to leave something to be desired. After the match, the PSV goalkeeper presented his opposite number with a gift of kit and I remember thinking, 'I hope there's some deodorant in there.'

"Also after the match, as was traditional, we had some whisky to give to the Dutch refereeing representative, but we had another bottle for ourselves. Alistair didn't take a drink so he spent his time writing a speech for George Smith's farewell dinner the following Saturday, while the rest of us had several whiskies and eventually got to our beds at 3.00 am. Our flight was at 6.00 am - the same morning - but despite the hangover it was a fantastic trip and the pinnacle of my career."

Just when you think you've retired…

"At 35 I had to go off the list. It was all down to the percentages and numbers, but there was a wee bit of puny politics too. The Secretary of the Aberdeen Association told me, "We're encouraging you to go on the committee." My task was going to be to sell raffles and sweepers. I said that wasn't for me, but that I would be happy to do other things, only to be told, 'it's got to be raffles or nothing - and if you don't do it then you can't go on the committee.' At the end of the season, someone on the committee got a few extra years on the list but I was taken off. I was appointed to the Reserve League Cup final for my curtain call, but essentially it was a letter saying,' thank you for your services, but you are now off the Senior list.' I carried on refereeing Juniors for two seasons after coming off the list, which wasn't great fun to be honest, but I also kept running the line in the Highland League, which I did enjoy.

"I stopped all my referee and linesmen duties in my mid-40s although I carried on attending Highland League games as a spectator most weekends. It's my league and I really enjoy the games and there is great entertainment. I was 48 when I did my last official game, as a linesman. It was at Inverurie Locos and I remember I got a Tannoy announcement and a round of applause after the game, as well as a special commemorative bottle of whisky. It wasn't made specially for me; they had commissioned 50 bottles to celebrate their admission to the Highland League and I got one of them.

"I never thought I'd get involved again, but in late September 2021 I went to see Inverurie Locos vs Brora. I got there early, taking up a place across from main stand. After a minute, the linesman in front of me went down in a heap and he looked unconscious and in distress. A lady doctor and the physios walked him off the park. Sure enough, the Tannoy came over loud and clear: 'can anyone help?' I hadn't run anywhere for about five years, so I hummed and hawed, then there was a second plea over the Tannoy and I thought, 'I'll throw my hat in the ring one last time.' I identified myself to the ref and he was fine about me taking over. I ran the line for almost the whole match, despite pulling my groin after 20 minutes. There is a stadium clock in the ground and I remember looking at it, thinking, 'get to half time,' then 'get to full time!'

"Fortunately, for me at least, there were no contentious decisions and the players were brilliant and complementary at the end of the game. That was a surprise to be honest, because the ref booked 14 players and sent off four! It was, it's fair to say, a highly competitive match. In my view, some were justified but the ref went over the top a bit. Then there was a stramash in the tunnel. However, I was chuffed when a Brora player said 'you were the best man on the park.' One of the Inverurie committee members called me and asked me to go along as their guest a few weeks' later. There is obviously life in the old dog yet!"

Herr Ziegfield said, 'you saw how not to referee last night…'
Brian McGinlay

Way back in the day, at Victoria Drive Senior Secondary School in Scotstoun, there were quite a lot of good footballers. One young lad, by his own admission, wasn't quite so good (*"I was useless"*), so one of the PE teachers gave him a flag and told him to stick it up when the ball was out of play. This boy was Brian McGinlay, who was to go on to have a major impact on Scottish refereeing, not just because of his ability to control games but also because he was the very antithesis of the older-style, jacket-wearing referee. However, before he got to that stage, he had had a lot of learning to do…

"In those days there were few referees for schools' football. Most of the games were controlled by the PE teachers and there were no linesmen. As well as my own school's games, I used to do matches involving Hyndland School and St Thomas Aquinas Secondary. I would often do two games on a Saturday morning, the first at 9.30 and the second at 11.00 am. These were generally Under-14 and Under 15 matches and as a result of my involvement I got chatting to other referees who suggested that I take the refereeing exam.

"In 1961 I took the exam and passed it, then moved on to doing the Glasgow YMCA League. My first Under-15 game in that league was between Possil YM and Sandyhills YM. Captain that day for Possil was a young lad called Kenneth Dalglish. I'd like to say that it was obvious he was going to be a star, but, in all honesty, I couldn't see it! However, Possil must have liked me as they asked me to referee various friendly games for them. I progressed from there and when I was 19, I got a call from one of the Glasgow Schools' officials asking if I could do an Under-15 match in Swansea. I was delighted. It was Wales vs England and one of the English team was a lad called Steve Perryman, who went on to have a very successful career with Spurs and had one cap for the senior England side.

"I felt I was getting a taste for refereeing and I seemed to be doing alright. I was getting invites to run the line for schoolboy internationals. These were usually played at Ibrox or Celtic Park. I started to progress up the Grades and then got another big game when, after Shawfield Juniors went bust, their ground, Roseberry Park in the east end of Glasgow, was bought by the Glasgow Schools FA. Bob Kelly, the Celtic Chairman, did the honours for the opening of the 'new' ground and I was the referee for the Glasgow Under-15 Cup final between St Mungo's and Holyrood. There was a big crowd and it was a good game. In those days, there was almost no dissent from the youngsters because their teachers were running the teams and they wouldn't tolerate any nonsense.

"By the time I was 21, I was getting more games. At Shawfield, referee Bob Wilson, who was a Grade 1 referee, seemed impressed and asked if I would like to move up to the Juniors. He gave me a West of Scotland cup tie. In those days, the invitation came via a postcard. It was between Port Glasgow and Maybole and, in the event, I got three games for the price of one, so to speak. There were two replays and the last match was in Maryhill. There, I met the

Secretary of the Scottish Junior League, who asked how I was doing and then said he'd give me a few more Junior games.

"My first league match in the Juniors was between Glencairn and St Rochs. There were no official linesmen in those days, at least not until the 5th round of the Junior Cup. Kenny Hope and I were placed with an experienced referee, Alex Currie, who was prominent in Junior football at that time, and we were then running the line at the later stages of the Junior Cup. There were huge crowds for these matches. I remember one tie between Johnstone Burgh and Greenock that finished as a draw. There were 7,000 at the first match at Keanie Park in Johnstone and 9,000 for the replay at Greenock."

At this point in his refereeing career, Brian began to take his fitness more seriously, although, as I discovered later, it was not his greatest strength…

"I began to go to the referees' training at Scotstoun Showgrounds. The Assessor, Andrew Fleming, took an interest in my progress. He had me assessed and I must have done something right because after two seasons in the Juniors I became a linesman in the Senior game. Ironically, Drew Fleming who was Class 1 at that time, fell down the ranks, creating the gap into which I stepped. At the age of 26, I was now a Class 1 referee, handling Senior matches, beginning with Stranraer at home to Brechin City."

It was very unusual to be Grade (Class) 1 at such an early age. However, this being the early 1970s, Brian brought some other traits associated with the younger generation of those days…

"Most referees at that time, almost all of them in fact, were strict, authoritarian even. Tiny Wharton, who was a great, well-respected, influence on us all, was the archetype. He was very helpful to me, especially when I ran the line for him in my early days. However, his generation was the one with the Brylcreemed hair, blazers, all-black boots and starched white laces, with no concession to what the players wanted. It was standard practice to refer to the players as 'Mr' followed by their surname.

"In contrast, I was all for modern, longer hair styles and I was quite happy to use the players' first names and try to communicate better with them. It wasn't absolutely frowned upon, but I was very much the exception to the rule. In particular, I was all for making sensible changes to the referees' kit. In those days, apart from Tom Wharton with his jacket, referees wore black tunics and if there was a 'colour clash,' say with Dundee, Falkirk or Raith Rovers, we had to wear khaki shirts. They were horrible things and I hated them with a vengeance. Because of the requirement to have at least two different shirts, we all had to buy the SFA badge and sow it on, or attach it with Velcro.

"I was officiating at a Hibs v Falkirk match, and obviously Falkirk's navy-blue shirts meant that we were supposed to change into the dreaded khaki. It just so happened that I had with me three red tops with SFA logos on them, so I suggested to my linesmen that we all wore them, adding, 'let's see if we get away with it…

"After the game, the Assessor (who, for reasons that will become obvious, will remain nameless) came into our dressing room. He was, unfortunately, rather old-school. His opening line was, 'by what authority are you wearing those shirts?' At that point, Tom Hart, the Hibernian chairman chapped on the door and asked to come in. Tom told us that he had been discussing our attire with his fellow directors and guests in the boardroom; then he said, 'I have to say, we all thought they were superb. It was so much easier to tell you and the players apart.' At this point, the Assessor chipped in, 'I was just telling Brian and the others that, Mr Hart…'"

Doug Yeats (of whom more below) also recalls being on the line with Brian and being given a red jersey to wear and, on another occasion, Brian introduced another, different coloured shirt. This also involved Falkirk, but this time they were at Airdrie (the home team changed colours in those days), so again there would have been a 'colour clash' and the officials were supposed to wear the hated khaki…

"Every year, at the Scottish Refs' conference in St Andrews, we were given SFA branded T-shirts. That year they were royal blue. The game at Airdrie was being televised, so I said to my linesmen, 'do you fancy wearing these shirts?', which we then did. After the game, George Peat, the Airdrie chairman, complimented us. A few days later, I got a letter, by first-class post, from Jim Farry. There were two pages about why I shouldn't have done this, blah, blah… I wrote back with my views, and he then replied and several more letters followed back and forth, but I gave up in disgust and stopped replying to him.

"It must be said that Jim Farry and I sometimes had differences of opinion. As I got to the end of my career, I knew I wasn't the fittest on the (referees') list, so I would use any excuse not to take the fitness test. I hated it, especially the 12 minute run. Anyway, Drew Herbertson, the Head of Refereeing Admin said, 'you know what Jim's like, you'll need to do it.' There was an absolute gale blowing, so I suggested I could take the test indoors, in the Kelvin Hall, which I did. That was on the Thursday but on Saturday the phone went and it was Drew, saying, 'Brian, there is bad news and good news. The bad news is there is a slight problem with your fitness test. It's come to Mr Farry's attention that you did it in the Kelvin Hall and he says you have to do it outside. The good news is that we've got a message from UEFA, saying you're doing the Under-21 European final between Sweden and Italy, with Hugh Dallas and Kenny Clark on the line and Hugh Williamson as the Fourth Official. However, Jim says you've got till Wednesday to do the test or he'll tell UEFA you're not available.'

"I had to go and do the test. Drew and Tom Wharton came to check that I did and I managed it, just… I never quite forgave Mr. Farry for that. However, we all went over and did the game and were given some rather nice gold medals as a momento."

Earlier in his career, Brian came across the influence that the Old Firm (allegedly) have over Scottish football…

"I had started doing some First Division games (this was when the First Division was the top Division in Scotland) when out of the blue I was earmarked for my first Old Firm game. Unfortunately, it didn't take place, or at least not when it was supposed to...

"What happened was that Rangers had played a European tie on the Wednesday night and wanted the game on Saturday postponed. The match was due to be at Hampden, because Ibrox was being renovated at the time. There had been a lot of snow, so I went and had a look at the pitch on the Thursday. It was thawing, but there were still some areas of snow, so the Queen's Park Secretary told me he'd get them cleared. I thought the game would be safe to go ahead at this point and said I'd come again the next day and inspect it again.

"Before I even went to inspect it, one of the young refs in my training area, called me to say, 'are you doing the Partick Thistle vs Rangers Glasgow Gup tie on Saturday? Willie Thornton (a director of Rangers) has called my Uncle Alex to say that he is going to the match and did he (my uncle) want to accompany him?' The implication was that Thornton knew that the Old Firm game was off. I wasn't best pleased and agreed that I would go and inspect the pitch again at 9.00 am the next morning (Friday). I went into the Scottish League office, which was near my work, and saw the Evening Times had a report which said the police had called the game off because the roads and ground outside Hampden were unsafe. Celtic were livid.

"I did get to referee that Old Firm match eventually. It was re-arranged to the end of the season. In the event, even though I gave a pen against Celtic, I had no problems with the match and Tom Wharton, who was at game as the Assessor, gave me a high mark for my performance.

"Another game in which Tiny Wharton was my Assessor was probably the biggest, most stressful one of my career. This was the 1991 League decider between Rangers and Aberdeen. It was the last game of the season and both teams were level on points and goal difference, but Aberdeen had scored two goals more. I wasn't actually down to do the game: Kenny Hope was, but he was injured so I got a call from the League and they told me that they were not going to announce who the referee was 'to give you some peace and quiet in the run-up.' Needless to say, the news came out pretty quickly and the peace and quiet failed to materialise. It was such a tense occasion and I'd be lying if I said I wasn't tense too. In truth, I was petrified I'd make an error and the league would be decided by it. Rangers won 2-0 and Tom awarded me 97 out of 100."

Success as a referee on the domestic front led, naturally, to international games - and a priceless souvenir of one of the world's greatest ever players…

"Jack Mowat was on the FIFA ref committee and I'm sure he was instrumental in my getting on the FIFA list. The first time I did a European tie was in Germany, between two German teams, Magdeburg and Schalke. Fredrick Ziegfield, an Austria referee, was the Supervisor and he picked me up from the airport and we went to see Bayern Munich playing Benfica that night. The referee for that match was the famous Clive Thomas from Wales and he had one

of those nights when nothing goes right. The following night, Herr Ziegfield said, 'you saw how not to referee last night...

"I was also very proud to be on the panel of referees for the European Championship in Italy in 1980. I was the youngest referee there and probably the last of the 12 refs to be used in a game. My match was West Germany vs Greece and I had Tommy Muirhead and David Syme as linesmen. At that time, UEFA wanted referees to work with an agreed group of linemen so we could all get used to each other's styles. Our 'team' did a famous friendly at Wembley between England v Argentina, which was possibly the first time the two countries had met since the infamous rammy in the 1966 World Cup. England had a host of famous names, including Ray Clemence, Ray Wilkins and Kevin Keegan. The Argentines had their own famous names, including Daniel Passarella, Alberto Tarantini and also a young man from Argentinos Juniors called Diego Maradona. There were 92,000 in the stadium to watch England win 3-1, but Maradona was amazing, with one run seemingly a forerunner for his more famous 'goal of the century' in the 1986 World Cup. After the game, he came in to the referee's dressing room and asked for the match ball. I was happy to give him it, but I asked for his shirt in exchange. I still have it – an outstanding momento of an outrageously talented footballer.

"I was also involved in the early North American Soccer League. Phil Woosnam, the Commissioner of the League, brought four European referees to the States to try to improve the standard and I was one of them. We had 30 games in 90 days and went all over the country, seeing all these fabulous players like Pele, George Best and Franz Beckenbauer. We did get some time off, but I was knackered. Then I got a call from Ernie Walker (the Secretary of the SFA at the time), asking when I'd be back. To cut a long story short, he said you need to get back for August because it's Jock Stein's testimonial and he wants you to referee it. It was Celtic v Liverpool, in front of a full house, with Danny McGrain captaining Celtic. The Liverpool captain was the young lad I'd previously seen playing Under-15 football for Possil. I've still got a photo of all of them taken at the game."

Another trip was to provide Brian with a bit of a headache...

"The North of Scotland Referee's Association was complaining their members weren't getting enough games, so we got all the FIFA refs together and it was agreed that we'd go and do Highland League games and they could do some in the central belt. I did an Inverness derby. Jim Leishman was the boss of Inverness Thistle and had just been done for drink driving. I was about to toss the coin at the start of the game when there was a wave of laughter. Here's Jim, riding a bicycle onto the track and waving at all and sundry. After the game, the linesmen and I were invited into the boardroom. One of the directors was the MD of Tomatin Distillery. It just so happened that it was my birthday that day and I'd arranged to take my wife to Dunblane Hydro. Unfortunately, we were in the boardroom for quite a long time and then they gave me a bottle of Tomatin and six cans for the train journey. Next thing I remember was being woken by the train guard, asking if I was going to stay on the train all night. I responded that I was getting off at Dunblane. 'That'll be difficult,' he replied, 'we're at Glasgow Queen Street now.' It's fair to say that my wife wasn't amused.

"Mind you, one other referee who was doing the Highland games didn't wake up until Newcastle. At this point, Jim Farry got to hear about it all and the experiment was stopped!"

And finally, Brian told us of the time he had to step out of the crowd to help officiate in a match. However, unlike those of us who have run the line on a Sunday to help our sons and daughters' teams on the local park, the time he did it was at a slightly larger venue…

"Rangers were due to play Aberdeen in the Cup final, but prior to that they had a league match at Ibrox. Before anyone starts any conspiracy theories, I was there as a guest of one of my business clients. Alan Ferguson was the ref and at half-time I could see that one of the linesmen was really struggling. Sure enough, an announcement came across the PA, asking if there were any qualified referees in the crowd. Well, there are usually about 50,000 people at both Ibrox and Parkhead who think they know what the ref should do but, on this occasion, I was probably the only one who could genuinely answer 'yes' to that question. They found me some kit and out I went. I have to say that when I came out of the tunnel, I got the biggest boo I've ever received in my professional career."

Debut Ref wins no friends at Gayfield
Sandy Roy

Most Scots will know Baxters of Fochabers, the famous family firm that makes tinned, traditional Scottish foods. However, most will probably not know that the firm is actually based in Mosstodloch, on the other side of the bridge from Fochabers. Baxters of Mosstodloch doesn't have the same kind of ring to it though…

At this point, you will be wondering what on earth this has to do with refereeing. Well, Sandy Roy began our conversation by telling me he was from Fochabers, before then confessing that he was actually born and raised in Mosstodloch. And, while perhaps not quite as famous as Baxters, Sandy's profile in Scottish football in the 1980s and 1990s was undoubtedly very high. Like many of the others interviewed for this book, he was keen on playing football. Unfortunately, also like many of the others, he wasn't, by his own admission, good enough to play beyond the juvenile and amateur levels.

As the oldest of five boys, when Sandy had the chance to go to university, he turned it down, concerned about the pressure it would put on his parents to make his siblings follow suit. Instead, he got a job…

"I was a trainee Chartered Surveyor and, because I didn't go to university, I had to do a correspondence course (there was no internet in those days), *so I sat in the spare room in our house, studying for four nights a week, six months of the year. In my first year, I only played juvenile football, but then played at amateur level after that. My weight fluctuated terribly: I put on two stones when I was studying, then lost them by playing – and did that on and off for the next six years until I qualified.*

"By this time, I was married and we'd moved to Fochabers. Every Saturday night, I'd go to the town centre and wait for the van to draw up and the bundled copies of the Green Final (Aberdeen Journals' weekend sports paper) *to be thrown out to the guy who sold them. Someone else who waited religiously for the Green Final was John Grant, a local referee, and we would chat away while we were looking out for the van. I'd ask him what game he'd done and he'd tell me about it. One day he asked, 'what are you doing about football – are you playing again?' I replied that I was hoping to get fit and start playing games. 'If you want to get fit, why not join us?' John said, 'there's six referees who train in Elgin every week and you'd be welcome to come along.'*

"I did that and then, of course, John suggested that I take the refereeing exam. My initial response was, 'no thanks, that's no for me,' but then he challenged me to say if I thought I could pass a test on the laws of the game. I was up for the challenge, so I did the course and passed it."

Despite having been led up the refereeing path, Sandy still wanted to get back to playing football. He was now captain of a local team, but he was also asked to run the line in the Highland League. At the end of his first season as an official, he was one of the linesmen for the match that would determine that year's Highland League championship, between (Inverness) Clachnacuddin and Elgin City. However, when he went to his manager and asked if he might not be considered for two midweek games due to his having to run the line in Highland League matches, he was disappointed to discover that he was subsequently dropped from the team…

"Basically, I took the huff and went into refereeing full-time. My career started officially in 1973 and, after that one season as a linesman in the Highland League, I had two seasons refereeing in Junior football and two years later was promoted to Grade 3a; then, in 1976, I started refereeing (as opposed to running the line) in the Highland League. I did two years at Grade 3a and then four at Grade 2, followed by 16 years at Grade 1, before retiring in 1998. They were called 'Grades' in those days, but nowadays the levels are called 'Categories' - it's the same thing really.

"My first game at Grade 1 was a League Cup tie between Arbroath and Alloa Athletic on 14th August 1982. I still have the headline from the Arbroath Herald, 'Debut Ref wins no friends at Gayfield.'"

Alloa, obviously, won, much to the delight of their young manager, Alex Totten, although in the years to come he would be less enamoured of one of Sandy's decisions in arguably the biggest match of his (Alex's) career. In the meantime, Sandy got on with gaining experience as a top-level referee and developing his career across Scotland – all the while getting to know and understand how football managers' minds work…

"Alex Smith did wonders for me. He was at Stirling Albion when they had just installed one of the first artificial pitches in Scotland and I remember arriving early, as I tended to do for most games. He saw me and asked me in for a cup of tea. Afterwards, whenever I was doing a game with one of Alex's teams, he'd always make a point of coming across for a chat. Some other managers are the same, including Jim Jeffries and Billy Brown, whose partnership I helped cement when they were starting out at Montrose, although they didn't actually think that at the time!

"Back then, if managers got into trouble with the SFA, there was an automatic £1,000 fine for the Premier managers, with a sliding scale of punishment down the leagues. Anyway, Jim and Billy were out of order that day, so I ordered them to the stand. However, they just climbed out of the dugout and sat in the front row and carried on instructing their team. Not long after, they moved to Falkirk and were given a Premier-sized fine, even though they had been at a lower Division club when it happened. Years later, I was at Dunfermline, acting as an Observer for the SFA and I took my grandson with me. We were in the boardroom, when Billy came in and I introduced him to the wee boy. Billy said that he and Jim recalled the incident frequently and they realised they had learned a lesson that day that helped them on their way as a managerial duo. Mind you, they weren't quite so polite on the day, and for some time afterwards. Today, though, if and when I meet them, it's all behind us and we get on as friends."

One other famous manager whom many referees in this book recall with affection (mostly) was Jim McLean…

"Jim McLean gave every referee zero points in his report to the SFA, but away from the match action he was a real gent. Referees always get two comps, and one day Jim spotted me when I arrived, early as usual, in my car at Tannadice. My wife and daughter were with me and they were going to use my complimentary tickets to get in, but Jim insisted that they come up to the directors' box. Jim must have had a touchline ban at the time, because when my wife and daughter sat down in the box he was there and they had to listen as he ranted and raved at me for the entire 90 minutes.

"Another time I was on the line at Tannadice and Jim, banned still (or again) from the touchline, was in a little glass-fronted box just above the tunnel. I was, as you have to, keeping an eye (and ear) on the United coaching team in the dugout as Jim was relaying his instructions by phone. Jim had sent a message, containing all the usual invective, about a substitution and the other coaches were outside the dugout trying to get the player ready. I could see the sub getting his track-suit off and knew I'd have to check his boots, so I made sure I was near the dugout. Unfortunately for the coaching staff, Jim had changed his mind and was frantically calling up the dugout again. In a state of total exasperation at the seeming inefficiency of his staff, he opened the glass window in his cubby-hole and bellowed, Will some **** answer that fucking phone!' I'm running up and down the line as this is going on, trying desperately not to piss myself laughing.

"One Highland League manager who became a great personal friend was Bobby Wilson. When he became Keith Manager, he stayed in the same housing development as we did and to get to my house I had to drive past Bobby's. One Saturday, on my way home from my match, I drove past Bobby's house as usual and then some 30 minutes later I got a phone call. 'Can I come for a word?' Bobby asked, 'and do you mind if Jessie (his wife) *comes too?' I said, 'of course,' and then the next thing I knew the milkman was arriving to deliver the milk, at 4.00 am. We've been friends ever since and after almost every match we'd meet up and talk football into the wee small hours."*

Sandy had to move to Aberdeen with his work. In Aberdeen, Sandy's career coincided with the great Alex Ferguson era at Pittodrie, but like most referees across the country, he was rarely scheduled to officiate at his local team.

"I only ever did one first-team match at Pittodrie. It was in 1984, my first season at Grade 1 and I remember it had just been announced that Gordon Strachan was leaving to go to Manchester United. The only other first team game I did involving Aberdeen was at Dundee, also in 1984. I was moving job from Elgin and starting on the Monday in Aberdeen. It was not one of my better games. Fergie said to me afterwards, 'it's a good job you'll not be getting Aberdeen games now you've moved.' Then, later that season, Maureen Cooper, who organised the referees' match schedules, called me at 4 pm one Monday afternoon, asking, 'can you help us out, there is a reserve game in Aberdeen tonight, against Dundee, but the ref has called off - can you manage?' I said I could, nipped home, got my kit - but didn't have

time for any tea - and arrived at Pittodrie for 6.00 pm. There I met Fergie, who said, 'I'm really grateful you've helped us out. I'm getting some of the reserve squad through into the first team and I want to see how they get on.' I was pleased to have been able to help him and when we got started the game was going smoothly, from my point of view at least. Then Dundee scored three minutes from half time. Nothing was said as we came off the pitch and I and the linesmen went away to our dressing room and the players went to their rooms. Inside Pittodrie, the away team dressing room is right next to the referee's so after the break, I went first to knock on Dundee's door to tell them to get out onto the field. I then went to knock on the Aberdeen door, opening it and saying, 'right lads, back on the park.' Alex Ferguson was standing over one of the players, lambasting him for having cost his side the goal. The last thing I heard was, 'your fucking wage is going to...' before he realised I was there and came storming towards me. I simply said, 'Mr Ferguson, just get your team out please.' While I was waiting for the teams Fergie was the last out. There are swing doors in that part of the corridor and he simply belted them, before telling me, 'you better get a grip.' I kept clear of him for a few minutes and nothing else was said during or after the game. Then, a few weeks later, I was out with my family for lunch and Fergie and his family were a few tables away from us. They finished their meal before us and he came across and said that he hoped we were enjoying the food. Once we were finished, I went to settle up, only to discover that he'd paid our bill. Some years later, in 1990, I went to Wembley to see Manchester United – they are my team - take on Crystal Palace in the FA Cup final. I had never been to Wembley and wanted to enjoy the whole experience, so we went down Wembley Way to see the teams arrive. All of a sudden, there on a balcony, I saw Fergie and Archie Knox waving down to me. Any time I see him, he'll come and speak to me, no matter the occasion: that's the mark of the man."

I then asked Sandy about his memories of one man many pundits reckon was one the greatest referees of this era – Willie Miller...

"I obviously didn't do many Aberdeen games, but know plenty of people who did. Willie was undoubtedly a moaner on the pitch, but the thing about players like him, or indeed managers like Fergie, and they'll all admit this, is that when they shout about a decision they are not really complaining about that decision. What they want to do is to try to plant a seed of doubt in your mind, hoping to get into your head for the next one. I think they really believe their complaints will register and they'll get the benefit the next time. I'm happy for them to think that: I don't believe referees act like this, not then or nowadays.

"Willie also features in one of my favourite stories about referees. Many will remember Andrew Waddell, who as well as being a referee was also a pathologist. According to legend, Andrew famously replied to Billy McNeil's angry comment of 'I'll see you later,' with the words, 'The next time I see you I hope it's in my professional capacity.' Anyway, I, along with every other referee in Scotland, had to go to Glasgow, or sometimes Wishaw, for the annual fitness test. We had to be there for 10.00 am, which didn't go down well with those os us from those areas of Scotland that are distant from the west. Part of the test involved shuttle runs and Andrew Waddell was brilliant at them. On being quizzed about why he was particularly good that day, Andrew pointed out that he had been reffing Aberdeen vs Celtic

the previous weekend and, 'I spent the whole game seeing Willie Miller coming at me and running in the opposite direction, only to then see Roy Aitken coming the other way and I'd turn and run back the way I'd come.'"

While in Aberdeen, Sandy met and became great friends with Gus Stewart, another Chartered Surveyor and, at the time, a director of St Johnstone. The two of them went to Perth to watch a game that became very famous and led to a black-bordered, front-page article in the Press and Journal…

"I went with Gus to see St Johnstone vs Aberdeen in the famous game where Saints went nap and won 5-0. Another friend from the construction industry, Stewart Milne, later to become chairman of Aberdeen, had just become a father. A few months later, Gus sent Stewart a specially designed Christmas Card, featuring five sets of nappies. Contrary to popular rumour, although I did travel in Gus's car, I wasn't the referee at that game.

"I have a lot of memories of Saints. I was the ref when Walter Smith and Alex Totten had their handbags dispute in the tunnel and the police got involved. Tayside Police had a reputation for interfering in football matches (as reported by other referees in this book). *That was a widely-reported incident, but it paled into insignificance with another match I refereed at McDiarmid - the famous game when Aggie gave as good as she got from Graeme Souness. I did the last ever match at Muirton too, when Ayr spoiled Saints' party by winning 2-1. At that time, there was a tradition at Saints that there were always three miniatures of Grouse in the dressing room for officials at the end of the game, but, perhaps because Saints lost, when we got back after that match, we discovered someone had been in and removed them. Geoff Brown wrote to me to apologise, but that was the only negative experience I had at Perth."*

Sandy also refereed one Highland League player who went on to become a referee himself – and to feature in this book…

"I refereed Alfie Smith and was one of only two refs to send him off! I don't know if that influenced him to become a referee. I never bothered whether I was popular or not; if you talk to Alfie he'll agree, but once he became a referee we got on very well and are friends to this day, so he obviously doesn't hold a grudge. The local Aberdeen Referees' Association was a really friendly group for the most part. We used to play games against the Moray and Banff Association and also the West Lothian refs. We would always get a Grade 1 ref to do the match and then had a dinner-dance afterwards."

Not holding grudges or worrying unduly about whether you are popular are probably very desirable traits in a referee. Certainly, in one case, this was true for Sandy…

"After his team won on my debut as a referee, Alex Totten then took me off his Christmas card list after the 1997 Scottish Cup final. In fact, I don't think he would go out of his way to speak to me to this day. I was on the line, with Hugh Dallas in the middle. Paul Wright had put Kilmarnock one up but in the second half Neil Oliver thought he had scored for

Falkirk, only for my flag to disallow the goal for offside. The Falkirk fans were jeering me for the rest of the game. Alex is Falkirk through and through and I think he still believes I was wrong. However, TV evidence shows that I wasn't."

Since retiring, Sandy, like many other senior refs of his era, has moved into supervising and assessing young referees as they make their way in the game. One key part of his advice is that there is no point crying over spilt milk, and that once you've made a mistake the game won't wait for you to think about it so you have to get on with the match. He's also confident that the future of refereeing is in good hands…

"Yes, I am confident about the refs coming through. We are more professional than we've ever been. It's time consuming being a referee because, unlike in my day, we have almost unlimited access to videos, DVDs, etc. You can look at footage of every match, but that's a good thing because you can learn quickly from watching lots of different scenarios from real games. Also, refs today are under more pressure compared to my time, especially with social media. They are also fitter. I trained twice a week officially and twice more unofficially, but they are all training at least four days a week now. There are no full-time refs in Scotland officially, but, in reality, they are more or less all professional. Willie Collum started when he was 14. I think Nick Walsh isn't even 30, but he's already at the top, doing international football. They both have a long time yet in the game.

"I wasn't a great player, but if I had been then my career would have been more or less over in my 30s. However, I was a Premier League referee and it extended my footballing career by decades. I didn't finish until I was 50, so I probably got an extra 20 years. I loved every minute."

Socrates made a point of giving me his jersey
Doug Yeats

Like many of those who got into refereeing, Doug Yeats (the Irish spelling of his surname is due to his Irish ancestry) was an enthusiastic footballer in his youth. However, football was not his first sport. Instead, he was a swimmer, and in particular a very good water polo player. For those who don't know that sport, it's very competitive, very physical, ruthless and aggressive and it involves a lot of off-the-ball skulduggery. It's probably ideal preparation for being a football referee…

"I played for the Dundee NCR water polo team and we were quite good, competing in the Scottish Cup, but I always had a hankering to be a footballer. I worked in Dewar's, in Perth. I was a cooper by trade and we had a works' team and a kickabout most lunchtimes. I played in the team and there were some good players, so much so that we moved up the local amateur and juvenile leagues. Unfortunately, I got a bad knee injury and knew I had to stop playing. One of the guys at work, whose name was Willie Young, was a referee (not the famous one from Ayrshire) and he persuaded me to go to the classes.

"The refereeing classes were held at Bell's Sports Centre and I went there on Monday nights and then refereed Under-18 matches the following Saturday. For those who know Perth, these were on the Inch. I always seemed to be on Pitch No. 6, refereeing teams like Jeanfield Swifts and Railway Athletic Under-18s.

"This was in 1971. I was a St Johnstone fan and at that time Saints, under Willie Ormond, had a great team, but once I started refereeing I was no longer an active supporter. I finished that first season doing Under-18s and then had two seasons doing Perthshire amateurs, making as few mistakes as I could. In my day, the amateurs were fairly respectful, but every new generation has different values and different ways of conducting themselves. It's very different nowadays.

"From about 1975, I started to do Junior football. I remember Stewart Duff, a left back with Luncarty Juniors. He was a constructive player who preferred to play the ball out of defence and not just lump it up the park. Years later, I used to meet him on the few occasions I refereed at McDiarmid Park, when Stewart was the St Johnstone Managing Director.

"I found the Junior game a bit more organised, not unnaturally, compared to the amateurs. The games – the play – was more structured, which made it easier to referee. I did a lot of Scottish Junior Cup ties, mainly in the west, including the Ayrshire derbies, and in 1981 I was delighted to be awarded the Scottish Junior Cup final. I found the Juniors not as bad as everyone says: there was certainly full commitment and they were far more physical than games in the east, but they were great games to referee and to watch. Another way thing that was different about going to a match in a place like Cumnock was the size of the crowd. The crowds for these Ayrshire games were a bit of a culture shock after the small crowds I was used to in the east. I had two years with the Juniors and then moved up to Senior level, as a

Class 3 official. I'd go and watch reserve football, which was often played on Monday nights back then, and I tried to pick games with refs I thought I could learn from. If you saw a ref who was good you tried to adopt some of his techniques and learn from the way he dealt with the players. Jim Renton and Bob Valentine were coming through at that time and I thought they were good – which they were!"

What, I wondered, was the difference between Junior and Senior football, from a referee's perspective?

"It's two different worlds. I really saw this as I was coming up the refereeing ladder, because at Category 3 level I was still refereeing Junior matches but also running the line for Senior games, doing midweek matches, reserves, everything. There was a lot more pressure, partly because I was still being monitored as a ref in the Junior games while trying to hone my skills as a linesman in the Seniors.

"It took me 10 years from when I started to get to Category 1. My first Senior game at that level was between the Glasgow and the Edinburgh Jags – Partick Thistle vs Meadowbank Thistle. Terry Christie, of duffle-coat fame, was the Meadowbank manager. He was fine with me, but he was, as all managers are, totally biased towards his own team.

"In your first season as a Grade 1 ref you get given lower league games and then, if you are considered to be making good progress, you are moved up to the top Division. The Premier Division was introduced in my time, in 1975-76, and for a referee it really was going into the big league. I'd describe it as like going from first gear to top gear in a car in one move of the gear-lever. For a start, the pressure from the top players is relentless and, of course, you are under far more scrutiny from the media. Even then, when there were fewer games televised, there were cameras at more matches in the top flight than at the lower Division grounds, so any mistakes were widely publicised. Of course, it's far worse nowadays: they have so many cameras and they play back incidents over and over again, in slow-motion. That's not how the referee sees it during a match.

"Once I got there, I had ten years at Grade 1 but then I had to retire at 50: those were the rules. It meant people were going off the list who were more than fit and had a world of experience. That, in my view, was wrong, because for referees there is nothing that can replace all their hard-won experience. Sensibly, there is no enforced retiral age now."

What did you do when you stopped refereeing?

"I am still involved, working with the SFA as a Referee Observer. The SFA allocate a game for me, usually on a weekly basis, and I go and watch - and assess - the referee. I had my share of doing Premiership and Championship matches, but now I'm more involved in the development of younger refs. It's important work, because the SFA needs to know who can move up a Grade, who needs to move down or who should stay where they are...

"As an Observer, you go along and watch the ref, then submit the report to the SFA and it is then distributed to the local Referees' Association. It's a bit of a long-drawn out process, but a lot happens at the local level. Every Referees' Association has a Minor Grade Advisory Panel and once an aspiring referee has enrolled and passed the entrance exam, their progress is monitored and their fitness checked. As young refs get more experienced and get better reports then they gradually get more difficult games and advance up the system."

Why, I wondered, do more professional players not go on to become referees?

"As I said before, nothing replaces experience and ex-footballers have that in abundance. In my day it was harder for a player to become a referee because the game was much more physical. Unlike today, they were able to make tackles - and were more than capable of doing so. This meant that if they tried to become referees, their interpretation of what was fair and what wasn't could be flawed at times. I remember the late Willie Coburn, who was St Johnstone's left back, tried to get into refereeing. Willie was a brilliant tackler: the proverbial hard but fair; however, when he was refereeing, he'd see a tackle and think, 'nothing wrong with that,' when he should have been giving a free kick. That applied to lots of different aspects of the game: ex-pros saw the match through the players' eyes, not through the strict requirements of the rules.

"Now, the interpretation of a tackle within the Laws of the game has changed completely. It only requires minimal contact and it's a foul. To my mind, the pendulum has swung too far. The concentration is on speed and physical fitness. And while football is a physical game, there has to be contact at times. Unfortunately, a lot of players don't know how to tackle today. It's a lost art. However, that means that, in some ways, it's easier for a modern player to become a referee.

"For example, last weekend (October 2021), I covered a game at Kirriemuir where there was a youngish referee officiating. It was Jamie McCunnie, who played for a number of clubs, including Dundee United, Ross County and Hartlepool before having a short career as a manager with Junior side Broughty Athletic. Having made the switch from playing and managing into refereeing he knew what was happening and you could see his ability to deal with any incident on the pitch. He was never flustered: he had been in these situations before, and at a higher level than the one he was refereeing, and you could just see his overall experience coming to the surface. He communicated so well with the players, on their, and his, level. It was a joy to see."

Given what he'd just said, I asked Doug how referees learn to communicate with the players.

"There is quite a lot of reverse psychology. Good referees know that the Laws are there for the guidance of wise men and the strict obedience of fools. If you go strictly by the rules there wouldn't be a game, you'd spend 90 minutes dishing out yellow and red cards. Man-management is vital and that's where experience comes in. If you watch a Premiership referee and then go to see a referee handling a Second Division match, you'll often see a totally different way of managing the game. Less experienced refs sometimes overreact.

"In my day, you got some respect and, believe it or not, there were still a lot of people who frowned on the use of bad language. Although we weren't supposed to, some referees would swear at players. Now, of course, they would get into trouble from the authorities. Of course, there was a lot of bad language in my time, but my tack was always to say something like, 'I didn't quite hear you - would you like to repeat that?' That usually did the trick. I remember Richard Gough, when he was at Dundee United, swore at me and I said, 'Richard, is that the best you can do?' It immediately put him on the back foot and he replied, "Sorry Dougie, I got a wee bit carried away there…'

"There were some guys who wouldn't be managed and you had to revert to yellow cards. Willie Young famously said there were some players he had an agreement with: namely that he never communicated with them apart from with yellow or red cards. There is a degree of truth in that. I had experience of certain players who seemed to be almost trying to get booked. Believe it or not, there were even a few who, once they'd received the yellow card, would say, 'thanks ref, I can now get on with the game.' Often, they would have been following their manager's instructions ('just sort out that centre forward early doors') but once they were booked it concentrated their minds and they could focus on playing.

"Of course, the managers were a different kettle of fish. They didn't always appreciate what you did for them though. I remember when John Blackley was manager at Hibs, I had to send him off. I had awarded what he thought was an offside goal: the linesman had not given it but I overruled him. John went berserk; basically, he lost it and the torrent of swear words was off the scale. I had to go into the technical area and tell him, 'you are up the tunnel.' When his case came up in front of the SFA, I was asked, 'did Mr Blackley swear at any time?' I replied, 'I never heard a swear word once.' John wasn't present at the meeting so he was unaware of this, but I saved him a £500 fine.

"Other managers presented different challenges but there were ones I had no problems with, including Jim McLean. He was absolutely superb. I often had conversations with him off the park, where he was a different guy from his public persona. Just before I was promoted to the Grade 1 list, I was running the line at a reserve game at Tannadice. Jim said to me, 'I hear you're being elevated to Category 1; as you live in Perth are we likely to get you as a ref?' I said, 'it's highly likely, but you may regret it.'

"Not too long afterwards, I refereed my first game at Tannadice. Now, as a youngster with Guildtown Amateurs, I'd played against Paul Sturrock when he was a young laddie at Vale of Atholl. I was in the United dressing room, inspecting the players' boots, when Jim chipped in, telling the United squad, 'This is today's match referee, he used to spend his amateur career trying to maim Paul Sturrock.' That was Jim trying his hand at referee management but it clearly didn't work because after the match, remembering my comment from the reserve match, he came up to me and said, 'you were right. I regret it.' Another sadly departed Scottish great was also at Tannadice. Walter Smith was an absolute gem and, like wee Jim, sadly missed."

Doug also enjoyed trips to Europe and further afield, where he learned that not every great footballer looked after his health as much as he perhaps should, although in the event, this rebounded to Doug's benefit.

"I was the senior Assistant ref to Brian McGinlay for a match between Fiorentina and Fenerbahçe in 1984 and we had just gone down the underground tunnel from the pitch that led into the dressing room to inspect the players' boots. Socrates, the great Brazilian midfielder, who was also a doctor incidentally, was smoking a cigarette. As I was checking his boots, he suddenly said, 'you take cigarette.' Giancarlo De Sisti, the Fiorentina coach, was coming down the tunnel, so I took the cigarette and, to my amazement, Signore De Sisti asked me if it was mine. 'Yes,' I said, 'Sometimes I get nervous before a game and have a cigarette.' After the match, which Fiorentina won, Socrates made a point of coming to the referees' changing room to give me his jersey, which I have to this day."

Being a local Perth boy, Doug rarely was on duty for matches involving St Johnstone. However, he did officiate for Saints in some notable games, and one especially crucial one…

"I remember a fixture at Muirton: it was one of the very few times I was allocated Saints. It was a match against Arbroath and it was in the season when the club were really struggling, just before Geoff Brown took over. I was asked to inspect the pitch the day before but it was brick hard and unplayable. However, the club said, 'we're playing tomorrow, so come back and have a look at it then as it may have improved.' I thought there was no way we could play the game: there was still hard frost and the forecast was for no change. Anyway, I turned up at the ground and the directors came to meet me. I said the game couldn't go ahead, but they took me to one side and said, 'it has to, otherwise the club will run out of money.' Then Arbroath turned up. Jimmy Bone was their manager and he, not unnaturally, asked me how the pitch was looking. 'It's fair,' I lied. Jimmy went out and had a look, before coming back in and saying, 'it's bloody terrible.' I explained the situation and he said, 'fine, we'll play.' Before the match, I usually had a chat with the linesmen, giving them any instructions necessary, but that day I simply said, 'whatever you do, don't fall on your arse – that will give the game away.' Fortunately, for the players and for St Johnstone, no-one was injured and the match was without major incident.

"I was delighted to be asked to do the friendly match between Saints and Manchester United – the official opening of McDiarmid Park. Although famous for the floodlight failure, on the park I had a wee problem with United's Mark Hughes. He wasn't really entering into the spirit of things and was, to put it mildly, rumbustious. He wouldn't take a telling and kept saying, 'it's just bumps and bruises.' After the match, Sir Matt Busby and Bobby Charlton came to see me. Sir Matt said, 'thank you Mr Referee for handling the game the way you did. We realise you could easily have sent off Mr Hughes so thank you for not doing so…"

At the end of the current (2021-22) season, Doug Yeats is retiring from football. He will then have been involved in one way or another in refereeing for 51 years - a fantastic achievement.

What do you mean, you've been shot?
Louis Thow

Ayrshire seems to have something in the soil that produces top class referees and footballers. Louis Thow's dad was one of the youngest, if not the youngest, lad to be capped for Scotland Schoolboys, at the age of 12, a fortnight prior to his 13th birthday. He signed for Ayr United at the age of 17 and played with them for three years prior to the war but, like so many other talented players of his generation, the conflict ruined his chances of a career in football. Latterly, he became a director of the club and then chairman and, equally importantly, he passed his love of the game on to Louis…

"I played youth and amateur football locally until I was about 22 or 23, but to be honest I wasn't particularly enjoying it, so I packed it in. I was studying for my Quantity Surveyor exams at the time and then there was a coup at Somerset Park and my dad was off the board, so football wasn't high on the agenda for a wee while. Then I got married at the age of 25 and about three weeks after our honeymoon I was told by my wife that there was a refereeing class in Kilmarnock, so I went and did it and the rest is history! The course was run by Bill Quinn and a Class 1 ref called Hugh Alexander. Both these gentlemen had a huge influence on my career. After six weeks I was given a match and I quickly discovered that going from a class to a game is like passing your driving test and then learning to drive on the open road. All of a sudden, the theory and practice are confronted with the reality of the big bad world and you have to learn fast.

"I began with school and youth games, often two on the same day, and then I suppose I just quietly made my way up the ranks. In some ways, it was just something to do on a Saturday afternoon, but I was enjoying it and in my fourth season I was given six amateur games, but to complicate things I'd also been put forward for some Junior matches by the Ayrshire Juniors' Secretary, Matt Speirs (who, after his death in 2019, was described by the 'Pie and Bovril' website as, "quite simply the best Regional Secretary Scottish Junior Football ever had"). *I remember doing an amateur game at Symington between two local teams and it was horsing down with rain. I saw this gent with a brolly standing by an oak tree at the side of the field and at the end of the match he tiptoed onto the park, telling me he was the Secretary of Ayrshire Amateurs and that he would take my name off their referees' ballot. I was then pitched into Ayrshire Junior football, with my first game at Glenafton, where Kello were the visitors, followed by a trip to Beith. I realised quickly that this wasn't amateur football, but I continued to make steady progress to Grade 3, which meant I was able to run the line in Senior games while continuing to referee the Juniors. I was then promoted to Class 2, which allowed me to referee the top-level Junior games. I did nine Auchinleck vs Cumnock games and once got hit on the head by a beer can at a Junior quarter final at Barrhead. I trooped off at half-time and was instructed by the Secretary to go to hospital get stitched up. The lad who threw the can was caught and got a £200 fine. I remember my dad telling me my head was never that valuable. There were a few games in those days where the Ayrshire Juniors lived up to their reputation. The match ballots for referees used to come by post and I recall one time I was put down for one game where the police had been called to a riot at the*

ground a few weeks before. My wife made a point of asking before I went to training that week if my life insurance was paid up...

"At the same time, I was trying to make my way in refereeing, I was also earning my living in the family glazing business. It was while I was on a building site one morning that I got my big break. Campbell Ogilvie , whom most people know from his time with Rangers but was then at the Scottish Football League, called and said, 'what are you doing tonight – can you do a game in Glasgow?' On being told that I could, Campbell then told me it was at Ibrox where there was a reserve match between the Old Firm.

As we shall see, that game went well, leading to more high-profile matches, but sometimes Old Firm games, even reserve ones, proved, literally, to be a pain in the backside

"The day after that match at Ibrox, I got a call from the SFA, this time from Peter Donald, who asked me if I was available to do another Old Firm reserve match as part of the same team of officials who had done the game at Ibrox. They had obviously thought that we did alright, so we went along to Parkhead and this time there was an incident that I'll not forget.

"It was just before half-time, when Rangers' Eric Morris, an Ayrshire lad who never really made it at Ibrox but went on to a good Junior career, ran up to me. 'I've been shot!' he told me. 'What do you mean, shot?' I asked, to which he replied, 'in my arse.' 'Are you taking the mick Eric?' I asked, and being assured that he wasn't I realised that I needed to investigate this alleged assault. The idea that someone had managed to get a weapon into ground was obviously very worrying. I got the managers out of the dugout, told the police who were there and then we had to investigate the source of Eric's pain... We found nothing and the game proceeded, fortunately, without further incident."

After refereeing at Class 2 level for three seasons, Louis then had three games as a trial for Senior football. He passed them with flying colours and in 1979-80 became a Class 1 referee, leading not just to top-flight Scottish games but also matches in Europe. Officiating on the continent meant receiving gifts from the clubs involved, some of which were well meant but not well thought out…

"My first game as a Class 1 referee was Stirling Albion vs Motherwell. Ally McLeod was the manager of Motherwell and Alex Smith was manager of Stirling. I can remember some of my games, but not all of them. My cousin, Willie Young, has a record of every game he's been involved in but I never recorded all my matches. I had 17 years at Class 1, including trips abroad as an Assistant as well as a referee. You usually got presents from the home team in Europe and I remember going to a match at KFC Winterslag, who are based in Genk, in Belgium. It's a coal-mining area and the club gave us a miner's lamp. It was very much a case of coals to Ayrshire: the pits were still open in Scotland then and miners' lamps were ten-a-penny,

Like every official from his era, Louis was fortunate to referee some of the exceptional talent that played in our country in the 1980s and 1990s and in doing so he saw some young lads coming through who would go on to become big stars.

"I remember doing a Hibs vs St Johnstone match in my second season. Ally McCoist was at Saints, just before his move to Sunderland and, although he was only 17, he was clearly already a very good player. I also remember doing a youth international match at Somerset Park between Scotland and Northern Ireland where McCoist was in the team along with Davie Bowman, Davie Moyes and Gary Mackay. There was only one lad in the Northern Ireland team who went on to make an impression, but it was certainly a big one. This was Norman Whiteside, who subsequently became the youngest player to take part in a World Cup as well as the youngest player to score in a League Cup and FA Cup final and, as if that wasn't enough, is the youngest player to score a senior goal for Manchester United.

"I did that game at Somerset Park because it was usually the case that a local referee would be given such matches. There was one season in England where, for some reason, there were weekends when a team didn't have a game and the northern sides would come up to Dumfries to play Queen of the South. I refereed a friendly in 1984 although the rain was chucking it down and we really shouldn't have been playing, but it went ahead anyway. There was a No. 8 for Newcastle who stood out: the Queen's players couldn't get the ball off him. I went into the Newcastle dressing room at half-time to get the teams out and he was being physically sick. I was slightly concerned and asked if he was suffering from hypothermia. 'No,' he replied, 'we have just come back from a trip to Mallorca and I had too good a time.' That was the second time I'd met Paul Gascoigne. The first time was when I refereed at the Ayr International Youth Tournament. He was playing for Cramlington, who brought a team up for the competition.

"There were some fabulous players on both sides of the Old Firm when I was refereeing. Paul McStay, Danny McGrain and Roy Aitken at Celtic and Davie Cooper, Peter Huistra and Butch Wilkins at Rangers. The latter was a real gentleman, always courteous on and off the pitch. Davie Cooper was probably the most skilful of them all in my opinion. I first came across him when he was breaking through at Clydebank, when I refereed a match very late in the season. I remember it was in early May and Cooper had his opposite right-back on toast. I particularly remember it because I was a right back when I played and I really felt for the lad! Davie was one of those players who are constantly at the referee. He wasn't foul-mouthed, but he really nipped my head sometimes.

"The one game which didn't go well was obviously the one with the Neil Simpson – Ian Durrant incident at Pittodrie in 1988, but I also did games that made the headlines for all the right reasons. Probably the biggest shock in any game I refereed was when newly-promoted St Johnstone hammered a star-studded Aberdeen side 5-0. In that match, I awarded a penalty to St Johnstone and there is a photograph in my archives of me running to position for the kick and Theo Snelders, the Aberdeen 'keeper, snarling at me while I'm doing my best not to pay any attention to him.

"The other big shock result I remember was when I refereed the game in which Forfar beat Hearts in the Scottish Cup. This match was in February 1982. The only goal of the game was scored just after half-time by Steve Hancock, who, ironically, had once been on Hearts' books. The Hearts' fans were not best pleased and even though they were at that time in the First Division (today's Championship), they were still expected to beat Second Division (and part-time) Forfar Athletic and I recall there were a lot of unflattering headlines in the press afterwards.

"There must have been something about the east, or more specifically the north-east, because there was one Hibs vs Dundee United game where I had a linesman from Stonehaven. He put his flag up and told me I had to send off two players. However, his Doric accent was so difficult to understand that I couldn't make out which players needed to go off. We eventually got it sorted and the right ones were sent off in the end. Being based in Ayrshire, I didn't do many games in the east, but I wasn't too upset at that as there was one supervisor there who, whenever he did one of my games, never saw me at my best."

We then discussed the relationship between referees and managers …

"In my experience, 99% of the time the players were fine and the people I met in football were really nice. During my refereeing career, I got on well with almost all the managers; there were only about two with whom I never really saw eye-to-eye. My view has always been to let bygones be bygones. I made it a rule to never ignore a manager and in return I don't think any ignored me. Like players, with managers it's all about man management.

"Managers too are obviously masters of man-management. I did the game at Dunfermline when Jim Leishman did his 'Martin Luther-King' speech, before they beat Celtic. Leishman is a good character, and you could certainly say the same about Walter Smith, Jock Stein, John Greig and Billy McNeil, all fine gentlemen. In those days, there was less pressure for managers to get sacked after a few bad results and consequently you got to know them over a period of years. There was a degree of mutual respect before and after the match. I ran the line for Jim McCluskey for the Old Firm match at Ibrox on the Sunday after the Dunblane massacre and Tommy Burns and Walter Smith came into our dressing room and said, 'great it's you Jim, we'll not have any bother today.'

"However, there is no doubt that a manager's attitude changes as the match starts. Because it was such a long journey, I used to leave early to get to Dundee United. Jim McLean would usually meet me at 1.00 pm and say come away in and have a cup of tea. We'd have a chat and I'd leave his room at about 1.30, by which time I could see he was starting to fidget. Right at the start of my career, I remember when Jock Wallace was at Rangers and I was doing a reserve game at Palmerston. I had gone out to inspect the pitch and Jock was out with his team, warming up. Normally, you might expect to exchange a few words, but he was adamant that wasn't going to happen. 'Right you lot,' he commanded his players, 'no fraternising with the enemy.'

"What's really good is that even after all these years you can still bump into players and managers from the old days. We all look out for each other. Just the other day, I met Archie Knox in Ayr and not long before that I met Craig Brown in the golf club. They are always happy to stop and chat. We look back on our time and reflect that it was great fun. I think there is a feeling though amongst some refs of my generation that we had the best of it and it's too serious nowadays, with too much pressure on the officials, especially from the (social) media."

Sometimes, managers can make a rod for their own backs…

"I was doing a Scottish Cup tie at Forfar in the early 1990s. It was against Ross County and the BBC were recording it for the television show that night. Before the match, I sat blethering to the Forfar manager, Tommy Campbell, over a cup of tea in his room. 'Do you know what I hate?' asked Tam, before going on to tell me, 'I hate those sleekit centre halves who will elbow the centre forward behind the ref's back.' I told him I wasn't too keen on them either. Sure enough, five minutes into the game, the Forfar centre half goes and elbows the Ross County striker. As I was sending him off, I noticed Tam with his head between his knees…"

Finally, given that he had spent many years supervising up-and-coming officials, I wondered what advice Louis might have for referees today?

"You have to earn the respect of the players. It is, as I've said, principally about man-management. That comes with experience. I keep saying that to young refs, you have to earn it, don't go in like a bull in a china shop. I remember I once had to send Tommy Craig to the stand on the advice of my linesman. I couldn't be seen to undermine him, but after the game I said to Tommy, 'I had to put you to the stand on the linesman's instruction, but if it was me on the line I'd have told you to sit on your backside and shut up.' A lot of this experience also comes from dealing with the world outside football. I was in the building trade, dealing with construction across the board with both public and private sector clients, with all the grief that goes with that. My experience in that tough world helped me in my man management and in my refereeing.

"There are not as many referees coming through now. Where they get scunnered is in the early days on the public parks. If we can keep them for three seasons, they usually go on to be good referees. I remember being an observer for Willie Collum when he was a young ref and you could see that he was going to be good. On another occasion, I was watching Don Robertson handling what I think was his first or second Junior game at Largs. Dougie Smith was his observer and I was mentoring Dougie that day. Afterwards, we both said that Don would go right to the top. You could see the way he was going about it, with sharp, clear signals, getting all the big decisions right, being respectful – and being very fit and getting about the park easily. We need more young refs like that."

I booked the Scotland manager in my first game in England
Joe Timmons

Joe Timmons is unique amongst referees in the history of the game in the UK. He is, to date, the only official who has refereed at the highest level in both Scotland and England. However, as we'll discover, it wasn't simply a case of crossing the border and being welcomed with open arms. The bureaucratic world of football administration doesn't work like that…

Like several of the refs featured in this book, Joe's passage into refereeing began with an injury which made it difficult to play football. *"I was a sprinter and could run like the wind,"* he told me, *"but when I was about 19 I had a cartilage operation and it meant that tackling put a lot of pressure on my knee. My brothers and the doctor both suggested that I should stop playing football, so I took up refereeing instead."*

By the time he was 25, he was refereeing the 1977 Scottish Junior Cup final while still only a Class 4 official, with two linesmen who were both senior to him in the referee's rankings. The following season, Joe was promoted to Class 3, then the next season to Class 2 and the season after that to Class 1.

"It was all quite quick, but what the game wanted above all at that time   and today of course – was competency. I had three seasons at Class 1, but then, during the third of those seasons, my employer, the Bank of Scotland, told me they wanted me to study for an MBA, which I did, but that ate into my time and I wasn't able to do many matches for a while. One I do remember was St Mirren against Hibs, when Jackie McNamara (senior) threw his jersey at me and was sent off as a result. I really didn't have time for refereeing at this stage of my career, but the Bank seemingly solved that problem for me by promoting me to Newcastle on Tyne."

Joe's last match in Scotland also involved St Mirren, this time away in front of a big crowd at Celtic Park. He recalls that he gave a yellow card to Frank McAvennie, who was making his name with the Buddies at this time. A few weeks later, Joe was in Newcastle and wondering if he'd be able to officiate in games south of the border.

"The FA had details of all my qualifications and references, but they said, 'you're in a new country now, so you've got to start again.' I didn't expect to have to go down the leagues, but that's what happened. I did my first game in the Wearside League at the end of 1983 in front of about 10 spectators. It was a far cry from the tens of thousands at Celtic Park for my previous match. You'll perhaps have heard of the famous Lindisfarne song, 'Fog on the Tyne?' Well, this was its close cousin, 'Fog on the (river) Wear.' I had to abandon the match because the haar came in after about 20 minutes and no-one could see.

"The next season, I was doing the Northern League, which featured some quite famous teams like Blyth Spartans and Gateshead. Just like my career in Scotland, I was promoted season

on season and the following year I was doing Conference League games, effectively the fifth tier of English football at that time. In 1986, I was again promoted, to the level of Football League linesman and the next season I eventually reached the top level for referees in England. This meant you could be called to do any game from the (old) Fourth Division to the First (top) Division. In reality, because I was living in Newcastle, the furthest south I went for a game was Birmingham.

"My first game in the First Division was interesting, because I booked the current Scotland manager! It was Sheffield Wednesday vs Chelsea, in 1988 if I remember rightly, and I gave Steve Clarke a yellow card. We both come from Saltcoats, which he was aware of as he remonstrated with me. I pointed out to him 'the guy you hit hasn't landed yet.'

"Steve wasn't the only Scot I came across. There were lots of others in the top flight in England in those days. I remember doing a game involving Manchester United in the Milk (League) Cup. Alex Ferguson and Archie Knox were in partnership at Old Trafford then and I think they were a bit bemused to see me. However, they were welcoming and pleasant before kick-off. By half-time, they had changed a bit and suggested, with some added adjectives, that they hoped my performance in the second half would be an improvement."

As the only man to have refereed in the top flight in both England and Scotland, Joe's views on the differences between the game in each country are particularly interesting…

"In England, the players were generally taller and broader. I think it's even more so nowadays, but in my time the difference in the players' physiques was noticeable. It's the same game, but obviously England is a bigger country with far more people, so from a referee's point of view there is far more competition at the top level. There were some good referees at that time: I recall men like Steve Lodge and David Elleray coming through.

"I general, I found the game was more professional in England. The club Secretaries were more efficient, even in the Northern League, where the standard is roughly equivalent to our Third Division and top Junior clubs, but they had better facilities in England, even down to the quality of the pitch markings. If the latter are not perfect you have to report the club, but I never had to do that in England, even in the lower leagues.

"Also, in England I was expected to give pre-match instructions to linesmen. These were usually fairly straightforward but it was necessary because there were different officials for every game, whereas in Scotland you usually knew the linesmen. At that time, giving instructions to the linesmen was more or less unheard of in Scotland, but it's accepted here now.

"When you went abroad, as I did for many European matches, including one in Sofia, Bulgaria, with Keith Hackett, who is recognised as one of the top 100 officials in world football, you found that English officials, or perhaps I should say officials from English football, were highly regarded, partly because the English game had higher status in those days because of the quality of their football. However, today UEFA and FIFA like smaller

countries such as Scotland and will promote good refs and make a point of using them in big, important games."

During his time in England, Joe refereed matches with some very big names, including, while on European duty, Mark Hateley and Glen Hoddle when they formed a dynamic duo at Monaco. Even in his lower league days he came across the odd player who was destined for the big time…

"I did a pre-season game between Blyth Spartans and Newcastle which featured an 18 year old called Paul Gascoigne. He was subbed late on and on his way off he asked if he could use the referee's room shower because the showers in the away dressing room weren't working. When the game was over, I went to my dressing room and he was getting dressed, pulling on his shoes but without any socks. He was a very cheery young man, albeit a bit wired to the moon, who was clearly also a very skilful player."

Joe had three seasons at the top level in England, but in 1989 he was promoted back to Edinburgh with the Bank of Scotland. He then lived in Musselburgh, but, unlike in England, he was accepted back straight away by the country's Football Association.

"Because I'd only been six years away and was at the highest level in England, the SFA accepted me at Grade 1. I got my FIFA badge and I refereed on the European scene for three years, but my knee was giving me serious bother and I retired in 1994, when I was 42.

"As those who live in west-central Scotland will know, my name is associated with one side of the Old Firm more than the other (for the uninitiated, it would appear to be a Catholic name). As a result, when I went to Celtic Park someone would inevitably say, 'Oh, it's you Joe, how about a penalty?' to which I'd reply, 'no bother, it will be in the 64th minute, so long as the ball is in the box,' followed quickly by 'aye, that'll be right.' Actually, I never refereed an Old Firm match, but I was the fourth official for a few. I also did the B&Q Cup final and a couple of North of Scotland and two South of Scotland finals, as well as about a score of international trips, both on the line and in the middle. I refereed at every senior ground in Scotland but my favourite was probably Tannadice. Generally, if you went to Angus or up north you were made very welcome and well looked after. Tynecastle and Easter Road were also good and when filled with 15,000 supporters they have a great atmosphere. I also did the opening match of St Johnstone's new ground (in 1989, against Clydebank), which was the first real step on the way to the modernisation of football grounds as we know them today. However, the biggest ground I ever did was Maine Road, Manchester City's old ground. It was a real, traditional, oval ground, a bit like the old Rugby Park in Kilmarnock before they re-developed it with all the new stands."

One of the perennial questions for football fans is how referees are assessed and whether they can be demoted. I heard this many times in my research for this book, usually in a question (or to be more precise a demand) from fans that implied that certain referees ought to be doing park football, if that. The reality, as Joe explains, is quite straightforward.

"After I finished as a ref, I did about four years as a Supervisor, assessing officials across Scotland. At that time, the officials didn't always know when they were being monitored, but today they have no excuse because you make contact with them at the game: you see them beforehand and usually have a short debrief afterwards. The referee then gets to see your full report, normally within three days of the match. The reason it can take a few days is that sometimes the Assessor/Supervisor wants to see an incident again and, in most cases, it's available somewhere on video.

"Premier and Championship games all have independent Assessors, but, unlike during my time, the managers don't do reports on referees nowadays. Back then, the clubs' marks counted for 50% of a referee's assessment. In England, club marks were regarded as especially important: they helped me get promoted there. I was only assessed a few times, until I got to the Conference, but I was also interviewed, face to face. I had to go to London, where they didn't know me from Adam but they knew my marks were good so they wanted to eyeball me. I was asked about my professional career in the bank and what I did away from football - what made me tick essentially. That doesn't happen in Scotland.

"All officials get a 'half term' and 'full term' report and if your marks aren't consistently improving then after a few years (usually two), you will be given more coaching and warned you might come off the list. Equally importantly, those whose skills and experience show that they are competent enough to make the step up are given the opportunity. Contrary to what fans might believe, every season there will be a couple of chaps downgraded. However, we try very hard to prevent that and the Referees' Associations are very quick to help improve those who are, for whatever reason, not quite where they ought to be. It's like players: no club wants to jettison someone who is having a slight dip in form, unless it becomes permanent. There is never a summary dismissal: referees who are not making it get two years' notice. It is, of course, very competitive at the top level. There are seven FIFA refs in Scotland and four or five other extremely competent refs, but only six Premier games, so even the very best don't officiate at a top flight game every week. It's the same all the way down the leagues, including at Junior level - referees are constantly assessed and helped to improve.

"Of course, it's much more difficult nowadays because of TV. The referees of my era were as competent as today's refs: we both made the same mistakes but my generation wasn't under so much scrutiny as the modern referee. Back then, as indeed today, so long as you didn't make frequent mistakes the SFA would support you. I had some poor games, controversial games where, rightly, I was criticised. You just have to accept this, in the same way fans accept that players have off-days.

"Fitness is far better today and all referees are very fit. I was fit, partly because I was a sprinter and because I trained hard, but some refs in my day were not really fit. My son-in-law is Grade 1 and he trains four or five days a week. The modern refs have quarterly fitness tests, plus BMI tests; they are, in effect, semi-professional. Body shape is vital today. You can't get a small chap whose body shape isn't good: you really need to be pretty lean to *referee. Referee assessors concentrate on fitness as well as ability and anyone with a fitness issue has to sort it. Tiny Wharton would have no chance today."*

Joe's last game was Queen's Park vs Arbroath at Hampden Park in 1994. There was a pleasing symmetry as his first senior match at Grade 1 was also at Hampden, for Queen's Park vs Stranraer. *"My retirement was unplanned really: it was my knee giving in so I just thought, 'that will do…' In the event it was a low-key game. I had just renewed by FIFA badge for the following year, so I was disappointed, but I look at the younger generation coming through and I think the game is in safe hands. If you are a young referee who is prepared to learn, the prospects are good. I saw three female match officials at Irvine Meadow recently and they were all really experienced and good at their jobs. For women like them, and young men too, if you stick in then the world's your oyster."*

The only referee to be cheered off the pitch
Duncan McKerchar

I'm indebted to St Johnstone fan Stevie Walker for the loan of his scrapbook, detailing the career of his grandfather, Duncan McKerchar (photo, right), from Stanley, who was one of the best-known Scottish referees in the post-World War II years.

Duncan began his refereeing career in the late 1920s and eventually retired, at the age of 48, in 1955. He began refereeing when he was 21, starting out in Perth City Boys football and then moving up the ranks of Juvenile, Amateur and Junior football, prior to his elevation to the senior game. As well as refereeing at the top level for many years, Duncan McKerchar also featured in one of the most inglorious episodes of the 1950s, the 'Battle of Brockville,' of which more below…

It's clear that he was much better than the average local referee. The scrapbook has a letter (shown below) from Tommy Muirhead, then the St Johnstone manager, but previously a famous half-back with Rangers and Scotland, in which he praises Duncan for his ability and recommends him for further advancement. The letter is not dated, but given that we believe

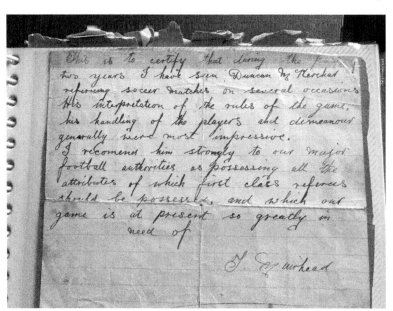

Duncan McKerchar began refereeing in 1928, and reportedly had his first senior match as a Grade 1 official in 1939, this ties in with the period (1931-36) when Muirhead was Saints' manager.

I have written 'reportedly had his first senior match as a Grade 1 official in 1939' because the press cuttings in the scrapbook have a number of different dates for Duncan's debut at Grade 1. Several cite the game in Dundee, between Dundee United and Leith Athletic on Saturday 2nd September 1939 as his first at Grade 1, but other newspaper reports quote him as saying he didn't actually make Grade 1 until 1942 and that his first match at that level was a wartime game between Dundee United and Raith Rovers.

One thing we do know is that, at the age of 74, he gave an interview to the Perthshire Advertiser in which he not only described his career, but also told them his fee for his first match at Grade 1 (which he said was in 1942) was four guineas – four pounds and four shillings, or £240 in today's money. In the same interview, Duncan said that his last senior game was between Hibernian and Dundee, on 10th December 1955. For his efforts that day in Edinburgh, he was paid… four guineas.

That same article in the Perthshire Advertiser also revealed the fees referees received for local matches in the 1930s. For a Junior game, they got 7/6d (37p, or c. £27 today) and for a Junior Cup final they received 10/- (50p, or £37 today), plus they could claim a third-class train fare to a game and also, so long as the ground was a mile or more from the railway station, a tram or bus fare.

The scrapbook is interesting for many reasons. As well as the cuttings from a number of matches, there are also several letters from clubs, thanking Duncan for the skill with which he handled their games and also recommending him for advancement in the refereeing profession. The one below is from 1947, from Dundee FC.

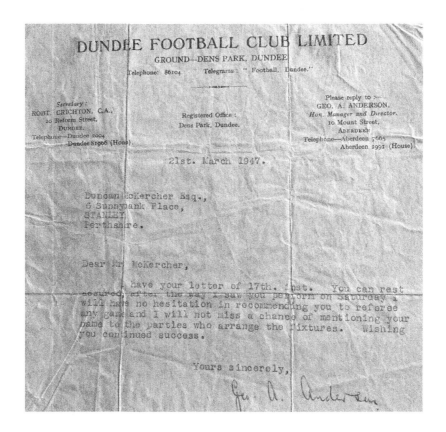

It wasn't only clubs who wrote to Mr McKerchar. There are also a number of letters from fans, lauding his performance in games they had watched. The one below, from a Mr Webster, presumably either a Hearts' or Hibs' fan, praises Duncan's resolute application of the laws and his refusal to be intimidated by large crowds.

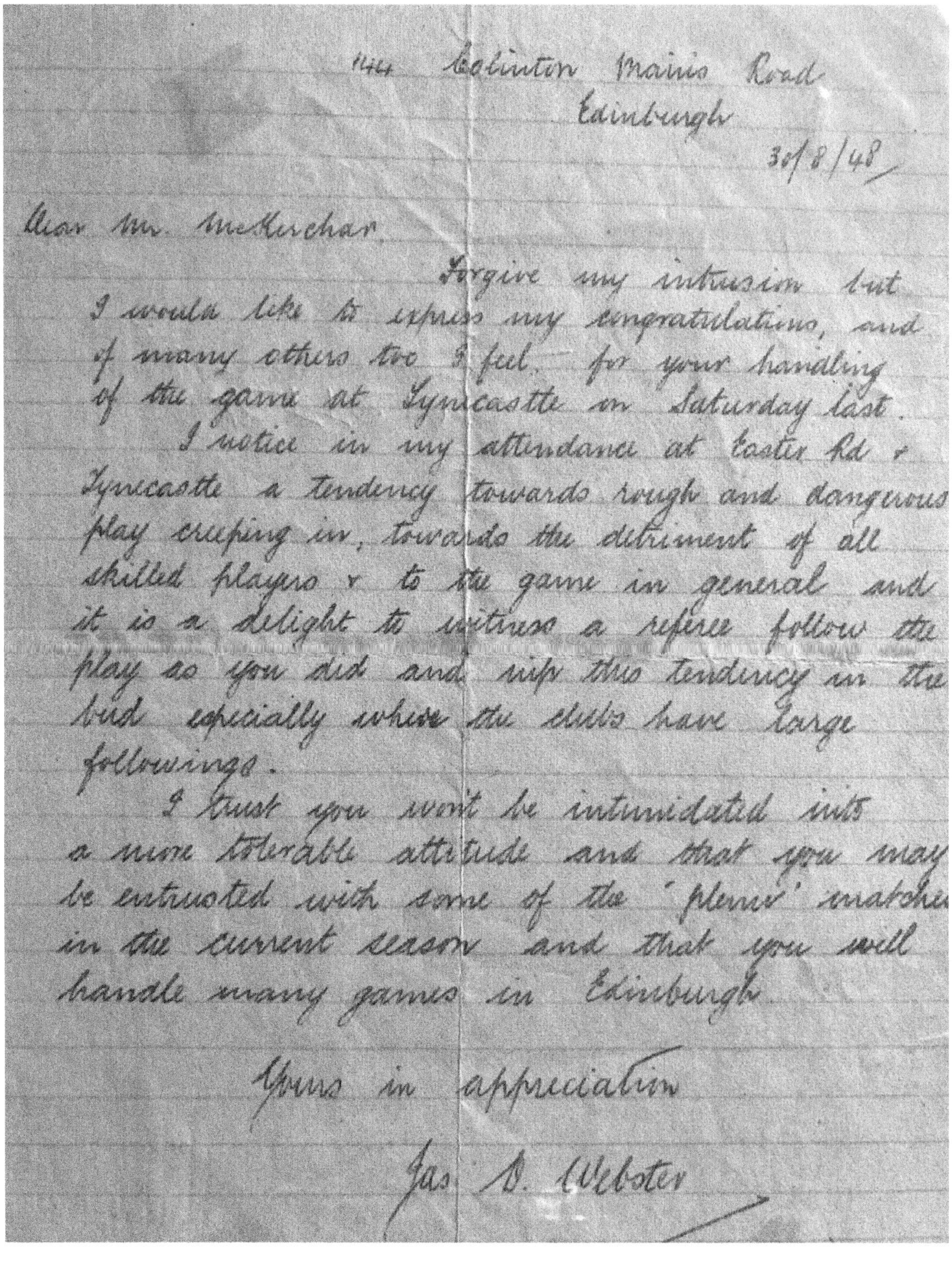

144 Colinton Mains Road
Edinburgh
30/8/48

Dear Mr McKerchar

Forgive my intrusion but I would like to express my congratulations, and of many others too I feel, for your handling of the game at Tynecastle on Saturday last.

I notice in my attendance at Easter Rd & Tynecastle a tendency towards rough and dangerous play creeping in, towards the detriment of all skilled players & to the game in general and it is a delight to witness a referee follow the play as you did and nip this tendency in the bud especially where the clubs have large followings.

I trust you won't be intimidated into a more tolerable attitude and that you may be entrusted with some of the 'plum' matches in the current season and that you will handle many games in Edinburgh.

Yours in appreciation

Jas. D. Webster

Not all games were straightforward though. Only a few months before the end of his career, Duncan McKerchar was the man in the middle for the League Cup match between Falkirk and Celtic, played at Brockville on 3rd September 1955. After Falkirk had gone ahead early in the game, fighting broke out on the terracing for several minutes. Hamilton, the Falkirk 'keeper was then felled by a thrown glass, having previously dodged a number of glasses and bottles thrown at him by the Celtic fans. Mr McKerchar stopped the game and spoke to the police, handing them some of the items that had been hurled. As is all too evident from the photo here, these were objects that could have caused serious injury.

Referee McKerchar with a glass thrown on to the field at Falkirk on Saturday.

Soon afterwards, Falkirk's Rae was sent off for a foul on Tully before Celtic equalised in the 68th minute. Then McIntosh of Falkirk was hit by an object and the police, obviously fearing more fighting, sent for reinforcements.

The press, unsurprisingly, reported the 'battle' in depth. The Celtic Supporters Association claimed to have gone on the pitch after the game and only found four glass objects. Consequently, the Celtic manager, Jimmy McGrory, said his club were being made scapegoats, and although there is no doubt that both sets of fans were involved in the fighting it seems to have been largely the Falkirk players who were on the receiving end of the missiles. Willie Maley, another grand old Celtic man, was less forgiving than McGrory, describing the perpetrators as *"Cowards and Curs,"* adding, *"That's what I call those thugs who throw a bottle or a glass from a football crowd."*

Fortunately, not all of Duncan's games were as feisty as that one. A few years beforehand, in 1952, he had officiated at the League Cup match between Hibs and Celtic at Easter Road. Today, most people would regard such a pairing as most likely having only one outcome, but this was the Hibernian team of the 'Famous Five' – Smith, Johnstone, Reilly, Turnbull and Ormond – who a few years later would become the first British team to compete in the European Cup. Hibs won 3-0 and Duncan was cheered from the park by the fans at the end of the game – probably the first and (to the best of my knowledge) certainly the last time this has ever happened in Scottish football.

Pope brings Peace to Ibrox
James Bee

All my conversations with former referees and managers were interesting for many different reasons, but my chat with James Bee was, in some ways, the most illuminating…

James grew up in Leith. Unusually for someone living in that area of Edinburgh he was a Hearts' fan. Being a Hearts' fan in Leith is a tough gig. Being the only Hearts' fan in your year at Leith Academy is even tougher. Being sworn at and spat at (and he says that was just the teachers) was, however, ideal training for becoming a referee.

"I was an out-and-out Hearts fan, but I also played football up to the age of 21. I wasn't great, getting only as far as the Under-21 side at Bonnyrigg and Poltonhall, but despite playing regularly in my youth I'd still get along to Tynecastle when I could. I used to get so exasperated at the referees and linesmen and then at one game, against St Mirren, the ref – Don McVicar - cautioned four Hearts' players for a botched substitution. Basically, the players and manager had cocked it up and technically it was a breach of the laws, but I went a bit scatty. It wasn't exactly a Damascene conversion, but for some reason, it occurred to me at that moment that if I was going to moan about the officials I should perhaps see if I could do any better.

"George Smith (recently deceased and one of the few Scots to have officiated at a World Cup – Italia '90) *lived quite close and one day I met him in the street and took the bull by the horns, asking him when was the next class for aspiring refs. I recall vividly the date the course began: it was the 12th September 1988 – my 21st birthday.*

Everyone, naturally, thought he would never go to the course that day, but instead of going to the pub he went to Boroughmuir High School, where he met two men who had a big influence on his formative year in refereeing…

"The coaches names were, believe it or not, David Pope and Peter Peace. David had once refereed a reserve game at Ibrox and Peter had run his line – Peter used to joke that the press ran a headline, 'Pope brings Peace to Ibrox.' I'm also told, and it is a sad reflection of our game, David was asked to consider changing his name so as 'not to bring attention to himself,' but, bravely, he didn't do it.

"David, especially, got me into refereeing You had to learn the laws more or less off-by-heart. It's a bit like remembering your times tables: 33 years later I can still recite huge swathes of the laws from memory. You had a mock exam before the actual one and the pass mark for the exam was very high. We then sat in a classroom to take the final exam. I got over 90% and then set off to learn how to do it for real…

"David Pope also got me Pele's autograph. This was in 1989, when the Under-16 World Cup was held in Scotland. For those who remember it, it was notorious for the Saudi Arabia

team allegedly fielding a few somewhat over-age players. Anyway, Pele was a FIFA Ambassador for the tournament and David Pope got call from SFA asking him to be Pele's driver for a few days. David is a massive Hearts and Armadale Thistle fan so he took Pele to Armadale! He also got the great man to sign lots of autographs. My nickname amongst the referees was, with a stunning lack of originality, 'Buzz', and Pele wrote, 'Buzz, Good Luck in your Refereeing, Pele.' Needless to say, it's one of my treasured possessions. I also have Eusebio's autograph. The late Portuguese superstar had attended a dinner which I was at with Stuart Dougal. We were amazed when Eusebio rattled off the entire Rangers team from the late 1960s/early 1970s. He knew them all, so we (naturally) asked why. 'I'm a Rangers man,' he explained, "and although I also know about Celtic, I could never support them because they play in green and white, like Sporting - Eusebio, of course, was famous for being a Benfica great and Sporting are their great rivals."

At 21 in 1988, James was considered a youngster (nowadays he'd be considered a late starter). He was told that the next step was crucial. The drop-out rate for referees is very high so if they are put into the 'wrong' level of match at the start then it can prove very difficult and they often give up. Consequently, James was given schools' football, starting with Under-10s, then moving up through the age ranges, 12s, 13s, 14s, then on to Under-16s, Under-18s and eventually Under-21s.

"The Under-21s were the last 'apprenticeship' level for me before I moved on to refereeing Junior football. I used to do matches with Hutchie Vale, Tynecastle Boys' Club, Easthouses and the like – all teams in and around Edinburgh. For these clubs, a Scottish Cup tie, even at Under-16 level, was a big deal as it meant they got to travel and play teams they didn't normally meet. For Edinburgh teams, a trip to Fife or Glasgow was a challenge. The romance of the Cup exists, even at that level, and both sides always seemed to raise their game. If, say, Dalkeith Thistle drew Port Glasgow Rangers at home, they almost wanted to get a draw so they could get a trip to the west. In some ways, it's like a European game for a senior club."

From age 21 to the Juniors, James was not subject to much supervision by an official referee Observer. However, once the local Referees' Association thinks a young ref is good enough to move up a level then he or she is watched by senior refs, with suggestions being made to try to help them improve. For James, that came relatively quickly…

"I had Observers like Bill Crombie and George Smith at some of the games I did to see if I was good enough to go to the Juniors. It took two seasons before they thought I had enough experience, by which time I was 24. Once I began to referee Junior football it was clear there was a significant jump in quality: you were dealing with grown men, including some veterans from the senior game at the end of their careers. Amongst others, I refereed Frank McGarvey (ex St Mirren and Celtic), and Wayne Foster (ex Hearts) and as a result I learnt a lot very quickly. These old pros were sometimes impossible for a young ref to deal with. They'd be elbowing people behind your back, giving you dissent in ways you hadn't experienced before, but it meant that you grew up fast as a referee."

Although James had begun his refereeing career comparatively early for those days, he didn't expect to make it to the top quickly. Today, referees come through the system very much more quickly, but back in the 1990s they were expected to have an apprenticeship of at least a dozen years before they'd get to Grade 1 level.

"George Smith told me, 'You have lots of time.' In those days, it was expected that a good referee would do about three years at each main level, moving up from Grade 3 to Grade 2 and then Grade 1. However, it all changed with the World Cup in 1990. I was only 23 and still refereeing youth club football but like everyone else I watched Scotland going down to Costa Rica then beating Sweden before losing to Brazil and going out. Unlike most others, I was also watching the officials, because George Smith was one of them. Like all World Cup competitions up to that time, there were no specialist linesman, so it was mostly older, highly experienced refs like George who were running the line. He hadn't run a line for at least 10 years! It was a disaster in terms of offside decisions and FIFA, having admitted they got it wrong, decided to fast track younger referees and came up with the idea of the Specialist Assistant Referee (SAR). Suddenly, I was told, 'you need to get a move on.'

"For me, and others like me at that time, not only had the whole field of play altered but the goalposts had moved as well. To give you an example of how much it's all changed, at that 1990 World Cup Peter Mikkelsen, the great Danish referee, became the youngest man (at that time) to referee in a World Cup. He was only 30 and was regarded as exceptional. But today, the SFA are looking for a boy to turn up at classes at the age of 16, to be out doing Juniors before they are even 20, then to become a Specialist Assistant Referee or a Category 1 ref at 23 and, ideally, get on the FIFA list by the age of 26 or 27 or younger! A lot of people, myself included, think that's too quick and that unless you are exceptionally talented, like Mikkelsen or Pierluigi Collina, you simply won't gain the experience necessary to become a really top-notch official in such a short time-scale.

"I was doing all right in the Juniors, refereeing low level games involving teams such as Stoneyburn and West Calder and gradually being given better matches with the likes of Linlithgow Rose. I also ran the line at Scottish Junior Cup matches and I remember a Dundee St. Josephs vs Auchinleck Talbot tie where the ref was Robert Wylie from Stirling. He went on to become a Premier-level linesman and, although he is best remembered for his involvement in the Les Mottram 'ghost goal' at Firhill, he was a high-quality official.

"In the Junior Scottish Cup quarter final between Pollok and Largs, I was running the line when I saw a player get head-butted by one of his opponents. I stuck my flag up and called over the ref, who promptly decided to ignore me and get on with the game. After the match, the referee committee demanded a full explanation. The referee and I were summoned to Park Gardens (then the SFA Head Office) to face the committee. I was 26 years old and on the other side of the table were Tom 'Tiny' Wharton, Bill Mullan, Kenny Hope, George Smith and Bob Valentine: as formidable an assembly of refereeing experience as you could imagine. Alongside them was the 'administrator's administrator,' Jim Farry. To give you an idea of how well-respected Bill Mullan was internationally, when Pele visited Scotland in

1989, one of his first questions, was, 'where is my friend, Bill Mullan?' As a result, the committee was, to put it mildly, nerve-wracking.

"We all had to give our accounts and at the end of the meeting the ref was struck off the list but I was commended for my actions. You might think this was good for my career, but what happened was that I was shunned by Junior football because the ref who got dismissed was a favourite of the Junior officials and secretaries. As a result, my career stalled a bit, but I eventually made it to Category 3 and then Category 2, which allowed me to referee at reserve league games.

"SARs came in for the 1994 World Cup in America. I was there as a fan and realised this was my future. Back in Scotland, I saw some of the guys who hadn't made it to Category 1 become Special Assistants and get their FIFA badge. I knew I wasn't going to make Category 1 so I set myself a goal of replacing David Doig on the SAR list in Scotland. David was a friend of mine who was one of the earliest Scottish SARs to get his FIFA badge and my aim was to replace him on the (FIFA) list when he retired. Consequently, I worked really hard, striving to be accurate with my offsides and other decisions.

"In 2003, I was told I was getting appointed to the FIFA list for 2003-2004. The FIFA year starts on January 1st, so that day I went to the FIFA website to see my name. It wasn't there! Two other Scots officials' names were though, so I thought it was just a mistake. On the 5th January I called the SFA and asked them to find out what happened. They admitted it was an admin error – FIFA had recorded my date of birth incorrectly and that's why I wasn't listed.

"At the time, I was devastated, but it did get sorted out and I was then on the FIFA list. This helped me get more big games, both across Europe and in Scotland. I stayed on the list until 2012 and did eight Old Firm matches, quite a few Edinburgh derbies, Rangers vs Aberdeen (even more fraught than the Old Firm at times), the Scottish and League Cup Finals as well as games across Europe. Before I got on the FIFA list, they gave me a UEFA Cup game in November 2003 to see if I was up to it. It was Slavia Prague vs Levski Sofia. I went to the game, thinking 'if I screw it up, at least I'll have done ONE European game.' Mike McCurry was the ref that night and I do remember he handed out two cautions to the same player but didn't send him off. I made a couple of good decisions, which I think helped cement my position on the 2004 FIFA list.

"My first FIFA appointment was an Under-17 level, mini-tournament in Spain, involving Spain, Russia and Hungary. There were two young Spaniards who really stood out: Cesc Fabregas and Gerard Piqué. I'd never heard of them before - no one had - but they did quite well later in their careers. I did Champions' League matches with the likes of Dinamo Kyiv and Sporting Lisbon as well as international games, including one between Brazil and Norway. Strangely, Brazil have never beaten Norway in five matches, including the one that night, which was drawn. I also officiated for the great 2008 Spanish team in a match against Latvia. That side had players of the calibre of Casillas, Puyol, Ramos, Iniesta, Xavi, Garcia, David Villa, etc. and they were so in control it was scary. As a linesman, you look along the defensive line and during that match it was as if I was part of it: Puyol marshalled everything *so well that it seemed that he had his own defence, the opposition attackers and me all on a string, which he pulled. I barely had to move and as a result the decisions were easier."*

International games bring their own challenges, not least being unable to understand the different languages. However, James explained that this isn't really a problem.

"I remember a Mexican referee said to us that if we heard a player saying 'Puta Madre' this is what it means… (its meaning can vary, but one of the most common translations is 'motherfucker'). *I knew one ref who made a point of learning 'red card' in all the major languages, but, in reality, there is a universal football language, which includes body language. This means I, as a referee or Assistant, don't need to know what the players are saying. You can tell if someone is angry, being overly demonstrative, or just not happy. Human communication is mainly non-verbal/non-audible. If there are guys screaming it could be in any language, but you learn how to position your hands, to smile and make calming gestures to de-escalate situations. However, the players know that even though we don't understand what they are saying, if they rattle something off in an inflammatory manner, that's enough for a caution or maybe more!"*

One of the really interesting things about speaking to James was to discover just how much work some officials put into improving their skills…

"The linesmen are there to assist the referee. It's not just offside and corners, but also watching out for off-the-ball stuff and, before the introduction of the fourth official, we had to manage the dugouts. That said, the main thing that causes everyone – officials, players and, especially, fans – grief is offside. It's an area where inexperienced Assistants need help because it is so hard to get right and experience makes a huge difference. And fans and players might find this hard to believe, but I would change my offside decision-making depending on whether I was on TV or not. That may sound terrible, but it's true…

"We all know that the Assistant signals offside by putting his flag up (this was before 'second-phase' offside), *but when the game is being recorded or is live on TV you know that if there are any controversial decisions you'll get pilloried by the pundits. It's a terrible feeling to see a former player or journalist, neither of whom actually knows the laws properly, point out your mistakes. Of course, they have the advantage, even without VAR in Scotland, of slow-motion replays and freeze-frames. After I had two or three high-profile errors highlighted in this way on television, I realised that I had to do something. I started to study the way in which your eyes and brain interact and discovered that 90% of what you 'see' comes from your brain, and only 10% from your eyes. It's an anatomical and physiological fact. The brain at times, also sees things 'further ahead' than your eyes.*

"After I worked this out, I started to keep my flag down if I saw a player marginally offside. Lo and behold, when I saw the game back on the television, it was invariably right to have done so. My decisions were becoming more accurate and therefore better.

"This really came home in an Old Firm game in 2011. Celtic's Emilio Izaguirre looked about three yards offside after a 'one-two' with Samaras, but I kept my flag down and Celtic scored. Unsurprisingly, almost the entire Rangers' team made a bee-line (no pun intended!) for me. Later, when I saw it on a monitor, it was clear I was right, as was 'confirmed' by the media that night on the telly.

"Having said all that, I discovered that if I did this for non-televised games, the fans, especially those behind me who could 'look along the line,' didn't know that this is how your brain works and would go mad at me. Consequently, if I was at, say, Montrose vs Brechin and saw a player seemingly offside, I did put my flag up, because if I allowed the guy to go on and score there would be mayhem, not just in the ground but in the Montrose Review's report of the match."

"Nowadays though, there are iPhone cameras and recordings of almost every match at every level of the game so there is no hiding place for the officials."

Although he is from Edinburgh, James said that the Old Firm was the one game all referees and linesmen want to do…

"The Old Firm is the one we all want to be on … you are terrified about the prospect but really want to do the game. Hugh Dallas was the ref for the first Old Firm match I did. Normally, the officials meet up in a hotel about two and a half hours before kick-off, but Hugh said he wanted us there at 9.30 am. I was up at 7.00 am, after about three hours sleep. There were scrambled eggs on offer for breakfast at the hotel, but I couldn't eat. Neither could the other 'rookie' Old Firm Assistant.

"That was pretty normal for a Rangers vs Celtic game. I felt sick in the morning, having had barely any sleep through worry, and then had to go out and perform at a very high level, despite having had no food, in front of tens of thousands of people.

"At an Old Firm match you can forget hearing the players: you can barely hear the whistle. In fact, all you hear is a big noise, where all the individual insults melt into one so you don't hear them. In contrast, at, say, Cowdenbeath you can hear everything. Doing the Old Firm is easier in some respects. In particular, you don't have to motivate yourself because your concentration and adrenaline levels are higher than for any other game. At the end of the match, so long as it has gone well, the relief is incredible. I know that fans of other teams will say that we should say that after every game, but to be honest there is a difference. For a start, if you get something seriously wrong in an Old Firm, you can be in the media spotlight for weeks and papers have been known to send journalists to an official's workplace or neighbours to try to 'find a story.'

Of course, sometimes the Old Firm games do kick-off….

"Most of them were without incident, but in one, after Celtic had lost, Neil Lennon, having already been shown a red card, really had a go at the ref, Stuart Dougal. I tried to defuse the

situation, but we all ended up at an official meeting in Hampden where both sides brought lawyers along and the whole thing took hours. If I had managed to defuse things, perhaps it wouldn't have escalated, but football is an emotive sport.

"One Celtic manager who I did manage to calm down (once!) was Gordon Strachan. Gordon is from Muirhouse, near where my Granny lived in Leith and when I was 10, she told me, 'my friend's grandson has just signed for Aberdeen'. It was Gordon, who went on to have a superb career as a player. However, several decades later, in a game at Falkirk that was live on television, it only took Gordon ten minutes to explode, screaming for me to explain the referee's decision. I'll be honest, I froze, unaware that a camera was zooming in on us. 'Explain this decision!' Gordon shouted again. I don't know why, but the only thing I could think of saying was 'my granny knew your granny.' He burst out laughing, and asked, 'which one?' 'Granny Carr,' I replied… and the referee's decision was forgotten."

Like every other former referee or linesman I have spoken to for this book, James wouldn't change anything about his career…

"It was fantastic. I saw about 45 countries in the years I refereed or was on the FIFA list, places I'd never have seen otherwise. Refereeing took me from the White House to The Kremlin. Equally importantly, I got a fantastic buzz from it and I think the vast majority of referees feel the same. Although I'm heavily involved in the referees' trade union and work hard to try to get a fairer deal for referees, I think that if you took the fee money out of the game, refs would still turn up and officiate matches …. that is the nature of the bug you get as a referee."

Finally, can you imagine refereeing a match with 22 referees who all know better than you?

James told me that fans "*might be interested to know that the hardest games to referee are games involving referees vs referees! Stirlingshire refs vs Fife refs or Aberdeenshire vs Edinburgh & District games were common up until about the early '90s and then they were banned because they were 'un-referee-able.' Even bounce five-a-side matches after Tuesday night training sessions in Edinburgh were banned due to knee high tackles, fights and an excessive number of injuries and bruises…"*

The rugby referees' view

There was this one lad who was the best cheat I've ever refereed
Malcom Currie

Malcolm Currie is a rugby referee development office and supervisor. Like many of his football equivalents (and also many rugby referees), he took up his whistle after injuries curtailed his playing career; in his case a dislocated knee followed by a snapped anterior cruciate ligament. Now, he helps bring through young and aspiring referees, supervising them during games in much the same way as football referee supervisors do in the round ball game.

"My job had taken me up to the Highlands and there is not much rugby there, but I played for a small team locally … and then dislocated my knee climbing in the Cairngorms. After three more seasons of playing, my ACL gave up during a Sevens' tournament. I was in my late twenties and I had the knee rebuilt, but it was a risk going back to playing. I still wanted to get back into rugby, so I looked at coaching and spoke to a couple of clubs but none was interested. I subsequently moved to Edinburgh and started playing touch rugby, where I got talking to one of the older refs who helped with these matches. He asked if I had ever thought about refereeing. Intrigued, I went along to a Level 1 refereeing course, run by Ian Thom, the Lothians' Referee Development Officer. I completed the course and then did my first game, at Haddington, for their 3rd XV. As they knew it was my first game, they were very nice to me, although it was still a very daunting experience. However, within a few weeks I realised I should have taken up refereeing years earlier. The main attraction was that I was totally involved in the game, running around the pitch but without any of the pain normally associated with a rugby match.

"Just like football referees, I progressed through the levels until I reached the third tier, which meant I was officiating at National Division One level, roughly equivalent to the Championship in football. Also, like football referees, my career in rugby refereeing took me around the world, to places like Russia, France, Spain and the Czech Republic. Everything was going swimmingly, until 2012, when I had a cycling accident and dislocated my shoulder. I was in my mid-40s at that point and had to have my shoulder rebuilt. That, in itself, wasn't the problem: my issue was not being able to get power into that shoulder for sprinting. It was obvious that I wasn't going to be able to get to a higher level, so I moved into coaching referees."

So far, this reads much the same as many of the interviews with football referees. However, as we all know, there are several, major differences between rugby football and Association football. There are also a few similarities, notably the way in which rugby refereeing is structured. Like football, rugby in Scotland has regional rugby referees' bodies and Malcolm is a member of the Edinburgh Society of Rugby Referees. There are six regional referees' societies and they all send representatives to the Scottish Rugby Referees' Association, which works with the SRU to organise rugby refereeing at all levels (elite/professional and amateur) across the country.

That apart, it's the differences that really interested me, the main one of which is, of course, the totally different attitude that rugby players take towards their referees. Just in case anyone doesn't know, all players are expected to (and do) call the referee 'sir,' and although they are allowed to (and do) question decisions, they do so in a much politer manner. One of the reasons for this is that if, after a penalty is awarded against them, they shout and swear at the referee in the way footballers do, the ref then moves the location of the penalty ten metres further up the pitch. By ceding ground, the penalty may become much more kickable or likely to result (from the next line-out) in a try, which is a strong deterrent to abusing the referee. This respect for the officials doesn't mean that rugby players don't swear, but they are much more careful to whom they direct their colourful language than their football counterparts.

Interestingly, as recounted elsewhere in this book, there was an experiment in Scotland during the 2000-01 League Cup (and also in some lesser competitions in England) with football referees being able to move a free-kick ten yards up the park if they received abuse after making a decision. Although popular with the referees and football authorities, the clubs were against it and it was not continued.

Another thing I learned from my conversation with Malcolm was the reason behind the difference in attitudes both of the players towards the referees and the referees towards the players. It is both practical and necessary, as he explained…

"In rugby, at the professional level, a solid tackle has been shown to be equivalent to the impact of a 40-mph car crash. A Scotland international like Johnny Gray will average around 15 such tackles per game. In a ruck or a maul, even at amateur level, the players will not all know what is happening and whether someone may be about to do something very dangerous – possibly even fatal – in the next second. Consequently, there is a trust in, and respect for, the referee to manage the game that, while allowing for the controlled violence and aggression that characterise rugby football, also means that everyone goes home safely at the end of the match. They will almost certainly be a bit bruised, but they will (usually) be in one piece!

"The management of the game by the referee in rugby is different. For rugby referees there is, naturally, a lot of focus on knowing the laws, but it's understanding how to apply them in match situations – principally the 'set-pieces' of the game such as scrums, mauls rucks and line-outs – that really matters. For example, in a game I supervised recently the referee was watching a maul and one team was complaining to him that their opponents were offside. However, he was, correctly, shouting to the players, 'it's not affecting anything, play on.' In rugby, the referees have to make far more frequent calls about what's not material – what won't affect the game even if it's a technical infringement – than their football counterparts. This focus on 'what's not material to the situation' is much bigger in rugby than football."

One area where rugby seems to mirror football is the art of cheating. As anyone who has read Michael Green's seminal 'The Art of Coarse Rugby' will know, gamesmanship has always been rife in the sport, but while in football diving is regrettably common, in rugby there seems to be more sophistication in the way players, sometimes with the connivance of their clubs and backroom staff, go about bending the laws. Admittedly, the complexity of the laws, and the proximity of the players to each other, can make it easier to hide what's going on, whereas in football most offences are in plain view.

One of the most famous examples of cheating in rugby was 'Bloodgate,' where a player used a capsule of fake blood to con the officials into allowing him to leave the field and then a player who had earlier been substituted and who was a better goal-kicker returned to the pitch. This is allowed in rugby for blood injuries (and there is more on it in the next chapter), but Malcolm told me that there is no real equivalent in rugby of diving for a penalty in football. That's not to say the players don't try it on...

"There was this one lad, who had better remain nameless, who was the 'best cheat' I've ever refereed. Not that he was actually cheating, or rather he would be doing stuff in the ruck or scrum that I wasn't quite able definitively to rule on. I used to think, 'I'll get you next time,' but he would then do something different. You could call that cheating, but I think what he was doing was playing me as a referee. He knew how far to push me, how to stay one step ahead. Often, the team that 'plays the referee' best is the one that comes out on top, partly because, in my experience, they get more 50:50 decisions. Conversely, the team that annoys the referee is likely to get fewer 50:50 decisions. You can see this in international matches, where different countries' referees have slightly different interpretations of the laws and the smart players note this and tell their team-mates."

Malcolm explained that the football and rugby refereeing authorities do compare notes and have had occasional meetings. The Edinburgh Society of Rugby Referees has also tried to learn from officials in other sports, with Malcolm telling me, *"We are great believers in the idea that there are more similarities than differences and we have had ice hockey umpires, cricket umpires and football referees speak to our Society. Calum Murray, the former FIFA list Scottish referee came to speak to us and was asked, 'why do you put up with all the abuse?' He said, 'I don't know, but it's not as bad at the top end of the game as it is at the bottom end.' Like most rugby referees, I am amazed at the way footballers speak to their referees.*

"Talking-back to the ref is such a bad thing in football and it just sends so many wrong signals, especially to young footballers. I do wonder why they haven't introduced a sin-bin for football: that would surely help stamp out a lot of the abuse and back-chat. It was introduced to Rugby League in Australia as far back as 1981 and brought into Rugby Union in 2001. The difference it makes to on-field discipline is remarkable because the players know if they step out of line then they'll be off the field for ten minutes. That, of course, puts added pressure on their team-mates, but, unlike a proper sending-off (which we do, of course, have for serious foul play), the sanction is only for a relatively short period. However, it's a period during which the team who are down to 14 are going to find it much more difficult. A sin-bin

in soccer would also help stop players in tournaments or cup competitions deliberately getting booked to make sure they only miss one game and are then available for a more important, later round."

My next question was simple: have you ever tried refereeing football? Malcolm's answer was also simple…

"No, I've never refereed a football match. I didn't play football much, but I did play a bit at school, at Alness Academy, where I was a centre half. Another local school had a young centre-forward called Eric Black. I wasn't that bad a player, but Eric was on a different level. His ball control and dexterity were exceptional. I wasn't surprised to see him play for Scotland and be a key part of the Aberdeen team that beat Real Madrid to win the European Cup Winners' Cup."

One of the other differences between the rugby and football is that unlike football, most rugby referees don't receive anything other than expenses for their trouble and it's only at the elite level that they are paid. Of course, one of the reasons for this (apart from the fact that there is opposition to the idea from both the referees and the local amateur clubs), is that there is less money in rugby, other than at the elite and international levels. Crowds outside those last two levels, are generally a few hundred, although a local Borders' derby, say between Selkirk and Hawick, will attract perhaps 1,000-2,000 people. Even here, there are differences between the two sports. In football, you can't imagine a referee ordering a spectator to move away from the pitch, but in rugby, the officials do indeed have that power, as Malcolm explained….

"It's not like football, but there can occasionally be some venom from the crowd. However, a rugby referee has control over the playing enclosure, including a few metres from the pitch. If a supporter is being excessively abusive, the ref can say to the home club that he'll suspend the game unless they remove that person from the enclosure. I have actually done this. The clubs don't like it, but not for the reasons you might think. Outside the professional ranks, there is still a strong spirit of amateurism and they don't want anyone to feel unwelcome, let alone threatened, so rather than taking aim at the referee they will move the offender away from the pitch-side.

"Moreover, clubs have to fit in with the game's protocols, so, for example, no-one from the club, whether players or club officials, is allowed to speak to referees for 15 minutes after the game. This is so everyone can calm down in the immediate aftermath of the match. Also, unlike football, referees have always been encouraged to go into the clubhouse after a game, speak to the players, committees and officials and answer questions. This is immensely beneficial for everyone. I remember during a game at Inverleith, a player asked, 'ref, what was that for?' I told him, but he said he didn't understand, so I said we could talk about it at the end of the game. After the match, he came up to me – he should have waited for the allotted 15 minutes but I wasn't bothered. I told him, 'Bottom line, I got it wrong!' I was then able to talk him through it and explain why I couldn't change my decision during the game, because a rugby referee is only allowed to change a decision under the advice of another

SRU appointed official – and there wasn't one at the match. He really appreciated that I had taken the time to explain it all and we parted amicably."

It does seem to me that there is much that football can learn from this. If it was rule that no-one from either club can approach a match official for 15 minutes after a game, we would be spared the unedifying sight of managers and players remonstrating with refs as they walk off the pitch, or waiting for them in the tunnel - or accosting them in their dressing rooms before they have even got showered. Similarly, if referees were allowed to speak to the players *privately* after the match and have a grown-up, discussion, with both sides' confidence being respected afterwards, they (the players) would almost certainly learn a lot more about the laws of the game and be more understanding of the way in which it is refereed. Why can't we introduce this? There are clearly some things that we, in football, should learn from rugby, as my next interviewee, a former international rugby referee, also made clear…

I refereed England vs France at Twickenham one week and the next week I did Primary 7 at George Watson's College
Jim Fleming

Of all the referees in this book, Jim Fleming has, unarguably, the most impressive track record. As well as officiating in 42 international matches, and running the line in a further 75, he has refereed at four World Cup finals, including two semi-finals and four quarter-finals, as well as the Women's World Cup Final in 1994 between England and the USA. He also officiated in the European Cup for six years, taking responsibility for four Cup semi-finals, one Challenge Cup semi-final and the 1998 final.

If you've never heard of him that's probably because you are a football fan rather than a rugby aficionado. He was recognised in 2004 by the International Rugby Board with their distinguished services award for refereeing and by the Scottish Rugby Union with their Lifetime Achievement Award in 2001. In 2002, he was awarded an MBE for services to rugby. Jim has been retired from active refereeing for some time now and is currently the Referee Performance Reviewer Manager at the Scottish Rugby Union. As a result, his views on the art of refereeing are extremely well worth reading…

Like many football referees, Jim became a rugby referee after he was unable to play, in his case due to concussion. Sadly, this was when he was only 18, back in 1973.

"I first realised I had a problem at school. I played for the first XV at Boroughmuir and I had a number of instances of being concussed. I saw a neuro-surgeon, who found a small blood clot at the back of my brain and consequently suggested that I should give up playing, which I did. I used to go and see Hearts at Tynecastle back in those days, but about two or three years after I'd stopped playing rugby my old gym teacher persuaded me to referee a first-year match at school and it really just took off from there. I was an exception in many ways: most people at that time went into refereeing after they had finished playing, usually in their early 30s. Mostly, though, it's a young man's game: I retired when I was 50 but most top refs now will be retired by their mid-40s.

"There were also more restrictions in my early days. Up until the late 1990s, as well as being a member of one of the local Referees' Society you also had to be member of a club, which meant that you couldn't referee games involving that club. It's changed nowadays, with young rugby referees starting at 14 or 15 and then coming through in their early 20s. Also, they tend to have played professional rugby, which wasn't an option in my day. For example, Mikey Adamson, who is one of our very best refs today, played Sevens for Scotland and 15-a-side for Glasgow Warriors. We now have four contracted, full-time referees in Scotland. Unlike football they will also act as touch judges and video-referees in some matches but, even though they are at the highest level, they can be – and are – asked to referee any game.

"To give you an idea of the range of games a top-level referee in rugby might do, in 1993 I refereed England vs France at Twickenham and the next week I was due to do a club game in Scotland. On the morning of that club match, I was going to watch my son, who was in Primary 7 at Watson's (School). His team were playing Edinburgh Academy, but before we left the house I got a phone call from the Watson's gym teacher, who told me they were toiling for someone to referee the Primary 7 game and would I help out? When I arrived, there were two masters from Edinburgh Academy with their team, both of whom were former referees. 'What on earth are you doing here?' one of them asked me. 'After my performance at Twickenham,' I said, 'they've told me I have to start again at the bottom!' This kind of thing doesn't occur very often nowadays, but it can still happen."

Like football, rugby has suffered a drop-off in the numbers of referees coming through the system. This, Jim explained, is partly because of the decline in the numbers actually playing the game, especially as a result of the Covid pandemic. Most young referees are still attached to clubs and there is a demand to fast-track the best coming through the six regional Rugby Referees' Societies. In his current post with the SRU, Jim and his colleagues are responsible for monitoring the up-and-coming officials in the senior, regional-level game across Scotland and they then feed these young refs into the selection panel (which he sits on) for promotion to the national set-up.

With such a long career in rugby refereeing, I wondered if Jim sees much difference between rugby as it was his day and the game today – and if there are any parallels with football.

"The game today is totally different from the 1960s. Obviously, the advent of professionalism in 1996 brought the biggest changes, but today the physicality of players, their speed and strength are far greater than back in the 1960s and 1970s. The defensive tactics in rugby have also improved massively, largely because of the introduction of coaches from Rugby League. In my day, the forwards did forwards' things – essentially competing for the ball with their opposing forwards and then feeding it to the backs. The forwards were bunched together and the backs were spread out across the pitch. Nowadays, everyone is spread out across the pitch so there is less room for a talented back to take on his opposite number. Also, it used to be the case when I was refereeing that there were major differences in the way the game was played across the world. When you refereed in New Zealand or Australia you realised it was different, so you had to adapt how you refereed down there. But now, most countries play a broadly similar style – with, as I noted, far less room on the pitch for the creative players to express themselves - and to that extent it's easier for the officials, albeit the pace of the game has increased so they too must be fitter. I knew it was time to give up when they asked me to wear a heart monitor! Nowadays, all the players and officials wear them, as well as GPS tracking vests so the coaches can see who is running the most."

Is this, I asked, a good thing for the game of rugby?

"Personally, and this may seem sacrilege to some, I think the game can be boring nowadays. Although there are far more, and longer, phases of play, there is less fluid movement and rarely does the ball get to the wing. Rugby has evolved far more than football, with the laws

also changing hugely and as a result I don't think it's as exciting a spectacle. The crowds seem to have changed slightly too. Not that long ago, on the day of an international at Murrayfield it was all rugby people, many of whom would have played in the morning before going to the game. A lot of people who go nowadays don't have rugby backgrounds and for them it's just another (corporate) day out.

"Another major issue is the size of the players and the serious injuries that are becoming more common. Although players are bigger, stronger and more muscled, the issue is that their joints can't get any bigger; their ligaments are the same size so when they take big hits they get more injuries. That's reflected in the number of players you need in your squad just to get through a game."

I found this really interesting, and in particular, the suggestion that as rugby players have got faster and fitter, there is less room on the pitch and hence less excitement for the spectators, with the game becoming bogged down into a territorial struggle. As a result, you commonly see minute after minute of a mass of players camped on the opposition line and a try only decided by (what seems like) four minutes of slow-motion video because ten huge bodies are all in a heap around the ball. As I argue elsewhere in this book, football is becoming like this and, in my opinion, is the worse for it. It may be offensive to the modern gurus of football science, but the old Scottish fans' demand to 'get it up the park!' tended, I believe, to produce more excitement – often from errors and the break of the ball - than the ball being passed side to side and little ground being made up – whether in football or rugby.

Of course, rugby introduced the TMO (Television Match Official) well before football came to enjoy the frustrating experience of VAR. Here again, Jim's views are pertinent, largely because they show the likely direction of travel for football

"The TMO in rugby began to be used properly, albeit in a basic form, after the Rugby World Cup in 1999. At first, like football, there was a straightforward focus on only a few key decisions. That was the original intention, but in time the TMO's remit expanded as rugby referees made more use of the technology. The problem, in my opinion, is that once the genie's out of the bottle he wants to explore more of the possibilities open to him. And that, of course, is what happened in rugby.

"Initially the TMO made the decision and there were no big screens for the fans and players to re-visit the action. Once that stable door was opened, it was pushed wider and wider and now the TMO sits in a van with the director and a couple of helpers in front of a bank of TV screens. Some of these screens have a five second delay, so they can see live and then re-watch five seconds later. A key issue for me – and I think this applies in football too – is that it all takes far too long. That's not good for the fans or the players – or the referee. In my view, if you have to rock and roll the video back and forth in slow-motion that implies that you are unsure and I believe that referees must be sure in their decision-making. If the TMO is not sure, then he should go with the on-field ref's initial decision. It's all about whether something is 'clear and obvious.' If I am assessing a ref and I think something is wrong, it's got to be a clear and obvious error, otherwise I'll always give him the benefit of the doubt. In

football, when I watch decisions being made by VAR, it increasingly seems to be getting silly – is a player's foot offside, or even just his big toe? This is creeping into rugby too: 'did the player brush the ball down deliberately or was it accidental?' Today, I watch rugby refs see what they think is a forward pass, but they let play go on and if a try is then scored they simply refer it to the TMO to check. I don't think I'd enjoy refereeing nowadays because the decision making is taken away from the on-field officials."

Of course, one of the biggest differences between the two codes is the attitude of the players towards the officials…

"Swearing at the referee rarely happens in rugby. It was slightly more common back in the day, but then referees began to be miked-up to the TV and the crowd could hear everything, so that tended to curtail any bad language.

"The year after I retired, I was invited to the SFA referees' annual conference in St Andrews to talk about the microphone technology we used in rugby. Tiny Wharton was main man and I spoke to the gathered masses, explaining how it all worked. I thought it was quite funny that of the 350 or so referees there only about 10 were in favour of using more technology in football. I posed the question, 'won't it help your game?' but the consensus was 'if we're miked up, they'll hear the players swearing at us…' Of course, I also explained that in rugby if that happened the penalty would be walked ten metres up the field and that also helped stop any problems with referees being abused.

"That's not to say that it doesn't happen. The English referee Wayne Barnes sent a French player off in an international game. He then called over the French captain to tell him what had happened, explaining, 'he had turned around and told me to fuck off.' Of course, being an international match this was broadcast not just to the crowd but live on the television. And before we were wired for sound, it wasn't unknown for a referee to turn to a player and tell him to 'fucking shut up.' Clayton Thomas was doing the Wales vs, Scotland game and one of the Scots' lads was giving him constant grief, so he got hold of the Scottish captain and said, 'if you don't get this bloody parrot off my shoulder, he's going to the sin bin.' The parrot then shut up…"

Of course, rugby is widely perceived to be a 'posh' game. Is the better behaviour of the players, I wondered, all down to social class?

"Historically, it probably was…. Many rugby clubs, especially in the central belt, are associated with public schools, so it's been mainly middle to upper class people who played the game. Although it's changing a bit, it's still noticeable that not many of the Scotland team went to a comprehensive school. Obviously, the public schools have an ethos of discipline and it isn't the done thing to question authority. However, attractive as this argument might seem, on the other hand, if you look at Rugby League it's always been regarded as a working-class game, yet it still has the same discipline as Rugby Union. It's bred into the players from the earliest possible age that it's always been the case that rugby players respect the referee."

I then asked if Jim had ever tried refereeing a football match…

"I've done football matches, including some of our office teams. I found it no problem but the office players reckoned I was too fit and too fast! I would like to have given it a bash at the senior level to see whether the same man-management skills are required. Quite a few years ago there was an experiment where a top rugby league team played against a top rugby union team. One referee did both games and got on fine. Admittedly, football is very different, but it would be interesting to see how refs from each code would get on doing the other game. On-field discipline would be the issue. In 28 years, I only sent 11 players off, but we didn't have yellow cards in those days. Those who are old enough to remember the famous All Black lock-forward Colin Meads being sent off at Murrayfield will remember what a stir that caused, but being dismissed is not frowned upon quite as much it was back in those days. Scotland had never had a player sent off until the late 1990s, when Nathan Hinds was dismissed. You have to remember that a lot of infringements in rugby are for technical stuff. There is an understandable, and necessary, emphasis on being very strict about dangerous tackling – but then it's a dangerous sport. I think the biggest problem would be that in football you have fairly consistent laws and very few have changed much, whereas in rugby they change the law all the time. If an issue crops up, they tinker and introduce something else – and then that becomes an issue and there is more tinkering. It is becoming silly at times."

While noting that some of the more recent law changes in football could also fall into the 'silly' category, my final question was what could football learn from rugby and vice versa, and has there been any attempt by the two codes to try and do so…

"As far as I know, there has been no contact between the SRU and SFA on this. I had a contact with the SFA Head of Refereeing at one time and we had informal discussions but it never came to anything. I suppose things like rugby's yellow card and sin bin would be worth looking at, as would the ten-metre rule for questioning a referee's decision. In rugby, we're even looking now at a change whereby after a player has been red-carded another player can be brought on after 15 minutes so it doesn't distort the game too badly. Then there is the moratorium in rugby on players and club officials approaching the referee for 15 minutes after the match. That might be a sensible thing to introduce into football. I am sure there is much we can learn from each other."

Chapter 2
Managers (and Media)

It is sometimes thought that if managers would only control their players or refuse to say anything derogatory about referees, a lot of heat would be taken out of football. Sadly, it doesn't work like that. In fact, I was told that when brothers David and Jocky Whiteford were the manager and coach respectively of East Stirlingshire, they tried to be nice to referees, hoping that it might result in their side being more favourably treated. It didn't, which suggests that referees really are unmoved by what's said about them by managers, or alternatively that the Whiteford brothers weren't nice enough.

One thing that does come out fairly loud and clear from my conversations with past referees is that, with only a tiny minority of exceptions, they all got on/get on well with managers, other than during the 90 or so minutes of a match when a switch is flicked and everyone goes into game-mode. Then, when the vultures of the press gather for the after-match press conference, hoping to elicit some incendiary titbit, the managers have to be very careful only to go so far in what they say, so as to avoid an email from the SFA's compliance person. However, it's fair to say that if there is one theme that managers have in their post-match comments about referees then it's consistency. *"Consistency - that's all we want!"* they cry, before launching into another thinly veiled critique of the unfortunate officials.

There is, in my view, only one problem with this: namely, that if the managers want consistency from referees, they need to display it themselves. It became apparent to me in researching this book and talking to many former referees that the refereeing community looks after itself. Although this applies to football in general, it seems to me that the bond is even stronger amongst referees. However, for a football manager, the 90 minutes of the game are almost the be-all and end-all. Emotions run high as their players strive to win. It's hardly surprising they get angry at what they perceive to be bad decisions. Similarly, they are delighted when decisions 'go for them' and they then win the match. Consequently, rather than there being unanimity over a poor refereeing decision, say a match-winning penalty that was clearly never a penalty, the losing manager will vent his feelings whereas the winning manager will mouth platitudes about *"I couldn't really see clearly,"* or *"The referee was better placed than me."* If managers want referees to be consistent then they need to do the same. Rather than saying, *"I will need to watch it back,"* or similar, they should come out and say, *"I've spoken to <the opposing manager> and we both agree it was never a penalty. Obviously, we were not going to turn down the chance to win the game and I'm pleased we did, but that doesn't detract from fact that the decision was, in my opinion, wrong. We need our referees to be consistently getting the big decisions right."*

Meanwhile, as hell refuses to freeze over, managers have their own opinions, a few of which, are given below. These are then followed by the thoughts of arguably the two most influential football fans in Scotland – Off-the-Ball's long-standing presenters Stuart Cosgrove and Tam Cowan, whose opinions on referees, in my view, probably reflect those of a great number of football supporters the length and breadth of the country…

The longer I've been in football management the more I appreciate the job the officials do for us
Tommy Wright

Tommy Wright's entire career has been in football, firstly as a goalkeeper with a string of clubs, including Manchester City, Newcastle and, internationally, Northern Ireland; and then as a manager, first in his native Northern Ireland and more famously at St Johnstone, where he and his players brought the Perth club their first major trophy. He was more recently at Kilmarnock, focusing on returning the famous old Ayrshire club to the Premiership but, in the current, febrile mood in football whereby directors and fans want instant success, he was not given the time to achieve that goal. Tommy has a depth and breadth of experience that few others can match and his views on referees reflect his knowledge and career to date. My first question to him was straight to the point…

Do managers and players appreciate the job the referee and linesmen do?

"I think players might not so much, but managers, yes, I think they do. Certainly, the longer I've been in management the more I appreciate the job the officials do and the challenges they face. When I look at the criticism they get, especially in Scotland, I have every sympathy with them – and that's coming from someone who has been known to criticise them himself. Scotland is a bit different in my opinion. In Ireland, managers seem to be able to come out and say what they think about refs, but here we have to be very careful. It's partly a result of the Old Firm and the religious divide that accompanies them: fans think that referees favour one side over another and it results in a lot of toxic stuff, especially on social media.

"I've always tried to get on with them. That said, things are different from my day as a player. Some would give you one-liners back, which they can't do nowadays. I remember having a go at Joe Worrall about one of his decisions when we were playing at Watford. He just retorted, 'You just fucking look after yourself. You're having a stinker.' To be honest, I didn't mind that: it was the give and take that you had to accept as part of the game back then, but he wouldn't be able to say it today."

Next, I wondered does a manager 'flick a switch' when the game starts?

"Yes, if we are all totally honest we do get involved in decisions we shouldn't. Especially unimportant decisions. We should just think, 'it's a throw in, get on with it…'

"At McDiarmid, the refs would walk past my office and I would make a point of trying to have a chat with them. I think that's important as it fosters relationships. Managers need to show respect but I often try to see the ref after the game. After I've made any point I wanted to make I try to move on … you can't have constant antagonism.

"I look at other sports, principally rugby, which is a very physical sport with a lot of aggression but there is total respect for the referee and we don't have that in football. That's disappointing. It goes all the way down to kids' football. It's really sad to see the local

paper reporting that a referee has been assaulted at a youth game. People in grass roots football need education to try to stop this, but I'm not sure how it can come about."

Like most high-profile managers, Tommy has had his fair share of shocking decisions. Perhaps the most notable was when Craig Thomson gave a penalty against St Johnstone in a game against Celtic when the ball hit Keith Watson's backside. It was a turning point in the game, made worse because Thomson had, not long before, turned down what looked a good shout for a penalty for St Johnstone, who were winning at the time.

"Craig Thomson rang me on the Sunday morning. He didn't have my number, so he must have gone out of his way to find it, probably from John Fleming, the referee supremo. Craig said, 'I'm really sorry, I've not slept all night.' 'Neither have I,' I replied, and we had a wee chuckle. He was man enough to admit the mistake, which was appreciated. The incident had been fully dissected on the TV on Saturday night and everyone agreed there was no way it was a penalty. I think John Fleming had encouraged Craig to get in touch."

I then wondered if managers should all be more honest about poor refereeing decisions, if they want consistency?

"Well, if you look at the recent decision by John Beaton to award a penalty for Hibs against St Johnstone (26th September 2021), it was clearly never a penalty. Yet I understand why Jack Ross, the Hibs manager, didn't say that. He was probably thinking he was supporting the referee. I have said sometimes that we were lucky to get a penalty so, yes, managers could help with what they say.

"That said, we do have be careful. The laws change almost every season and for older managers, brought up with, say, the understanding that a handball decision for a penalty can only be justified when it's deliberate handball, it's hard for us to get our heads round the current 'unnatural position' interpretation. The managers all meet with the officials once a year to be updated on the law changes, but it's only an hour's meeting and it's unsurprising that we don't always fully grasp every last nuance of the latest change.

"The players and the fans don't know all the rules either, which is largely why they go mad when they think they'd been hard done by. Last season (2020-21), when Alfredo Morelos was sent off at Pittodrie, the supporters and media hammered the ref, but the law had changed from the previous season and so his interpretation was correct. Above all, unless you have actually tried refereeing, I think we should cut referees some slack. Ask any trainer or manager how they find refereeing training matches and you'll soon discover that no-one thinks it's easy. For the really critical decisions, the ref has only a split-second to get it right. He doesn't have the luxury of a slow-motion playback and a leisurely studio discussion."

Finally, I asked Tommy how referees could improve their relationships with managers?

"Sometimes, they react according to the book rather than judging a situation on its merits and using their common sense. When I was at St Johnstone, we had a game in which several

players were dismissed. Along with Paul Smith, then Saints' Football Administrator, I went to see the referee after the match and he was sitting with a towel round him and asked us to give him a few more minutes. I suspect he was thinking about how to handle us, but when we returned, he promptly told us that we should sit down and he would listen to what we had to say – but if we disrespected him then the meeting was over. As I was explaining my view, there was a rap on the door. Not surprisingly, Paul and I turned out heads to the noise. 'Right, that's it, you've disrespected me, meeting over.' We just left, shaking our heads…

"On the other hand, there are refs I do like more than others, usually because a decision has gone for us. Willie Collum isn't every fan's cup of tea, but he made one of the best decisions ever when he didn't penalise James Dunne for a high foot in his challenge that led to Stevie May's equaliser in the 2014 semi-final against Aberdeen. There were a number of challenges from Saints' players that could easily have led to a yellow card that day, but I think Willie realised that the chance of getting to the Cup final was such a big deal for a club like St Johnstone that he took that into account and was more lenient than he might otherwise have been. That's common-sense refereeing."

If Tiny said something you didn't dare question it.
Jim Jeffries

The name Jim Jeffries is intertwined with Heart of Midlothian. As a player, he spent 14 seasons with the club: as a manager, across two separate spells, six seasons. However, Jim also managed a host of other Scottish clubs, notably Falkirk and Kilmarnock and, in partnership with his assistant, Billy Brown, he has made an indelible impression on the game – and, as various of them describe elsewhere in this book, its referees.

As a player, Jim played under referees like Tiny Wharton, arguably the biggest name in the history of Scottish refereeing. However, as he recalls…

"It was very different in those days to now. The tackles we did, well, you'd never be on the park today. Referees were far more lenient back then and you had to do something serious before you even got your name taken. We knew we'd get away with a lot: it was all part and parcel of the game. However, players knew how to look after themselves and quite a few were cute, knowing how to delay a tackle so you'd feel the weight of it. There were a lot of hard men (my great hero was John Cummings, as hard a man in training as you can imagine) but there weren't many who were deliberately dirty.

"I'd love to know how many sending-offs there were in those days compared to today. I see players being sent off now for a fairly innocuous foul and I think, I've put in harder tackles than that, but instead of being sent off the fans were cheering and the ref waved play on. I was sent off a couple of times in my playing career, but I suspect it would be more often if I was playing today.

"Another change since my playing days is that now we are always at refs, whereas I think it was easier to get on with them in days gone by. Most would call the players Mr. followed by their surname, but some would call you by your first name. You got to know who was strict and who wasn't. You knew what you could get away with and what you would not. Then, after your playing career was over, you meet up with these people, referees, linesmen and supervisors - and the banter is great.

"That said, some were very strict, John Gordon was one I always though was very officious. These types wouldn't speak to players during the game unless they'd done something to incur their displeasure. But we all respected Tiny Wharton, who was not just a big man but was also a really big presence on the pitch. It was generally accepted that if he said something you didn't dare question it.

"Today, referees are under tremendous pressure, not just from the players and managers, but also from social media and the pundits who play back the contentious moments of games in super slo-mo, a facility that isn't available to referees. This introduction of technology, of which VAR is a part, is something that I don't think helps the game as much as its advocates say. Referees only see tackles and fouls in real time."

Next, I wondered about Jim's relationships with referees when he was a manager…

"There were a few who weren't my cup of tea. They could be nice guys off the pitch, but on it they didn't have a good attitude towards the players and the managers. I think that's essential in a good referee. For example, Brian McGinlay and I got on fine, even though a lot of controversy followed him round. The thing about Brian was that he had a good manner. He'd tell you to go away (he didn't actually use those words) or he'd ignore you if you were shouting at him during a match, but afterwards he'd explain his decisions, telling you why he'd made them. That's how it should be.

"Kenny Clark always mentions me in his after-dinner speeches, usually referring to me as Jim Jeffries MBE, which he says stands for "Miserable Bastard from Edinburgh.' When I was a manager, Kenny used to annoy me more than any other referee. Similarly, Willie Young and I have had many battles over the years but, like Kenny, I get on fine with him now. Both of them could be good at winding you up, but they were also fair. I remember when I was a Kilmarnock and we were drawing 1-1 with Celtic and the game had gone well into injury time. Willie was the ref and Billy Brown and I were screaming at him to blow his whistle. At a break in play, he walked towards the dug-out, beckoning to us both with his finger, so we had to go to see him, like naughty schoolboys. Which is obviously how he saw us, because he then said, 'you two are acting like a couple of schoolkids. We'll be here all fucking night until Celtic score if you don't shut up.' Billy and I just looked at each other, but soon as play resumed, he blew the whistle for the end of the match.

"Willie was also more than happy to help you to wind up others. He refereed the 1998 Cup final and gave us a penalty in the first minute, which Colin Cameron converted (Hearts went on to beat Rangers 2-1). Rangers had a good claim for a penalty just before the end which looked like it was going get them back in the match, but it wasn't given. After the game, Willie told me, 'The rule is that if the linesman runs to the corner flag it's a penalty, in which case I'd have given it, but because he stayed level with the 18-yard box I knew the foul was outside – so it wasn't a penalty.' Meanwhile, Walter (Smith – the Rangers' manager at that time), McCoist and the rest of the Rangers players and staff were still going daft…

"I get on well with Walter and Coisty and they always bring up Willie's performance in that game. Some months after the match, I was playing golf at the Renaissance in North Berwick when I saw Willie in his car there. I walked over and we had a chat. Then, when I went into the clubhouse, standing at the top of the steep staircase was Walter and his wife. I turned round and here's Willie coming towards me. Hoping Walter was still at the top of the steps, I said to Willie, 'I'll put my arms around you as we go up the steps,' to which he, not unreasonably, asked 'why?' and I simply replied, 'you'll find out in a minute.' Anyway, there's Walter at the top of the steps, looking at us coming up arm in arm, to which he responded, 'I fucking knew you two were in cahoots….'"

How, if at all, I wondered, do managers' attitudes to referees change over time?

"You get to know them a lot better, which does help. There is so much passion in the game and once the whistle blows the pressure and adrenalin start pumping. However, over the course of my career there were plenty of incidents where you do wonder…

"For example, early in my managerial career I was at Berwick Rangers. We were playing at the old Montrose ground and Sandy Roy was the ref. Billy and I were shouting abuse at the linesman, giving him stick about an offside decision and he must have shouted to Sandy to come and have a word. Sandy came across and sent me and Billy to the stand. Well, if you remember the old Montrose ground, we were able to just step over the fence and carry on from about two feet further away than we were in the dugout. The authorities didn't like that: they wanted to set an example and, as they saw it, tone down the managers' aggression, so when I then joined Falkirk as manager I was banned to the stand for a year and fined £1,000. I was a part-time manager at Berwick (probably getting £30 a week if I remember rightly) and I couldn't really afford the fine. To make matters worse, Falkirk didn't win any of our first five games in charge, so we got pelters from the fans around us in the stand. For a long time after that, I used to pull Sandy up every time I saw him.

Do managers plan for the referee?

"Most managers ask who the ref is well before the match. You start to think, 'did I fall out with him the last time we had him?' or 'will he hold something against me?' You get gut feelings about certain situations. When I was managing Hearts, I remember one very famous referee who, in my view, overstepped the mark. I must have said something about him on the radio after a previous match which he didn't like, because he said something before the game which he shouldn't have. Unfortunately for him, he said it in front of the fourth official (who was Sandy Roy, ironically!) and the two linesmen. 'What are you saying?' I asked, 'are you going to be against us today?'

"I went and reported his comments to my chairman, who said, 'keep a note of what happens during the game.' Of course, nothing happened and it was probably one of the best games that referee had with any of the teams I've managed. We all make mistakes and now I get on fine with that particular ref (who is well retired).

"Linesmen, who, like Fourth Officials, are often in more direct contact than the ref with managers during the match, are fair game. You're always trying to get a wee edge, claiming for anything and everything. You have to understand that they don't get everything right. It's a heat of the moment thing: you are always looking for someone to blame when things go wrong. I know it's not an easy job… You have to remember that you need referees or there is no game – and, of course, you have to remember they are only human."

Do the Old Firm get more favourable decisions at Celtic Park and Ibrox?

"You get people saying, 'you're paranoid,' but every manager will tell you that when you go away to the Old Firm, with 50,000 plus in the stadium, hardly any of them away fans, it happens too often… You think, why does it happen and then you realise, as I've just said,

referees are human. The place will go mental if they get something wrong against the home team. There is no doubt that the crowd can have an influence on referees and I include all the bigger crowds – in Edinburgh and Aberdeen too – in this. It's the sheer volume that is intimidating. Every manager I know has the same complaint and it will often feature in their team talks before an Old Firm match. When I was Killie manager, Ian Durrant was on the backroom staff and he told me, 'you know, when I played for Rangers I used to think everyone was paranoid about this, until I came to Kilmarnock when I realised what everyone was on about.' If you get a break at Ibrox or Parkhead then you've earned it, so take it and get out quick! Someone should do some statistical analysis on this: I'd be surprised if it didn't show that the home teams get more favourable decisions at Parkhead and Ibrox."

Do referees ever apologise?

"I've only had two apologies from refs over my entire career."

What makes a good referee today?

"There are some good referees about today, but latterly my personal view is that because of all the pressure they are under it's increasingly hard for them - much more than it was when I was playing. There are a couple of the current crop of refs I'm not wild about, but I know it's not easy, especially, as I said earlier, because of the TV replays and social media. However, the best referees are the ones with a good attitude towards the players and the personality to take players with them, using common sense and not always sticking to the letter of the law. Unfortunately, that's difficult, because in the same way that football is now full of stats the referees too are judged by stats - and the guy watching them in the stand. Most of the football stats we increasingly see on Sky are useless as the only statistic that matters is what the score is at the end of the game. This also applies to too many of the stats on a referee's performance. Statistics don't tell you about the personality a referee brings to the game. The players today will tell you that some of the refs' attitudes are not great. I wonder if they are told to be like that? Of course, they are making tough decisions, but if they make any slip-ups they get reported back to the football authorities, so that's one of the reasons why some behave the way they do. The problem is that if referees are perceived of as arrogant, they upset the players who are then more likely to become angry and get sent off. That's not good man-management. That said, there are still some you can talk to and they are generally, in my opinion, the better ones."

I have been known to apologise occasionally to referees
Dick Campbell

After a lengthy playing career with a host of clubs, notably Brechin City, Dick Campbell embarked on an equally lengthy, and continuing, career as a manager with Cowdenbeath, Dunfermline, Brechin, Partick Thistle, Ross County, Forfar and now, since 2015, Arbroath, whom he led to successive promotions to the Championship and from which they arguably should have been promoted to the top flight in May 2022. Well-known as a colourful, larger-than-life character, an image that was reinforced in our conversation, Dick's views are honest and straight to the point. For example…

"You asked me what I think about Scottish refereeing… well, I don't think it's difficult. For a start, their fitness levels in Scotland are a disgrace; they run a couple of laps and do a few stretches and think that's enough. They need to stop being controversial, keep up with the play, have a good rapport with managers and players. Get the decisions right, it's not hard – we all know whether it's a foul or not. OK, you might make the occasional mistake, we can all accept that, but just get it right. That's all managers want.

"What we don't want is all these rule changes that don't make any difference. Over the last ten years or so there have been six new changes introduced and not one of them has made the game better. There's the six second rule for goalkeepers – are you kidding me? Then there's the second phase rule for offside – ridiculous. Also, explain to me why I'm only allowed 30 seconds to make one sub but two minutes if I want to put two subs on? As for VAR, don't start…"

At this point, I cautiously ventured the idea that the players might not know all the rules…

"I know the rules, because I did my coaching badges. It's a simple game, not rocket science. I've had an up and down relationship with Scottish referees over the years, but would say that things are different from when I played. It's definitely more difficult for referees nowadays. When I was playing it was much easier to have a laugh with them. I remember Kenny Hope, who'd be giving you a lecture, wagging his finger in your face and the fans were thinking he was laying in to you, but what he was actually saying was, 'you'd better be buying me a pint after this.' They couldn't get away with that today. Nowadays, they have supervisors watching everything they do and they can't use their common sense, but there are a few egotistical ones who think the fans are there to watch them.

"To be fair, we obviously do need them. As I get older, I have better rapport with them than I ever did and I don't think there are bad referees, although there are some ordinary referees. Overall, I wouldn't say that Scottish referees are any worse than any other country's refs. And there are also some very good ones – they are the refs you don't notice. In my playing days, people like Kenny (Hope) and John Rowbotham – they were refereeing in Europe and you don't do that if you're no good.

"You might find this hard to believe, but I have been known to apologise occasionally to referees. However, I don't recall any apologising to me. If there is a controversial decision and you question it after the game, they say they'll get back to you, but they never do."

I then wondered if everything is forgiven and forgotten after a match…

"I often would say to them, 'I had hoped you would be better today than you were the last time you were here.' The smart ones say something like, 'well, you weren't too great either.'

"You can have some fun with them though. I remember being with my (twin) brother Ian at a posh restaurant in Tenerife. We were having a nice meal and I noticed that Willie Young and his brother, John, were in the far corner of the restaurant. The waiter brought us this note that Willie had written. It said, 'John and I are sitting in the corner; can we join you after the meal? I got hold of the waiter and got him to bring me a pen and paper and sent a note back saying, 'with respect why don't you go …. yourself.' Fair play, he wet himself. I see him on the after-dinner circuit these days and we have a good laugh together. I remind him that you have to have a good personality to be a great referee, which is why he never was…

"Another story involving Willie was when he was doing a match at Cappielow. Strangely, it was a sunny day in Greenock and he was out warming up with the linesmen before the game. This wee boy ran on to the pitch with an autograph book and a pen, but referees are not supposed to sign autographs so Willie refused him. All the fans were booing and the players were telling him, 'go on, sign the wee boy's book.' So, Willie called the boy back, picked up the pen and found that it was one of these joke electric pens that give you a shock. The crowd and the players were killing themselves laughing.

"I could write a book on John Rowbotham. I remember one game he gave a penalty that wasn't even two inches outside the box; it was about 20 years outside the box. I see John on the after-dinner circuit too and I know he uses a lot of stories about me, so fair's fair.

"Probably my favourite story though was with Kenny Hope. It was when I was managing Brechin and we were playing Kilmarnock. John Ritchie, a real Brechin great, was still on the coaching staff after he retired, but for this game he was banned from the touchline and was in the stand, so we were using walkie-talkies. There was a blatant penalty that Kenny didn't give, so I'm giving him pelters and I could hear John on the walkie-talkie trying to calm me down. The fact that he was sitting next to the chairman, David Will, who at that time was a Vice-President of FIFA, and also Craig Brown, former Scotland manager, might have had something to do with it, but I was having none of it. I'm running up the touchline, shouting at Kenny, 'you … and John's shouting in my ear, so I said to Kenny, 'and that's not all, here's John Ritchie wants to talk to you….'

"I suppose you could say I have a love-hate relationship with them..."

Gordon saw that Pele and I were next to each other and blew the final whistle
Tommy Craig

I remember Tommy Craig more as an Assistant Manager (notably at Hibs, Celtic and Aberdeen) and manager (at St Mirren) than as a player. Part of the reason for that, as I discovered when I looked up the details of his playing career, was because he spent most of his time south of the border, principally with Sheffield Wednesday, but also with Newcastle, Aston Villa, Swansea and Carlisle. He also has one cap for Scotland. In other words, Tommy was more than a decent player as well as a manager, although, as he admitted when we met, *"coaching rather than managing was my forte."* However, it is his experience as a player and in management across the UK that makes him such an interesting person to talk to about referees and refereeing. We began our conversation by discussing the differences between players and managers' attitudes to officials. More specifically, I asked *do players know the rules and, more importantly, do they understand them?"* Unwittingly, I had hit upon probably Tommy's most embarrassing moment as a coach in football.

"It was at a game between Celtic and St Mirren at Love Street in Paisley when I was the Assistant Manager at Celtic. Frank McGarvey was playing up front for St Mirren. For almost the entire 45 mins of the first half I berated the stand-side linesman, because every time St Mirren had a goal-kick, Frank was 10-15 yards offside. I was yelling, 'Look at him, he's offside, get your flag up' but all I got was a dry look. I waited till half time, followed the ref and linesmen up the tunnel and demanded to see them. In their dressing room the stand-side linesman just stared at me. I was incensed, telling the officials: 'that's 45 fucking minutes you've been letting them away with offsides. What's the story?' Calmly, the ref replied, 'you cannae be offside from a goal kick.' I went down on my knees in supplication; I was sweating and confessed, 'I can't believe I've given you such a torrid time.' Considering the abuse I'd been giving them, they were very decent about it and we just got on with the game in the second half, but it taught me, as if I didn't know, that players and managers really don't know the rules as well as the referees and linesmen.

"That said, in general, I think that managers are more aware than players, largely because they are giving instructions to their teams and constantly trying to gain an advantage, so it does pay to have a look at the rule book. Fergie, who has a great memory, is one of the best, but I doubt many managers will know all the rules."

Next, we discussed the differences between officials in England and Scotland.

"In my experience, the top refs were quite similar in both countries. The best referees are brilliant in the way they manage footballers, especially how they defuse a situation that threatens to blow up. It is really all down to excellent man management. There were two in England who come to mind, both standouts. They were Jack Taylor and Gordon Hill, both of whom refereed in different ways but got the same results. Jack Taylor, who did the 1974 World Cup final, managed players with his eyes, like Collina. He didn't have to say anything, he would look at you and that look said, 'Tommy, you've got one more.' Gordon Hill, on the

other hand, was the arm-on-shoulder type. He would not berate you, but let you know, getting close and quietly saying 'no more!' He was the type who would give as good as he got. I remember one game when I was at Sheffield Wednesday and I told him, 'Gordon, you're having a nightmare,' and he came right back at me with, 'from where I'm standing, you're not doing so well yourself.' I wasn't, so I shut up.

"One thing I did experience in England which didn't occur in my time in Scotland was that a few referees would actually compliment you on your game. The likes of Gordon Hill would say, 'good pass son,' as they ran past you. Some may not like that as it suggests favouritism, but I think they knew that they were getting you on their side and less likely to do anything to wind them up.

"Really, a lot of refereeing is just down to common sense. Lots of people remember the incident with Gazza when he picked up the ref's yellow card and brandished it at him, only to get a proper booking in return. It would have been wonderful if the ref had played it out and given back the card to him, pretending he should referee the game. The fans would have loved it and it would be remembered for all the right reasons.

"In Scotland I liked Kenny Hope as a referee. I remember he was refereeing Celtic vs Hibs just after I had joined as player-assistant manager to Sloop (John Blackley) at Easter Road. I was never the best tackler in the world and there was a long ball into the corner for Davie Provan, the Celtic winger, to chase. It was a race between us and I got there a wee bit late. Davie, ended up on the trackside. We were right next to the Celtic fans and, as you can imagine, they were giving me a lot of abuse. Kenny rushed over and beckoned me away from the corner flag. He carried on wagging his finger at me throughout, so the fans thought I was getting a real telling-off, but what he was actually saying was, 'I know that's not your style, but welcome back to Scotland. I'm giving you a yellow card, but I could easily have given you a red.' Of course, the Celtic fans were delighted, though they might have been less pleased if they'd heard the conversation. Kenny Hope knew I wasn't that sort of player and, more importantly, he knew I wasn't out to get Davie Provan. Davie patted me on the back and got on with the game. In my view, that was good refereeing: he removed me from the potential flashpoint with the fans, gave me an appropriate punishment while making it clear that it could have been worse and, to cap it all, finished it with a joke, telling me, 'I refereed your brother John at Partick Thistle, last weekend and he was much worse than you.' Everyone was satisfied at the end of the incident; Kenny handled it brilliantly.

"There were other refs I liked too. George Smith, who was Edinburgh based, was quiet and, although he had a superior manner he was demonstrably in charge and didn't lose control of a situation. Crucially, he didn't take action too quickly but seldom got it wrong, much like Jack Taylor and Gordon Hill.

"Unfortunately, nowadays the hierarchy (the football authorities) *don't seem to want any banter between officials and players. The referees all seem to stick together, which is great, but I would like to see some more flexibility and common sense at times."*

120

Turning again to Tommy's time as a manager and assistant manager, I asked if he thinks that once the game starts, a switch flicks on and the manager and his team, driven by their professionalism and will to win, act differently from how they normally behave?

"Yes, I think that's true, but it depends on how the game goes. The will to win is intense; that's how players and managers get to the top. The ref doesn't want to be seen to be swayed by either dugout and he knows he obviously can't influence the fans, but he will, naturally, demand respect. In theory, there should be no foul language, but in the heat of the game people get away with the odd obscenity. For the ref, the challenge is to let them know you're in charge. They need to stand their ground when the going gets tough. The psychology involved in being a ref is considerable. I remember at Parkhead when Andrew Waddell once summoned Billy McNeil to come to the touchline for a dressing down. Billy got out of the dug-out and walked to the touchline, inflating his chest and drawing himself up to his full height. Andrew had to walk across to him, psychologically getting smaller and smaller while Billy seemed to get bigger and bigger. It looked comical at the time.

"Sometimes the hierarchy could do with showing some common sense too. I got sent to the stand once when I was at Celtic and came up before SFA committee. I remember Alex Miller of Rangers was up before them the same day. They asked me a number of questions, including, 'Did you encroach on to the pitch?' 'Did you swear?' I said, no to both. It was apparent that the committee couldn't say that I'd actually transgressed, other than the fact that my left foot was on the pitch. That was enough for them, so I got a £1,000 fine. Two weeks later, I met one of the committee members outside Hampden. He came over and said, 'Hi Tommy, I'm really sorry about the punishment, you and Alex Miller are two of the nicest guys in Scottish football.' In that case, I replied, 'can you get the fine rescinded?' Unsurprisingly, the answer was no…"

I have asked a few referees what it's like doing the Old Firm derby, with some admitting they didn't sleep beforehand. What is it like, I wondered, from the (assistant) manager's viewpoint?

"There are very few people who genuinely transcend the Old Firm divide. Ally McCoist and Tommy Burns are probably two of the few who were respected and liked by the opposition fans, but for referees it must be very difficult. There have been so many incidents over the years, including the infamous one where Terry Butcher et al got sent off. Of course, the fans think the referee is against them. At Celtic, I remember one of the club's most experienced backroom staff saying, 'we'll need to win 1-0 just to get a draw,' but in truth I don't believe that stuff. But to referee an Old Firm game you really have to be a strong personality. I remember one ref, who I'll not name, for obvious reasons, and when he came to inspect the boots the sweat was dripping off him. It was five minutes to three and he looked as if he would rather be anywhere but in that dressing room. Billy McNeil and I looked at each other and Billy asked if he was OK."

Sometimes, referees must wonder about the behaviour of spectators…

"When John Blackley was manager of Hibs, he was out on a Sunday and, seeing a game in progress on a local park he stopped to watch. To his amazement, one of his squad, Joe Tortolano, was playing. Sloop started shouting, 'what the fuck are you doing, get your arse off that pitch!' The referee must have wondered who this lunatic was, but Tortolano just ignored him. John kept on shouting, 'get off that fucking park right now!' until the referee stopped the game. Tortolano came across to John and told him that he wasn't going to stop playing because he was Mario, Joe's twin brother..."

On other occasions, referees would go out of their way to help...

"When I was at Sheffield Wednesday, Santos, with Pele in their ranks, were on a European tour and they were scheduled to play us. The game was on a Wednesday afternoon and a full house was expected. All over Sheffield there was a rash of gran's funerals. The referee was to be one of my favourites – Gordon Hill. I spend the entire fortnight before the match thinking how I could get Pele's shirt. Although there have been some fabulous footballers since then – Maradona, Messi and Ronaldo amongst others – for me Pele still just shades it as the best of all time. I was racking my brains for a cunning plan, 'how do I get his shirt?' Then it came to me. At half time, when we were in the tunnel, I buttonholed Gordon. 'Can you do me a favour please?' I pleaded. 'Can you let me know when you're going to blow the final whistle?' Gordon was perplexed and asked me why I wanted to know this. 'Well, I'm not going to be playing against Pele again...' so the light dawned on him and he agreed he would let me know. It was getting very close to the end of the second half and we were attacking. However, I was standing on the halfway line, encouraging our full back to get forward in my place! Sure enough, Gordon saw that Pele and I were next to each other and blew the final whistle. I made a bee-line for Pele and we swopped shirts. I still have it, framed in the house.

"Pele was very difficult to play against, even in a friendly. It was very hard not to be a fan; you were just watching him on the park, almost saying, 'come and beat me,' and he did! I felt like applauding. It was an honour to be on the same pitch. After the match, he showed what a gentleman he is. He was an hour late for the post-match reception because he was sitting there and signing autographs for fans."

And, despite what some might think, players and managers are prepared to socialise with referees...

"I remember being at the Under-23 tournament in Toulon with Scotland. John Rowbotham was the only Scottish referee there, so we asked him to come along and share a meal with the squad, which he did."

Finally, Tommy was happy to admit that his own experiences of refereeing made him realise just how hard it is...

"Like all managers and assistants, I've had to referee training matches. You find out just how difficult it is…you are instantly, in a split second, calling a foul, or not as the case may be. You give a foul, then you think, 'hang-on, was it really a foul?'

"We need, as players and managers, to remember that referees and their linesmen are doing a job that most people would never want to do. Refs are trying to keep a grip on the game while all around them are the players who all desperately want to win for their team. Then there is the crowd, who obviously want their team to win too. The referees are the ones out there in the middle and they haven't got anyone on their side. Because of this, I have never refused a referee's hand after a game. I'd never not look a ref in the eye, even when, especially perhaps when, I didn't agree with him. I understand the pressures, they are under. No-one deserves to be jumping in his car after a game of football and fearing for their safety. We owe it to our referees to treat them with respect."

You're only allowed to complain about the ref if your team has won…
Tam Cowan and Stuart Cosgrove

'Off-the-Ball' is, I think it's fair to say, a Scottish football institution that is now embedded in most fans' pre-match rituals, whether driving to a game or settling in for an afternoon of 'Open all Mics' on Radio Scotland. On the air for 28 years now and going out live every weekend in the hours when fans are travelling to the grounds, each programme attracts well over 100,000 listeners and receives a mountain of tweets and emails over the course of a normal show - some of which are even suitable for being read out live on air. Stuart Cosgrove and Tam Cowan, the show's long-standing presenters, are famous for being supporters of St Johnstone and Motherwell respectively and are respected for bringing a genuine fan's perspective to the key issues of the day in Scottish football, both trivial (mostly) and (from time to time) serious. They have slightly differing views on a number of aspects of referees and refereeing, with Tam generally regarded as being perhaps more sympathetic to officials than Stuart. By way of an opening question, I wondered why that is…?

TC – *"I do have a lot of sympathy for referees, probably more than most fans, because my close pal, Jim Walker, was once one. Jim was destined for the top of the refereeing fraternity until he sustained a really bad knee injury and had to give up. He reached the level where he was running the line in the Premier and I remember him telling me about a game in the early 1990s, where he brought the referee's attention to an off-the-ball incident involving Hearts' Justin Fashanu, who had elbowed an opponent off the ball and as a result was sent off.*

"It annoyed him when one fan suggested that that the £850 or so that a ref gets per match today is great pay for only an hour and a half's work. As Jim noted, that hour and a half is the tip of the iceberg: there are many, many hours, days, weeks and years required to get to that level and even when you get to Grade 1 you have to train very hard for several days every week. Like all referees, Jim had to start right at the bottom of the tree, refereeing BB games and then slowly rising up through amateurs and Junior football and he opened my eyes to the immense work that referees put into their careers and how they are pilloried, frequently unfairly, in the media. I also remember one season when the Sunday Mail ran a feature on 'The year's 10 biggest refereeing blunders.' Jim pointed out to me that they had got three of them wrong!

"As I developed my own career in media, I realised just how little most fans (and journalists) actually know about referees and refereeing. Various newspaper and broadcast media have had (and continue to have) some form of "Ref Watch" feature, some of which scored the referee's performance in each game. Some refs got zero

points, but strangely, none of the players in any game were ever awarded such a derisory low score. I always say that in my 42 years of having a season ticket for Motherwell, I've seen a lot of shite teams and, although I'll give the ref stick when I think he deserves it, I will always say that it's not the referees who costs us the most points over any season - it's the players.

"In addition, we've had a lot of referees on the show over the years – Hugh Dallas, Kenny Clark, Willie Young, Stuart Dougal etc. – and talking to them you realise they are all intelligent men who really do love football, so when you hear the crap they have to take it's shocking.

"Of course, we get Old Firm supporters who think the dice are loaded against them, but I always point out that Celtic and Rangers both won nine-in-a-row, so if there was a conspiracy for or against them then it didn't work very well."

SC – *"I think that one thing that brought it home to fans that our referees are actually not that bad was when the (referees') strike was on and we had refs and linesmen brought in from Europe. When they went home, everyone realised that there wasn't really much difference between our home-grown officials and those elsewhere.*

"Another problem for refs is that whenever there is a dispute over any major incident, the media do like to keep it going. From a journalist's point of view, that's not a problem – it's their job - but I'm not sure it does referees any good in the short or indeed the long term. The current referees, as we know, don't really speak to the media, other than when a game is called off and then they sometimes agree to speak on air about their reasons for doing so: other than that, they don't often communicate with us. Again, I'm not surprised as on the few occasions when sports journalists do get to speak to the officials they tend to treat them differently from players or club officials. For example, it's fine for a manager or a player to make a joke in an interview, but it would be a brave referee who did so. They would be demonised and social media would be all over it."

As a conduit for fans to make their feelings known, I wondered if Off-the-Ball provides a sort-of safety valve for supporters to vent their feelings?

SC – *"It's in the fans' psyche to have a go at the referee for almost anything. We do, obviously, get a reaction to big incidents, both on and off the park, but in in general I think that fans have an expectation of how the game should be managed, even if they don't know the rules themselves. Of course, what colours their opinions most is whether their team has won or not."*

TC – *"yes, and that's why we have had this sort-of rule for years on Off-the-Ball that you can only criticise a referee if your team has won...."*

Do you know the laws of the game yourselves...?

SC – *"Yes, about 90% of them I think."*

TC – *"I'll happily admit I don't. Neither do most players and managers in my experience. My mate Jim Walker said that when the managers of all the senior clubs were invited (regionally) to the annual meeting with the local refs to learn about any changes to the laws, hardly any of them went. That was the case in his time and I suspect it may still be true today."*

Will the introduction of VAR be a good thing?

TC – *"Yes, I'm all for it. However, the average football fan wants to argue about incidents in the game and no amount of VAR is going to stop him or her doing so."*

SC – *"I'm not sure: I have reservations. If you look at the way some of the rules have made players change their behaviour, I think this will only get worse with the introduction of VAR. For example, the incident when John Beaton wrongly gave a penalty against* (St Johnstone's) *Jamie McCart at Easter Road for 'handball' earlier this season has made McCart even more determined to force his arms behind his back when he's defending crosses. With VAR that will be even more the case, but how can he, or any other player, actually play the game with his hands and arms in such an unnatural position?"*

Is there anything that refs do that annoys you personally?

TC – *"I have a go at refs for minor infringements. It really annoys me when they give a free kick in your half of the field, then make the player retake it because it wasn't quite in the right place or the ball has moved a fraction just before it's kicked."*

SC – *"I think some refs adjust their behaviour during the game. For example, at the start, they let players away with murder, then if the game becomes testy later on, a sub can come on and get booked after 30 seconds for a tackle that went unpunished in the previous seventy minutes..."*

PART II

Chapter 1
Whose idea was that…?
The development of the Laws of the game

While working with my good friend Brian Doyle (the man who knows more about St Johnstone and the club's statistical record than anyone else) on our first edition of the club's official history, I spent many years traipsing back and forth from Glasgow to the Sandeman Library in Perth before the book was published, in 1997. I was fortunate in having the privilege, not accorded to every football club's historian, of being given complete access to the Saints directors' minutes. This was provided by John Litster, who, as noted above, is not only one of the most knowledgeable people on the subject of Scottish football history, but was then St Johnstone's General Manager/Secretary. John not only encouraged me but also allowed me to take away and reproduce some of the very old photographs the club owns, including the one shown on this page of a game against Arbroath at the Recreation Ground in Perth in 1887. It depicts a throw-in being taken by an Arbroath player and, as John pointed out, it's being taken one-handed.

Picture courtesy of St Johnstone FC

At that time, I had no idea that throw-ins were ever taken in this manner, assuming that the two-handed throw-in had been in place since the dawn of time. As I began to add to my knowledge of St Johnstone's history and, by default, about the history of the game in general, it was clear I had a lot more to learn.

I knew that Saints played their early games on the South Inch, a large public park in Perth, but it took us until the updated version of the official history to work out where exactly these matches took place. Initially, we thought they were on the Lesser Inch – the smaller area on the other side of the Edinburgh Road for those who know Perth. Later research for the updated club history in 2015 revealed that the club began playing on the main body of the Inch, in the area nearest the railway. For the first edition we had a photograph taken of the pitches which were still there on the Lesser Inch, complete with the goalposts and crossbar. However, although I knew that the crossbar wasn't officially introduced until 1888, some years after St Johnstone's formation in 1885, I, and I suspect most others, just had this hazy

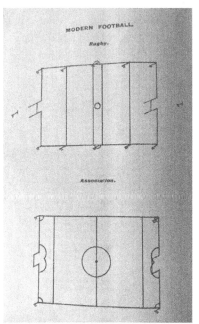

notion that the proto-footballers of Perth and Perthshire, playing for clubs like Erin Rovers, Caledonian Rangers, Tulloch, St Johnstone, Dunblane, Auchtergaven (Bankfoot) and Blairgowrie just turned up and the posts and pitch markings were already there.

The truth is that I simply don't know who was responsible for laying out the pitches in those days. I do know what the pitch markings were like (no penalty box or penalty spot and two wee arcs where today we have the rectangular goalkeeper's box – and just a tape for the crossbar). The reason for the arcs was simply that a goal kick had to be taken six yards from the nearest goalpost to where the ball went out of play. While it seems that the matches were sufficiently well-organised that there was more to it than simply putting jumpers down for goalposts, one wonders if the local authority, watching as this game of Association football became more popular, marked out the pitches and erected permanent goal-posts, as they did when I turned out for Craigie Primary School on the South

Inch in the 1960s. Or (much more likely) did the clubs employ a man who would come along before the game and set up the posts and make sure the pitch was marked out? I know that the first St Johnstone team bought their own goalposts, but were the pitches they played upon marked out with sawdust or was there some form of whitewash used?

In the course of researching St Johnstone's history, I acquired a rare book called *"Football in Perthshire,"* published in 1898 and written by Peter Baxter, one of the very earliest members of the Perth club. The line-drawing from this book, shown here, illustrates how pitches were laid out in the late nineteenth century. As you can see, there are no rectangular penalty or goal areas, but the centre circle and corner quadrants are already standard. The two other lines across the pitch were 12 yards from the goal, introduced after the penalty kick was brought in to the game in 1891. Penalty kicks were then taken at any place along that 12 yard line. Subsequently, a further line, 18 yards out, was made on the pitch, within which an infringement resulted in a penalty. In the photo from the 1901 FA Cup Final shown here, the 12-yard line is easily distinguished but the 18-yard line is barely visible. Today's modern penalty area and penalty 'spot' were introduced in 1902. All of which made me realise that the furore today about VAR and other changes to the rules is nothing new. The men who played through the last decade of the nineteenth century and the first decade of the twentieth must have had just as much change to cope with as the modern-day footballer.

The more I researched the subject of the early development of the pitch markings and the rules more generally, the more fascinating (to me at least) it all became. As the game developed in the nineteenth century, different people came up with different ideas and interpretations of how best to make it all work. For example, someone decided that having those six-yard arcs around the goal was a good idea. Similarly, someone else decided that awarding a penalty for serious breaches of the rules was also a good idea. Others had the ideas for goal-nets, corner flags and that most vital piece of equipment, the referee's whistle. In 1866, there was the sensible introduction of a tape between the posts to mark the height of the goal at eight feet, followed by the replacement of the tape with a solid bar, officially approved in 1883. The latter innovation is claimed by both Sheffield FC and Queen's Park, although the latter may have been first, introducing a wooden crossbar in 1875. Even the replacement of the tape by a solid bar didn't stop arguments. In the 1905 Perthshire Cup final, played at Crieff between Dunblane and St Johnstone, the Saints' 2-1 victory was rendered null and void when Dunblane complained about a shot that had struck the bar. The referee subsequently measured the goal and discovered that the bar the ball had struck was one-and-a-quarter inches lower than the regulation height. As a result, the game was replayed, at Stanley. On that occasion, the crowd were incensed by a refereeing decision and invaded the pitch, leading to a third match, again at Crieff, where Dunblane won 3-1. In some respects, crowd behaviour towards referees has possibly improved (a little bit) since then…

Back in the nineteenth century, there were many unknown and consequently unsung heroes who came up with suggestions for important changes to the way in which football is played and its infrastructure organised. To them, we all owe an enormous debt. The success of football is largely because of its innate simplicity, but even simple games require some structure and rules. In the last decades of the nineteenth century, as the differing formats and rules came together to become one, universally accepted set of laws, it was evident that this was a sport which didn't require a lot of effort to understand and, crucially, was a game which was exciting both to play and to watch. Once the laws were standardised, it was clear that the essence of football was as near perfect as makes no difference: as demonstrated by the fact that, despite the slow process of change and the gradual introduction of many new facets and interpretations, the essential elements of the game are still much the same today as they were then.

There are only 17 laws of the game, although as any good referee will tell you there are actually 18, the eighteenth being, *"use your common sense."* Like the first 17, this *"law"* is not always applied. However, how there came to be these 17 laws is a longish story…

Although various forms of football can be traced across Europe from medieval times, the game has a long history in the British Isles, with contests played annually, often on Shrove Tuesday or at New Year, essentially involving mobs of men from opposing villages competing, frequently with considerable violence, to carry and propel a ball – often an inflated pig's bladder (to which we shall return) – to a place or mark that constituted a goal.

Sometimes referred to as 'mob football' (those who remember BB – Boys Brigade - football may empathise with this concept), this proto-form of the game had very few rules. It was violent and dangerous. To get from there to today's VAR-dominated and, some would argue, increasingly (and excessively) regulated game required a lot of change and ingenuity.

In my research for St Johnstone's official history, I came across lengthy descriptions of some of these early games, notably the 'Ba' o' Scoon,' which was referred to in several books of Scottish customs and pastimes. The actual origins of this contest are lost to antiquity, but we know that it was held annually, at (Old) Scone, just outside Perth. Originally it was held at a Mayday festival but latterly it took place on Shrove Tuesday. It was a competition between the married men of the village in one team and the bachelors in the other. The objective for the bachelors was to 'drown' the ball three times in the river Tay, whilst the married men were to place the ball three times in a small hole in the moor. Given the size of the Tay compared to a hole in the ground, this seems somewhat unfair and there were frequent outbursts of violence, but the prevailing atmosphere of the contest was summed up in the local proverb, *"All was fair at the Ba' o' Scoon."*

Similar 'marrieds' vs 'single men' competitions were popular in the seventeenth century, with many games played on the North and South Inches (the public parks) of Perth on Eastern Eve (Shrove Tuesday) but the eighteenth century, with its Jacobite risings, saw much less football played in Perthshire, probably because the government, not unnaturally, was suspicious of large gatherings of men, especially in country areas where landowners were supporters of the cause of *"the King over the water."* The nineteenth century saw two brief revivals prior to the later decades when the modern game took off in Perthshire. These games demonstrated how relatively little football had changed since the Middle Ages.

The first of these was in the 1830s when, at a meeting of the Literary and Antiquarian Society of Perth, Lord Stormont and Lord Provost Pringle arranged a challenge match between Perth and Scone. This game was played on the 8th of January 1836. Each side consisted of 50 men, playing across the full extent of the North Inch and watched, it was said, by an improbably large crowd of some 14,000.

The game ended when, with the Perth side pressing hard towards their opponents' goal, the spectators interfered with play. As a result of the confusion this caused, the umpires decided that the match was drawn. The spectators were not happy and a riot broke out, with it being reported that some of the Scone players had to seek sanctuary in the nearby houses.

The next upturn came in the early 1850s, as a result of a number of keen Irishmen in the town who would pile their coats, or heaps of stones, to form goals (something all of us can remember doing in our childhood). These games became regular Saturday events and sometimes the spectators would join in, leading to matches between teams of up to 30-a-side.

In 1853, a challenge match took place on the North Inch, again between married men and bachelors. The stakes were 1 shilling (5p) per man and a crowd of around 2,000 watched around a 'pitch' measuring almost a mile in length. The married men scored the only goal and the game ended, by mutual consent, after two hours' play. Unlike the match in 1836, there appears to have been no undue violence, but despite this mid-century revival, football in Perth died away until the start of the Association game in the early 1880s.

These stories from Perthshire can be replicated across Scotland. Generally referred to as *"the Ba' game"* and with records going back hundreds of years, this 'football' is still played today in Kirkwall, Jedburgh, Roxburgh and Duns. I also came across an article on the Robert Gordon University 'Jobs Blog' (of all unlikely places) which explained that Aberdeenshire can lay claim to having an interest in this proto-football, with records from the early 17th century showing that in either 1633 or 1636 (opinions differ as to which is the correct year), there is some evidence of schoolboys in Aberdeen playing a football game. The original source is in Latin, but roughly translated it suggests that handling of the ball was allowed, as was charging into the opposition, and the ball may have been 'passed' from player to player. The word used for the goal in the original source is (in Latin) *"metum,"* which was the pillar at each end of the circus course in a Roman chariot race. As any Spanish scholars out there will know, the word for goal in that language is *"meta"* and a goalkeeper is a *"guardameta."*

In their book on the Edinburgh Foot-ball Club, of which much more below, Scottish football historian Andy Mitchell and John Hutchison wrote of their discovery of a doodle in an Edinburgh University students' jotter from the early 1670s. This shows two men (in what look like Mexican sombreros!) playing a game that involves kicking a ball. This is the first known illustration in the country of a football-type game. The goals shown in the drawing have three traverse bars set between two posts, a bit like a farmer's gate stuck on the top of two poles. As the authors concede, there is no way of knowing exactly what is going on, but the ball seems to be roughly the same size as a modern ball and it very much looks like some form of football. There is some speculation that the location of this kickabout – namely Gallowgreen, where the Edinburgh city gallows were – might have led to the old Scots' term 'hail' becoming 'goal' as a result of the corruption of the word 'gallows.' However, as Hutchison and Mitchell note, *"these are fanciful ideas awaiting positive proof"* and, as I'll explain below, there is possibly another reason for the use of the word 'hail' in this context.

Gradually, the more extreme violence associated with medieval football was removed from the game as it began to be codified during the nineteenth century with the introduction of a more formal structure and rules, principally introduced by the public schools in England. Nevertheless, before 1863, 'hacking' (essentially kicking an opponent to the ground) was accepted by many as a key component of a manly game.

It is widely (and correctly) accepted that the main developments in the codification of the modern game of Association football were made in England and initially involved the famous public schools and universities of that country. However, as we shall see later, Scotland does have a very good claim to be the first to provide a set of rules for an organised football-like sport. Furthermore, the reality is that the development of the modern game on both sides of the border in the latter third of the nineteenth century demonstrates that both countries, in differing ways, played their own parts in the formulation and development of the modern sport, albeit with England playing the major part as far as the laws were concerned…

In the nineteenth century, several English public schools played a form of 'football.' The rules differed from school to school and area to area. As they became more unified, there were, naturally, those who dissented and wished to play according to their preferred set of laws. As a result, today we have several different modern games all derived from the nineteenth century variations in football rules. These obviously include rugby – whose origins are famously traced to the mythical day when William Webb Ellis allegedly caught and carried the ball in his hands at Rugby School in 1823 - and also Irish Gaelic football and, further afield, American football and Australian Rules football. Interestingly, Aussie Rules has more than a passing connection with some elements of the field game as played at Eton College, notably the two additional, shorter posts at the side of the main goal posts (making four posts at each end in all). Also in Aussie Rules, the early football rule that there is no limit to the height the ball can be as it passes through the space between the posts and still be counted as a goal still applies. For those interested in learning more about the similarities between the various forms of football played across the globe, I recommend Tony Collins' book, *"How Football Began."* However, these particular sports, while very popular in these countries, have remained minority interests across the world at large and it was Association football, aided by the growth of the British Empire in the nineteenth century, that spread across the planet. That it's a very simple game to play and understand also helped…

As the English, Scots, Irish and Welsh left our shores to seek fortune and fame under the auspices of the Empire, they took with them not just football (and cricket) but also cultural influences, which, like football, became embedded in countries throughout the world; a phenomenon trenchantly summed up by the much-quoted remark of Sir Richard Turnbull, a senior British colonial official who was Governor of Tanganyika between 9th December 1961 and 9th December 1962. Sir Richard famously said, "*When the British Empire finally sinks beneath the waves of history, it will leave behind it only two memorials: one is the game of Association Football ... and the other is the expression 'Fuck off'.*" The two may, of course, be related…

The nineteenth century public schools' attempts to find a mutually agreeable set of rules by which to play 'football' was to prove a long and wearisome task. The debate between the schools about the format of the game continued and it took several meetings until it was decided once and for all that football was a dribbling-kicking game played exclusively with the feet and not a catch-and-run game played with the hands. From the late 1830s there are references in local histories of a game of 'football' being played that seems to have progressed slightly from the unregulated mob football described above. It is highly probable that some forms of rules were printed in various locations in the country but unless and until they turn up, we are none the wiser as to what they were.

Until 1863, carrying the ball with the hands was still practised in several schools. A first attempt to bring together a collection of rules that might be used everywhere that football was played was made in 1848 at a meeting in Cambridge (there is evidence of "Foot-Ball" being played at Cambridge University in 1710). Representatives from various British schools attended and the meeting resulted in an agreement, called the 'Cambridge Rules.'

There is no extant copy of the original 1848 Cambridge Rules, but a copy of a further revision, made in 1856, does exist and it is believed by some football historians that these later rules were identical, or at least very similar, to the 1848 version. These 1856 rules were as follows:

THE LAWS OF THE UNIVERSITY FOOT BALL CLUB

1. *This club shall be called the University Foot Ball Club.*
2. *At the commencement of the play, the ball shall be kicked off from the middle of the ground: after every goal there shall be a kick-off in the same way.*
3. *After a goal, the losing side shall kick off; the sides changing goals, unless a previous arrangement be made to the contrary.*
4. *The ball is out when it has passed the line of the flag-posts on either side of the ground, in which case it shall be thrown in straight.*
5. *The ball is behind when it has passed the goal on either side of it.*
6. *When the ball is behind it shall be brought forward at the place where it left the ground, not more than ten paces, and kicked off.*
7. *Goal is when the ball is kicked through the flag-posts and under the string.*
8. *When a player catches the ball directly from the foot, he may kick it as he can without running with it. In no other case may the ball be touched with the hands, except to stop it.*
9. *If the ball has passed a player, and has come from the direction of his own goal, he may not touch it till the other side have kicked it, unless there are more than three of*

the other side before him. No player is allowed to loiter between the ball and the adversaries' goal.

10. *In no case is holding a player, pushing with the hands, or tripping up allowed. Any player may prevent another from getting to the ball by any means consistent with the above rules.*

11. *Every match shall be decided by a majority of goals.*

Interestingly, and with regard to the divergence of different codes of football noted above, it is worth comparing Rule 8 above with the *"playing rules"* of modern Gaelic Football which state: *"The ball can be carried in the hand for a distance of four steps and can be kicked or 'hand-passed,' a striking motion with the hand or fist. After every four steps the ball must be either bounced or "solo-ed", an action of dropping the ball onto the foot and kicking it back into the hand. You may not bounce the ball twice in a row. Players may contest for the ball by playing it with the hand or by shoulder charging an opponent side-to-side."*

A year after the first Cambridge Rules were devised, Surrey FC (an offshoot of Surrey Cricket Club) printed a set of rules (in 1849, and published in Bell's Life in London, as shown here). The connection with the cricket club meant that they played their games at the Oval

"THE SURREY FOOT-BALL CLUB.

"1. The club to consist only of such gentlemen as are members of the Surrey Cricket Club, the Surrey Paragon Club, the South London Club, and the Union Club.

"2. That a subscription of five shillings by any one of the above-named gentlemen shall entitle him to all the privileges of the 'Surrey Foot-ball Club.' That the money so subscribed shall be appropriated to the defrayal of the expenses of the club, namely, the cost of the balls and ropes, and the payment of a person who shall keep the balls, &c, in proper condition. The members shall dine together at the end of the season, and any surplus of the subscriptions which may then be in hand, after the payment of all expenses, shall be applied to such dinner.

"3. That the days for practice be (weather permitting) every Wednesday and Saturday in the afternoon, commencing the first week in October, and continuing until the last week in April in each year, the play to begin at three o'clock.

"4. That the sides shall consist of not more than twenty-two each; but if that number of members shall not be in attendance, then of any smaller number, to be arranged by those present.

"5. That wilful kicking shall not be allowed.

"6. That the ball shall be tossed up in the centre of the ground, and the game be determined in favour of that side which shall first kick the ball over the "goal rope" of their opponents. Should the ball be kicked over the fence on either side of the ground, then the ball, when regained, shall be tossed up in the centre of the ground in a line with the place where it went over."

Cricket Ground in London, where in due course, the early FA Cup finals were played. Only half of the six rules actually deal with the playing of the game, but nevertheless we do see the injunction *"that wilful kicking shall not be allowed"* – an anti-hacking sentiment that is shared by almost all the other early, formal rules for a kicking rather than a handling game.

While the cricketers, varsity students and public school boys were debating their rules, football as an organised sport was also gaining in popularity in towns and cities. First and foremost were the men of Sheffield FC. This club still exists today and its website proudly claims (erroneously in my view) that it is the world's first football club and the home of football. It would be fairer to say that England – with some significant input from Scotland – is the home of football, with no one city or club really being able to claim to being the sole genesis of the modern game. Indeed, the cross-fertilisation of ideas from different nineteenth century sports was central to the creation of the various 'football' games we enjoy today.

Sheffield and Perth are two very different cities, but there is an obvious parallel between the foundation of Sheffield FC and St Johnstone. The latter came into being when members of the St Johnstone Cricket Club decided they wanted some exercise during the winter of 1884-1885 and began kicking a ball around prior to the football club's actual founding on 24th February 1885.

Preceding them by some 28 years, the members of Sheffield Cricket Club similarly took up football, albeit of a somewhat primitive kind, as a means of keeping fit outside the cricket season. To this end, matches would be arranged between those with surnames beginning from A-M and those whose surnames began from N-Z, or bachelors against married men. These games were described as being played from 2.00 pm until it grew dark and, as in Perth, an interest in the winter game was kindled that led to the foundation of a proper football club.

There were many other connections between football and cricket in those early days. In the UK, these included (Sheffield) Wednesday who came out of the eponymous cricket club in 1867, while north of the border, Clydesdale Cricket Club, formed in 1848 and still a major force in Scottish cricket today, produced Clydesdale FC, who played between 1872 and 1881. As well as producing several Scottish football internationalists, Clydesdale FC also contested the first ever Scottish Cup final, losing 2-0 to Queen's Park. In addition, Andy Mitchell has written about the birth of Partick Football and Cricket Club in March 1872. This was not the same club as today's Partick Thistle, but of interest to fans of the latter may be his discovery of a Partick Thistle Cricket Club who were playing in 1875.

Coming from the same area of Glasgow, but in rugby rather than football, West of Scotland were formed in 1865 as an off-shoot of the West of Scotland Cricket Club, which was itself formed in 1862. The rugby club played at Hamilton Crescent in Partick which is, of course, where the first official international football match was played, as were several other subsequent internationals and the 1877 Scottish Cup final.

Interestingly, in 1880 The Times newspaper reported that there were probably more than twice as many rugby union players as footballers across the UK, but by the end of the century the round ball game was dominant. This was partly because rugby was inherently more violent and dangerous (in Yorkshire in the late 1880s/early1890s several men died as a result of injuries sustained at rugby) but also quite possibly because soccer was a far easier game to understand and play. This was graphically illustrated by the fact that when the FA Rules were first drawn up in 1863 there were only 13 laws for football, but when the Rugby Football Union was formed in January 1871, they devised 59 laws for their sport. Today, this has decreased to only 21, but the game itself seems to have become far more complicated for both players and spectators.

It is, to my mind at least, strange that nowadays there seems to be a gulf between cricket, rugby and football in Scotland, with the first two frequently described as 'posh' sports while football is, for many people, thought of as a 'working-class' game. In reality, those who initiated and developed the modern version of these sports were often (although not always) from the middle/upper classes. The spectators, on the other hand, reflected a wide cross-section of society. An interesting insight comes from David Drummond Bone's 1890 book of

"Scottish Football Reminiscences and Sketches," where, under a chapter titled *"The Patrons, Spectators and Popular Players,"* we can read…

"At a cup tie or International match, it is quite a common thing to see the Convenor of an adjacent county, the city magnate, the suburban magistrate, the Free Kirk minister, and the handsome, matronly lady, standing side-by-side with the horny-handed mechanic, the office-boy, the overgrown schoolboy, and the Buchanan Street 'swell.' They all watch the game and surroundings in their own particular way."

However, there was also…

"…the low, vulgar fellow, whose collarless neck and general coarseness of exterior and language indicates that he possesses all the vices but none of the virtues of the 'honest working man.' … it is he who, by his foul tongue and very breath, contaminates the atmosphere he breathes, and brings some of the matches into disrepute."

As football games became more popular, their appeal quickly broadened and people from all walks of life enjoyed their sport in the nineteenth and early twentieth centuries – as indeed they do today. In our era, however, foul tongues are the lingua franca of football crowds and coarse language regularly emanates from the mouths of the suburban magistrate as much as the horny-handed mechanic.

More specifically, the early exponents of football were happy to participate in (and spectate at) all sorts of different games, with sportsmen playing cricket in the summer and then football in the winter and with local sports' days featuring all manner of athletic and other sporting events. Indeed, in the first ever match played by St Johnstone, two of the side, Harper Wood and D M Stuart, played after having walked from the North Inch where they had just taken part in a game of rugby.

Returning to Sheffield, we find that, despite the city's industrial image as the steel capital of England, the two founding fathers of Sheffield FC were very much from the middle-classes. William Prest was a wine merchant and captain of Yorkshire County Cricket Club and Nathaniel Creswick was a solicitor. Some football historians believe that the public school rules played a part in influencing the rules produced by the Sheffield club but others, perhaps with an underlying political motive, disagree. Either way, the formulation of the Sheffield Rules was a seminal moment in the development of football.

Looking at them today, the Sheffield rules are clearly not quite football as we know it. For a start, there are only 11 of them, compared to today's 17. Moreover, they also have more than a passing resemblance to rugby in places. There were several drafts made before they were finally agreed, at a meeting in the Adelphi Hotel in the city on 28th October 1858, as follows:

1. Kick off from Middle must be a place kick.

2. Kick out must not be from more than twenty five yards out of goal.

3. Fair Catch is a Catch from any player provided the Ball has not touched the ground and has not been thrown from touch and entitles a free kick.

4. Charging is fair in case of a place kick (with the exception of a kick off) as soon as the player offers to kick, but he may always draw back unless he has actually touched the Ball with his foot.

5. Pushing with the Hands is allowed but no Hacking (or tripping up) is fair under any circumstances whatsoever.

6. No player may be held or pulled over.

7. It is not lawful to take the Ball off the ground (except in touch) for any purpose whatever.

8. The Ball may be pushed or hit with the Hand – but holding the ball (except in the case of a fair kick) is altogether disallowed.

9. A Goal must be kicked but not from touch nor by a free kick from a catch.

10. A ball in touch is dead. Consequently the side that touches it down, must bring it to the edge of the touch, & throw it straight out at least six yards from touch.

11. Each player must provide himself with a Red and dark blue flannel Cap, one colour to be worn by each side.

The importance of the Sheffield Rules lies in the fact that, despite the continuing links with a rugby-style game, their insistence on what we now recognise as the key elements of modern football was a major change. For example, as rule 9 makes clear, a goal could only be scored by a player kicking the ball. We can also see that they had a throw-in when the ball went out of play (rule 10), but the player threw it in using only one hand and he had to hurl it at right angles to the touch-line for a distance of at least six yards (as is, more or less, the case with a line-out in rugby today, although the distance is now five metres). In addition, the rejection of hacking (rule 5) created clear blue water between Sheffield and some of the public schools, such as Rugby. In 2021, a copy of the Sheffield Rules fetched £56,7000 at an online auction carried out by Sotheby's, its value presumably boosted by its claim to be the earliest, official (and printed) guide to the game. In fact, as noted above, Cambridge University's rules (1848) and Surrey FC's rules (1849) predate Sheffield's, and Cambridge's rules were preceded by printed rules from Rugby School in 1845 and Eton College in 1847. However, as we shall see, none of these was the first: that particular honour lies north of Hadrian's Wall.

Despite Sheffield putting down their marker, there was a problem in that lots of other clubs played to their own rules. This made it difficult for anyone attempting to officiate and it was obvious that for the sport to prosper some unifying body and standardised regulations were going to be needed.

In October 1863, a meeting was held at the Freemasons' Tavern in London (on Great Queen Street, near the current Holborn tube station) to discuss the issue and it was agreed that evening to form the Football Association. This initially consisted of the dozen London and suburban clubs who attended that night. These clubs, which included several public schools, then met a further six times over the next 44 days to formulate a set of rules. These are shown below. The original, hand-written laws are now in the English Football Museum in Manchester.

1. Kick off from Middle must be a place kick.
2. Kick out must not be from more than twenty five yards out of goal.
3. Fair Catch is a Catch from any player provided the Ball has not touched the ground and has not been thrown from touch and entitles a free kick.
4. A goal shall be won when the ball passes between the goal posts or over the space between the goal posts (at whatever height), not being thrown, knocked on, or carried.
5. When the ball is in touch the first player who touches it shall throw it from the point on the boundary line where it left the ground, in a direction at right angles with the boundary line.
6. When a player has kicked the ball any one of the same side who is nearer to the opponent's goal line is out of play and may not touch the ball himself nor in any way whatever prevent any other player from doing so until the ball has been played; but no player is out of play when the ball is kicked from behind the goal line.
7. In case the ball goes behind the goal line, if a player on the side to whom the goal belongs first touches the ball, one of his side shall be entitled to a free kick from the goal line at the point opposite the place where the ball shall be touched. If a player of the opposite side first touches the ball, one of his side shall be entitled to a free kick (but at the goal only) from a point 15 yards from the goal line opposite the place where the ball is touched. The opposing side shall stand behind their goal line until he has had his kick.
8. If a player makes a fair catch he shall be entitled to a free kick, provided he claims it by making a mark with his heel at once; and in order to take such kick he may go as far back as he pleases, and no player on the opposite side shall advance beyond his mark until he has kicked.
9. No player shall carry the ball.
10. Neither tripping nor hacking shall be allowed and no player shall use his hands to hold or push his adversary.
11. A player shall not throw the ball or pass it to another.
12. No player shall take the ball from the ground with his hands while it is in play under any pretence whatever.
13. No player shall wear projecting nails, iron plates, or gutta percha on the soles or heels of his boots.

Definition of Terms

A Place Kick: Is a kick at the ball while it is on the ground, in any position in which the kicker may choose to place it.
A Free Kick: Is the privilege of kicking at the ball, without obstruction in such a manner as the kicker may think fit.
A Fair Catch: Is when the ball is caught after it has touched the person of an adversary, and before it has touched the ground or one of the side catching it; but if the ball is kicked from behind the goal line, a fair catch cannot be made.
Hacking: Is kicking an adversary intentionally.
Tripping Is throwing an adversary by the use of the leg.

Knocking on: Is when a player strikes or propels the ball with his hands or arms.
Holding: Includes the obstruction of a player by the hand or any part of the arm below the elbow.
Touch: Is that part of the field on either side of the ground, which is beyond the line of flags.

As you can see, these rules are not particularly different from the Sheffield Rules made only a few years earlier and there are several similarities with rugby, such as law 8 which involves what is still called 'making a mark' in Rugby Union today. It's also worth noting that a goal was awarded if the ball went between the posts at any height. There was also no use of the word 'offside,' which wasn't introduced until 1866. Interestingly, the FA rules still subscribed to the idea that football would be (as the FA website explains), *"a blend of handling and dribbling. Players would be able to handle the ball: a fair catch accompanied by 'a mark with the heel' would win a free kick. The sticking point was 'hacking', kicking an opponent on the leg, which Blackheath FC wanted to keep."*

In Scotland, the rules of the game in the 1860s were notably different in one area in particular. In England, only the goalkeeper was allowed to handle the ball, but in Scotland the outfield players were still allowed to use their hands at this time. However, the 1860s did see some key changes, notably the introduction of a tape stretched between the goalposts at a height of eight feet to form a complete goal (before this, as noted above, a goal was awarded simply for the ball passing between the uprights, no matter at what height). In 1866, the first offside rule was introduced and a few years later, in 1869, goal-kicks were introduced.

It's important to realise that despite its seemingly all-encompassing title, the FA was pretty weak in its early years. In the Official History of the Football Association, published in 1991, the author, Bryon Butler, wrote: *"The FA's early influence on the game at large was not dramatic or even widespread. Its membership was small and its authority and laws were often challenged and sometimes ignored. But its motives and ambitions were so honourably based that, like growing ripples on a still pond, its standing grew perceptibly. It was a period of high ideals and ready compromise."*

Even after the formation of the English Football Association in 1862, the development of a unified set of rules was a slow process, as demonstrated by the work of football historian and academic Andrew Harvey. He researched the rules for all types of football as used by universities, public schools, local regions and counties and also what he referred to as *"Scottish variants of rugby."* He concluded that in 1868 there were 105 different versions and this number increased every year up to 1873, by which time there were 275. Of course, over time, this number withered away as the different branches of Association and Rugby football went their separate ways and their rules became codified and agreed nationally, but their common origins are plain to see.

What these different regional codes meant in reality was that games, especially those between the London clubs and those from the north, were often played to the rules of the home side, or alternatively one set of rules was played in the first half and another in the second half. Sheffield FC, despite joining the FA in 1863, continued to use their rules. This did little to standardise matters. There was lots of experimentation and gradual change and, in both England and Scotland, a small number of organisations came to the fore. In England, the Football League was formed as a separate organisation in 1888 but never acknowledged the FA as 'the ultimate authority' until the FA Premier League was instituted in 1992. The formation of the Football League had created a 12 club competition which began in 1888-89. Such a competition in turn required consistency of regulations and, in due course, a body of referees to try to apply the agreed laws consistently and fairly. Arguably, it was the introduction of the FA Cup in 1872 that did most to bring all the clubs together and the FA's rules subsequently became the dominant national – and, eventually, international - code. However, it was still the case that for much of the latter decades of the nineteenth century football was, in some key respects, still far removed from the game we watch today.

As I have had cause to mention before, I learned so much during my research for this book but one thing that constantly stands out is the extent to which there were differing rules and interpretations of the rules in different areas of the country. Like, I suspect, most football fans who have grown up with the game in the post-war period, I assumed the laws were more or less set in stone from the beginning. However, as I have demonstrated here, although it is possible (and some do try) to make a case for one part of the country (usually England or Scotland) as being the most important in the development of the modern game, it's clear to me that the credit should be shared around.

In Scotland, the SFA, founded in 1873, had competition from the Scottish Junior FA, founded in 1886, with the latter's clubs taking no part in the Scottish Cup at this time. Pre-dating the formation of the SFA, Queen's Park, the oldest Association football club in Scotland, was formed in 1867, followed by Kilmarnock in 1869, Stranraer in 1870 then Dumbarton and Rangers in 1872. Although there were "Scotch" versions of the rules, the bulk of the work in creating a set of laws that could be applied universally was, as described above, done in England. However, several decades earlier, there was a club in Scotland that, while not playing what we now call Association football, was most definitely a football club within the wide range of sporting styles of the game that persisted throughout the early and middle nineteenth century. Moreover, much to the chagrin of those in Sheffield (and Cambridge), this club also produced a set of rules, which have survived and predate anything similar from south of the border.

The club was called simply The Foot-Ball Club (of Edinburgh) and it began life in 1824. Although the archive containing all the information about this club was first discovered by social historian Dr Neil Tranter, the full story is told in detail in the book *"The World's First Football club (1824): John Hope and the Edinburgh footballers: a story of sport, education and philanthropy."* Written by John Hutchinson and Andy Mitchell and published in 2018, it tells how Edinburgh student John Hope established this club in 1824 and it carried on for another 17 years. Fortunately, the club's records have all survived and show, in immense detail, the membership lists, accounts, letters and personal reminiscences. In addition, there is a set of rules of the game, dating to 1833 and, as shown below, these (much like their later, English equivalents) suggest clearly that the game played was certainly not football as it is played today, but rather (a bit like the Sheffield Rules) a game that mixed handling and kicking, with holding and pushing allowed but no tripping.

Edinburgh Foot-ball Club Rules

1. *Single-soled shoes, no iron*
2. *No tripping*
3. *Ball to pass imaginary line*
4. *A place kick if ball out of bounds*
5. *Pushing is allowed. Holding not illegal.*
6. *Allow the ball to be lifted between fields*

Below this list of rules, John Hope added his own thoughts on the attributes of the game, viz, "*Aff* (affirmative) *Fun, air, exercise, Neg* (negative) *No tripping.*"

What we have here is, at the time of writing, the first known set of written rules of football of any kind, including rugby football (whose first rules were not written down until 1845). They clearly pre-date the first written rules from England and, I suspect to the annoyance of many in Sheffield, the existence of the Foot-Ball Club in Edinburgh suggests that the Sheffield FC's claim (on its website and on the club crest) to be *"the first football club in the world"* and *"the home of football,"* is somewhat tarnished.

The claim of the Steel City to primacy is further diminished when we learn, again courtesy of Hutchison and Mitchell, that John Hope also produced a printed guide to playing football some four years before the Sheffield rules were published. In 1854, John Hope financed and created the 'Stockbridge Playground' – a public park in Edinburgh, complete with a fully-laid out football pitch. To help the park's users, he had printed and published that same year, a set of rules which include the following:

Rules for the Stockbridge Playground

"The Game of Foot-Ball is strongly recommended as giving most exercise and fun in a short time. There must be no kicking of the shins, nor tripping – for these are apt to produce quarrels and hurts, and do not form part of the game. The ball is not "hailed," unless it is sent between the posts, by one of the side whose duty it is to send it through, and unless it touch the ground. If the ball is sent through by one of the other side, it is not "hailed." The ball should not be kicked out of bounds. When this occurs, it should be lifted up by the hand, and brought within bounds. The party thus lifting it, is entitled to a "free kick," but the ball must not be lifted by the hand from the ground at any other time. The British League Cap, to distinguish sides, cost 2d, is recommended. Beware of kicking the ball over the fences."

Compare these instructions with the Sheffield Rules described above and it's clear that Hope's game set the parameters first. That said, we can infer from both Edinburgh and Sheffield that the emphasis was on playing the game within a defined set of boundaries, between two teams with different colours (the caps) and the requirement to avoid handling the ball and not to hack the opposition are also familiar to us today (although the odd hack is not uncommon in the twenty-first century).

I didn't appreciate until I read Hutchison and Mitchell just how important a role Edinburgh played in the development of not just football but a number of other sports. Today, we tend to think of Scottish football as having originated in the west of the country, with, as noted above, Queen's Park being the first Association club, closely followed by Kilmarnock, with Rangers, Celtic, Dumbarton, Vale of Leven, Clydesdale and Renton – all from the west - also being prominent early winners of the Scottish Cup and Football League. In fact, much to my surprise, I discovered that Vale of Leven have won the Scottish Cup more often that St Johnstone. And although Hearts and Hibs did soon make their mark on Scottish football in the nineteenth century, most people, I suspect, would consider the Greater Glasgow area as the crucible of our game. However, as Hutchison and Mitchell tell us, it was actually Edinburgh that was home to *"the world's first football trophy, printed rules, organised games for girls and the first inter-school football matches."* From their research, I also discovered that goalposts were originally referred to in Edinburgh Foot-Ball as *"hailing sticks"* and at that time the verb *"hailed"* was used to signify the scoring of a goal.

John Hope's Foot-Ball Club lasted for some 17 years, eventually running out of members in 1841. Latterly, he became a man of considerable influence in Edinburgh and he then turned his hand to other sporting and leisure related projects, all underpinned by his insistence on abstinence from *"alcohol, tobacco or opium."* However, while the Foot-Ball Club lasted it counted many notable young gentlemen (a few of the 300 or so members were as young as 12 and 13 and the vast majority were in their teens or twenties), principally from Edinburgh but also from across the United Kingdom, including several Englishmen and lads from places as far apart as Barra, Shetland and Herefordshire. These young men, invariably from wealthy backgrounds, would go on to play important and influential roles in many different areas of Scottish and British life, both at home and overseas. Significantly, they seem to have carried their interest in football and other sports on into their later lives and, as we shall see, played their part in the development of the game of football that we know today.

That said, and as I have inferred previously, the evolution of the current rules of the modern ball games of football, rugby, Gaelic, Australian and American football, can all be traced back to the nineteenth century and the school and university clubs in England, Scotland and Ireland. Across the Irish Sea, Dublin University Football Club, founded in 1854, still exists today and has a good claim to be the longest standing football club of any code of football in the world. It is closely followed by Edinburgh Academy Football Club, founded only a few years later in 1857 and still going strong today, albeit very much in the rugby union tradition.

There are, for perfectly understandable reasons, many who wish to seize the crown of being the world's first, but when looked at dispassionately, it's obvious that those who make such claims forget that the modern versions of football, rugby etc. were moulded and formed by a diverse range of people over the years. As these games and their associated rules changed over the nineteenth century, so they have changed over the twentieth and twenty-first centuries as the patchwork of different rules and interpretations slowly came together to create the modern game.

To give an idea of how late-nineteenth century football was only part-way to its modern incarnation, consider this description of an 1880-81 FA Cup match between Old Etonians (twice winners of the FA Cup) and Stafford Road, the Great Western Railways works team. This is taken from Andy Mitchell's book on (Lord) Arthur Kinnaird, the Scotsman who was one of the game's leading figures in the nineteenth and early twentieth centuries. It is actually a quote from a report of the game by one of the umpires.

"During the game, Ray, the Stafford Road goalkeeper, fell on the ball after saving a shot. Macaulay had promptly fallen on top of him and soon a regular Rugby scrimmage was formed, with all the players assisting. After this had been in progress for some minutes (my emphasis), *Kinnaird, who was buried in the thick of it, was observed to be wriggling out backwards, and when free he rushed to the referee saying 'I claim hands! Somebody must have handled the ball.' Receiving a negative reply, he immediately buried himself in the melee."*

It's abundantly clear from this and many other match reports that this was not yet the game we enjoy today. Football in England had evolved at this time into, at times, a non-handling version of a rolling maul in rugby, whereby teams hunted in packs. Football historians believe that the game there was played principally by players surrounding the ball and attempting to dribble/shepherd it towards their opponents' goal.

In contrast, in Scotland the players seem to have spread out more across the field and each individual would attempt to run with the ball at his feet. When they were tackled, the ball might break to a team-mate or, alternatively, it could be passed to him. The Scots' style of play was closer to football as we know it today, but it should be emphasised that, as described below, the state of the pitches and the boots used were such that passing the ball accurately must have been difficult. Moreover, all bar one of the contemporary reports of the first football international between Scotland and England in 1872 make no reference to the ball being passed but instead emphasise the dribbling of both teams.

That said, there is no doubt that the Scots did lead the way in passing the ball in a more modern manner and matches played between Scottish and English clubs, and the export of players to play for northern clubs in the FA Cup, spread this style down south and had a significant influence on subsequent refinements of the rules. Similarly, the introduction of payments to players – with mill towns in northern England offering work to talented Scottish footballers (often referred to as the *"Scotch Professors"*) led, in time, and despite strong opposition from both the FA and SFA, to professionalism both south and north of the border.

The most famous Scottish club at this time was, of course, Queen's Park. Avowedly amateur (until 2019), Queen's Park is the mother club of Scottish football and in their early years they were active in travelling around the country and encouraging others to take up the game. Famously, they demonstrated the game in Alexandria and as a result Vale of Leven FC was formed in 1872. The Vale's ground was opened with a match against Queen's Park which ended 0-0, partly because the game was stopped several times while the Queen's players explained the rules to the new-boys.

They also took part in the first few FA Cup competitions, including the very first one in 1872. They made the semi-final that year, but, after drawing 0-0 with Wanderers, they had to scratch because the club couldn't afford to travel to London for the replay. Despite their financial embarrassment, Queen's Park did subsequently make the final on two other occasions, in 1884 and 1885, although they lost both times. As well as Queen's Park, a number of other Scottish clubs joined the English FA and Cowlairs, Hearts, Rangers, Partick Thistle, Renton and Third Lanark all played in the FA Cup (with Rangers reaching the semi-final in 1886-87), but as the game grew in Scotland they left the FA and joined the Scottish football firmament, specifically the SFA and the Scottish Football League. They were strongly encouraged to cut their ties with England by the SFA, which passed a rule in May 1887 forbidding its clubs from being a member of another national association, under penalty of expulsion.

With increasing interest in football both north and south of the border, it was inevitable that games would be arranged between the leading clubs. Queen's Park was the first Scottish club side to host an English side. In front of a crowd of 10,000, this match was played in October 1875 at Hampden (this was the first Hampden stadium, not the current – third – one), and the visitors were Wanderers, with whom Queen's Park had drawn the 1872 FA Cup semi-final referred to above. Queen's Park had never lost at home up to that point and they routed their English visitors by five goals to nil. The Glasgow side's superiority was such that their goalkeeper reportedly did not touch the ball once in the first half.

Matches between the top clubs in Scotland and England over the next few years usually demonstrated the superiority of the Scots at this time. In addition, there were a series of matches played between Sheffield and Glasgow – in effect between the two Cities' Football Associations (and thus initially featuring mainly players from Sheffield Wednesday and Queen's Park). The first of these was at Bramall Lane in Sheffield, on the 14th March 1874, and they continued regularly for nearly 90 years, with the last being played on 16th November 1960 at Celtic Park. In total, 68 matches were played, with Glasgow winning 33 times, Sheffield 23 times and with 12 draws.

Further evidence of the strength of the game in Scotland came when the Scottish Cup holders, Vale of Leven, travelled to London in April 1878 to play FA Cup winners, Wanderers. This ended in a 3-1 win for the Scots and was one of the first instances of the demonstration of the superiority of the Scots' passing game as opposed to the reliance on individual dribbling that characterised the English approach to football.

In the following year, a tour by the Old Etonians to Scotland matched the then FA Cup holders with Vale of Leven, holders of the Scottish FA Cup, and resulted in a 5-2 drubbing for the English side. This match was played two days after Christmas, in the teeth of a gale which worsened over the next 24 hours and, on the following day (28th December 1879) led to the Tay Bridge Disaster. At the end of that 1879-80 season, the Old Etonians hosted Vale of Leven at the Oval in London and once again lost. Interestingly, the match reports make it clear that the first half was played under Scottish rules and despite this the Etonians were winning at half-time. However, Vale adapted better to the FA rules in the second half than the Etonians had to the Scottish rules in the first half and scored three times to finish the game as deserved victors.

At this time, all teams were amateur and club players were largely drawn from the surrounding local area or were Old Boys of a public school. However, the existence of a Scottish sporting diaspora meant that when FA Secretary Charles Alcock issued a challenge, via adverts in newspapers in Scotland, for the Scots to put up a team to play England in London, there were sufficient players in the capital to form a team. This, the first match between the auld enemies, is not considered an official international because of the lack of home-based Scots (neither were four subsequent games, played on a similar basis, considered as official contests), but of particular interest in this first match is the fact that the Scottish captain that day was James Kilpatrick. His father, Charles, was a member of the Edinburgh Foot-Ball Club between 1831-32 and it seems had passed on his love of the game to his son. Francis Moncrieff, another son of a Foot-Ball Club member (James Moncrieff, who played from 1832-33), was the captain of Scotland in the first ever rugby international played, against England at Raeburn Place in Edinburgh in 1871.

A year later, the first ever official international football match, between Scotland and England, was played at Hamilton Crescent in Glasgow. As a child, I remember being given picture history books about football, almost all of which contained a series of famous line drawings made by W Ralston of this match. At that time, I was slightly perplexed by the caption on one of these drawings (shown here), which read, *"How's that umpire?"* This was a phrase I associated with cricket and, of course, I knew that football didn't have umpires, rather referees.

I subsequently discovered that in the nineteenth century, the early football matches were officiated by umpires, one for each side. It was only when the umpires could not agree that they referred the decision to a third party, who, for obvious reasons, then became known as the "referee."

Other illustrations from this era also reveal some interesting aspects of the game at this time. There is a drawing from the 1879 England vs Scotland game at the Oval in London (shown overleaf – and like all the illustrations in this section publicly available via WikiCommons), where we can see players obviously vying to head the ball. This picture also shows the close-quarter combat that still characterised a lot of football at this time, with players running together in packs.

THE FOOTBALL MATCH AT THE OVAL—ENGLAND v. SCOTLAND.

No-one knows when teams began to head the ball regularly, but there is evidence that it was being done in the early 1870s. The Field magazine reported on a match between Wanderers and Queen's Park in 1872, noting that both sides indulged in "driving the ball with the head." There is another engraved picture from the same year which clearly shows a player heading the ball. Drummond Bone's 1890 reminiscences book, referred to above, records that Queen's Park and Scotland captain, Guyana-born, Andrew Watson, who had begun playing 12 years before that date, "was a rare 'header-out.'" Did the Scots 'invent' heading? We can't say definitively, but it seems that we were certainly instrumental in making it a key part of the game. One thing we can definitely say though is that Andy Watson was the first black footballer to represent - and captain - any international team, gaining the first of his three caps for Scotland (as captain) in the amazing 6-1 defeat of England in London in 1881.

Another aspect of Ralston's drawings from the first international match, which can be seen in the picture here as well as his other one above, is the shape of the ball. It is most definitely not round. If you'll indulge me for a moment, we'll have a wee diversion about the football itself (and why it is round). By way of pre-amble, here is the modern law (Law 2) of the game concerning the ball.

All balls must be:

- spherical.
- made of suitable material.
- of a circumference of between 68 cm (27 ins) and 70 cm (28 ins)
- between 410 g (14 oz) and 450 g (16 oz) in weight at the start of the match.
- of a pressure equal to 0.6 – 1.1 atmosphere (600 – 1,100g/cm2) at sea level (8.5 lbs/sq. in – 15.6 lbs/sq. in).

SOFT FALLING, FORTUNATELY —

There are few differences between the current rules regarding the ball and those set out in the nineteenth century. The only substantive one is in the weight of the ball, which was increased from 13-15oz to 14-16oz in 1937.

That change apart, the structure, materials and manufacture of footballs remained virtually the same for nigh on a century. I remember as a small boy in the mid-1960s being given a football for a birthday present. It was leather, with a vulcanised rubber bladder which was pumped up via a tube in the bladder. Access to said tube was via an opening in the leather panels which was secured by a lace. Untying the lace, blowing up the ball through the tube, tying a knot/lace around the tube to seal the air and then tucking the secured tube into the opening before tightening the lace all took ages. Heading the ball, especially on the lace, was decidedly painful. None of these things were any different to those experienced by the late nineteenth century pioneers of the game. However, even in the 1960s there were better, more modern versions of the ball than the one I was given. In particular there was the one that every boy wanted – the one without the lace!

Now everyone who has seen the film of the 1966 World Cup final will remember that the ball was orange, but, apart from the colour, the differences between it and those used in the first seasons of League football in Scotland and England were minimal. In fact, the difference between that 1966 ball and those used in more recent World Cups is far greater than the differences between England's World Cup-winning ball and those of the 1880s. Also, although we all remember the colour, can you remember who made that ball?

The answer is Slazenger: a firm more associated today with tennis, cricket and golf. And Slazenger, like a few other famous names associated with football is a very long-established company, tracing its origin back to 1881, when brothers Ralph and Albert moved from Manchester to London and set up a shop selling rubber sporting goods.

Another famous sporting goods maker whose name is still around today, albeit associated with rugby rather than football, is Gilbert. William Gilbert (1799-1877) was the boot and shoe maker to Rugby School. He had a small shop in the town and by 1823 he was already supplying the school with rugby balls. Like the balls we observed in the drawings from the first official football international, the original rugby balls were much more plum-shaped. The reasons for the evolution of the shapes of the modern football and rugby balls are interesting. In the kicking game, there were obvious advantages in having a spherical ball. In contrast, in rugby the ball evolved to improve passing and handling. The biggest problem with the original leather casing with an animal bladder inside it was, as we have seen, that it was a pig to inflate and equally hard to stop from bursting. However, both codes were helped significantly by the invention of the rubber bladder (and a pump to inflate it), by Richard Lindon in Rugby in 1875. This in turn was made possible by Charles Goodyear's invention in the 1830s of the process for vulcanising rubber, which itself was an improvement on the use of natural rubber (aka latex, also called 'india-rubber').

Another celebrated football maker is Mitre, whose balls have been used in top flight football in Scotland for decades. Founded by Benjamin Crook in Huddersfield in 1817, Mitre is now based in Wakefield and makes footballs and other sporting goods and is the official supplier for many Leagues around the world, including the SPFL. Should you wish to purchase a Mitre Delta Max, the ball used by the Scottish professional game, it will, at time of writing and according to the company's website, set you back £115. In contrast, the copious records kept by John Hope of the Edinburgh Foot-Ball Club, contains receipts from 1836 for the leather outer and hundreds of bladders. The bladders cost 3d (1p), a tin pipe for inflating the ball 2d (1p) and the leather casings 3/6d each (17.5p). In the course of one of these early football matches, as many as five bladders would burst and a boy was employed to blow up new ones and thus ensure a steady supply of balls for the players. Interestingly, given that these early football players would get through up to five balls per game, the total cost of the footballs used in a match in 1836 is, in today's terms (and assuming they had five outer casings available per match - and also allowing for paying the boy to blow them up), roughly £116 – more or less the same price as the modern Mitre Delta Max.

One of Mitre's rivals was Thomlinson, of Partick in Glasgow. From the late nineteenth century, they made shoes, saddles and "buttonless" footballs (although these still had the laced-up slit for the bladder to be inflated) at their Greenbank Leather Works, on a corner of Dumbarton Road. Thomlinson was most famous though for the invention of the "T-Panel" ball (see picture, courtesy of Andy Mitchell),

made from 11 T-shaped panels of leather and used, for decades, by most top-flight clubs. Google *"Football Factory, 1946,"* and you'll find a film about the company which shows the manufacturing process by which a skilled man could make 20 footballs a week.

The manufacture of footballs has a long history in Scotland. We know this because the oldest football in existence is Scottish. It consists of a pig's bladder encased in a leather shell and it was made in Stirling and discovered in 1981 behind the panelling of the Queen's Chamber in Stirling Castle, which was decorated in the 1540s. This was the time of Mary Queen of Scots, who recorded a game of 'football' in her diaries while at Carlisle Castle, after fleeing from the Battle of Langside. It was said that 20 people from her retinue played a game for her amusement for two hours. However, the ball found in Stirling, while obviously related to the modern ball, is considerably smaller, being only 14–16 cm (5.5–6.3 in) in diameter and weighing 125 g (4.4 oz).

Football histories refer to the use of a pig's bladder as the core element in a football, but there are also many records of ox bladders and sheep bladders being used. The difference between the different types of bladder possibly has more importance than many people realise. Most books and articles on the history of the football suggest that it was the introduction of new technology (i.e. rubber) and the changing demands of the different codes for handling or kicking that resulted in the shapes of the modern ball in rugby and football. However, in the frontispiece of *"Football in Perthshire,"* author Peter Baxter's showed another reason why a football is round and a rugby ball is oval. The answer, as you can see here, is all to do with the shape of the animal's bladder from which the first balls were formed. The ox's bladder is more of an oval shape, leading to the rugby ball, and the sheep's bladder is more of a sphere, leading, naturally, to the modern football. It's interesting that Baxter, who was writing in the late nineteenth century, uses an illustration of a sheep's bladder rather than a pig's bladder, however, this may be a reflection of a long-held aversion in Scotland, especially Highland Scotland, to pigs (something else I had never heard of

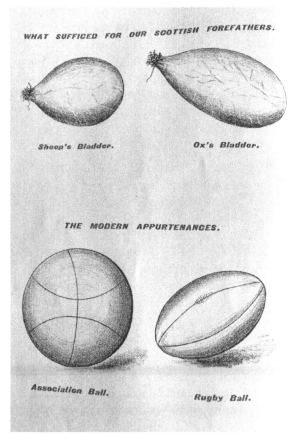

until I started to research football refereeing!). That said, this phobia had, by and large disappeared by the nineteenth century, so it may be that Perthshire's earliest footballers didn't have many local butchers dealing in pork…or just that there were a lot more sheep locally.

By the start of the twentieth century, the inner bladders of footballs were made with a strong rubber that could withstand a lot of pressure. The outside of the ball was made up of leather that was formed of eighteen sections. There were six panels with three strips on each panel, all brought together by stitching on one side of the ball. Invariably the leather was dyed dark brown, not for any obvious reason other than uniformity. The ball might have been good for kicking, but the stitching, as well as the fact that the leather would absorb water, meant that it was very uncomfortable to head!

One little known fact about the importance of the football involves the World Cup final of 1930. Argentina was playing Uruguay and no consensus could be reached regarding which country's ball design to use. In order to make things as fair as possible, the Argentinian ball was used for the first-half and the Uruguayan one was used in the second-half. Argentina was 2-1 up at half-time, only for Uruguay to run out 4-2 winners by the end of the game. Would the result have been different had the Argentinian ball been used for the full ninety minutes? Doubtless the South American neighbours have differing views on this…

Unfortunately, lessons weren't learnt from that match. Different countries continued to play with differently sized balls, causing all sorts of problems when it came to international games. During the 1954 World Cup match between Brazil and Yugoslavia, the referee was Scotland's Charles Faultless and one of the linesmen was the Englishman Arthur Ellis, whom older readers may remember as the referee in the TV gameshow 'It's a Knock-Out.' After the ball had been kicked over the touchline, Ellis saw the Brazilian coach returning a smaller ball onto the field. It was known that the Brazilians, who were one goal down, preferred playing with a smaller ball.

In the wake of the Second World War, material began to be used in between the outer leather facade and the bladder inside. Obviously, this offered a degree of cushioning and also ensured that the ball could maintain its shape more easily. By the time the 1950s came around, the colour of the ball from the spectator's point of view began to be taken into account. Initially this was because of the introduction of floodlights, with a decision taken to white-wash the leather in order to allow the ball to be more visible to the crowd. Then, when it snowed, an orange ball was used for the first time. Older fans will remember the orange ball being used in Scotland, but for the younger generation it is a relic from history, largely because it's so unusual for a game to be played in snow these days.

Amazingly, FIFA didn't actually introduce a proper 'Quality Programme for Footballs' until 1996. The balls themselves underwent numerous developments before that, with the most significant being the design of a revolutionary ball by Eigil Nielsen, who played in goal for Denmark between 1940 and 1951 but still found time to create his company, Select, in 1947. In 1962, Nielsen launched his new football, which had 32 panels rather than the usual 18.

Subsequently, Richard Buckminster Fuller, the American architect who had invented the geodesic dome, came up with a ball that consisted of 20 hexagonal and twelve pentagonal surfaces which were sewn together to create a near perfect sphere. Introduced in the late 1960s, it was christened, with stunning originality, the "Bucky" and first came to international recognition when it was made by Adidas. Formally named the "Telestar," it was the first "official" ball to be used at a World Cup, in Germany in 1970. I remember that at the time it was a sensation: a totally new look for a football and, with its combination of black and white panels (specifically white hexagons and black pentagons); a most striking design that every boy of that era wanted.

The pace of development in ball technology ramped up after the 1970 World Cup. In the 1982 World Cup in Spain, Adidas introduced the Tango, to my mind the most iconic and memorable football design ever. This was the last time the World Cup would feature balls made of natural leather, but with a polyurethane coating and rubber inlaid over the seams to try to stop water seeping in (probably not too much of a problem in the Spanish summer). Water ingress had been the perennial problem for all footballs since they were first made, with the older style of ball gaining considerably in weight during wet matches. Former St Johnstone goalkeeper Bill Taylor recalls that in the early 1960s the club used to have 'Beat the Goalie' competitions for the fans, but gave the supporters a ball that had been soaked in water overnight. Unsurprisingly, the fans could hardly shift it off the penalty spot. Bill would then say, *"ah well, that's the difference between you and us professionals!"*

With today's multi-coloured balls, it may seem incredible that the first football with a colour other than brown, black and white wasn't used in an official tournament until the World Cup in France in 1998. Red, white and blue were introduced then, but when the competition was held in Japan and South Korea in 2002 gold-coloured balls were unveiled, and since then football designers have been able to give full rein to their creative impulses.

More significantly (after all, who can remember the colour of the ball after a goal is scored?), one of the most important changes came in 2006 when Adidas launched their Teamgeist ball, with 14 panels rather than 32. This made the ball rounder than previously (footballs are never true spheres) and the panels were moulded rather than stitched as had been the case since John Hope's Edinburgh Foot-Ball Club days. The much-reviled Jabulani ball that was used in the South Africa World Cup in 2010 had just eight panels. It's fair to say that it was not popular, especially with goalkeepers, due to the way it swerved and dipped, seemingly contradicting the laws of physics.

From the introduction of the first synthetic balls in the 1960s and replacement of natural leather for synthetic leather in the 1980s, the science and aesthetics involved in the design of footballs has continuously developed. The football itself – that vital, yet arguably least appreciated part of the game - has been on a long journey, from those leather-encased pigs' bladders via india rubber and vulcanised rubber to today's synthetic spheres. Moreover, it's a journey that is unlikely ever to be over…

Right, that's enough balls. Let's return to the subject of referees and, in particular, the laws of the game, starting with the single most significant event in the development of a unified set of rules for the game across the UK and, in time, worldwide.

Founding of IFAB

On 2nd June 1886, two representatives from each of the four home nations (i.e. Scotland, England, Wales and Ireland) met and agreed to form a body that would oversee the rules for all. This was the International Football Association Board, referred to thereafter as IFAB. It's worth noting that this was several years before the founding of the Scottish Football League, so the laws that applied in the first league season in Scotland were, in effect, the same as those that applied across the rest of the UK (remembering that Ireland was part of the United Kingdom in those days). There is an excellent blog by German archivist/historian Petra Tabarelli, called Nachspielzeiten.de (Nachspielzeiten means "Extra-time" in German), where all the key changes to each of the laws of the game made by IFAB are set out in easy-to-follow timelines (in English). For those really interested, this is far and away the best guide to the evolution of the rules by which football is played.

In 1904, as the game became more popular across the world, seven nations came together in Paris to found the Federation Internationale de Football Associations (FIFA). At this time,

Great Britain was at the peak of its global power and this, allied to the fact that the modern game's origins clearly lay in the British Isles, meant that FIFA agreed from the outset to abide by the rules as laid down by IFAB, although they (FIFA) didn't actually join IFAB until 1913. However, the agreement to use IFAB's rules was crucial: it allowed matches to be played between any club or country across the world. This global standardisation of the laws, combined with the basic simplicity of the game (with a ball of some kind being the only essential requirement for a kickabout), led to football becoming – and remaining to this day - the most popular sport in the world.

As described above, the Scottish FA had, in 1887, prohibited its members from playing in the FA Cup and the separation of the two countries' footballing systems continued with the formation of the Football League in England in 1888. Interestingly, Bob Crampsey's Centenary History of the Scottish Football League records that William McGregor, the Aston Villa committee man, FA stalwart and native of Perthshire, who proposed the formation of the Football League, deliberately chose not to call it the English Football League because *"his hope was that in the future Scottish clubs could be admitted to membership."* Such hopes were dashed with the founding of the Scottish Football League in 1890, but it is intriguing to speculate what might have happened if Scottish and English clubs had formed a British League. For a start, it would have saved Celtic and Rangers from all the efforts they have made in recent years to join the English League system…

The founding of IFAB also meant that, as far as Scotland and the football authorities here were concerned, changes in the laws were now universal and clubs were able to leave behind the time when 'Scotch Laws' and regional English laws made football games between the respective countries' top clubs difficult to referee. Moreover, the SFA continued to put forward ideas to IFAB for changes to the laws. The majority of these were not accepted, or were withdrawn before a vote, but some critical ideas were advanced and accepted, demonstrating Scotland's continuing influence (albeit waning in the modern world of football politics?) on the Association game. I am indebted to Petra Tabarelli for sending me her compilation of all the SFA's proposals to IFAB from 1887 up to 2009 (this list is shown in the Appendix). Even allowing for Scotland's leading position as one of the four founding (and permanent) members of IFAB, it's clear that the country has, in many respects, had considerable influence in formulating the Laws of the game. Overall, the SFA made 181 proposals to IFAB between 1887 and 2009. Of these, just over one third (66) were accepted, although quite a few of these were technical alterations (e.g. in 1924, *"The penalty clause for infringements of the throw-in law is deleted,"* or in 1969, *"The passage is changed so that the game is restarted with an IDFK [indirect free kick] for the opposing team instead of dropping the ball."*). To give you a flavour, here are my own personal favourites …

In 1892, the SFA proposed that a player could only strike the ball once from a penalty kick, or, as the wording had it*, "repeated touching of the ball by the player taking the kick is prohibited."* This was accepted and it still the law today.

Also, on the subject of Law 14 (the penalty kick), each year from 1898 to 1900 the SFA proposed a *"Change of the place of performance to a place on twelve yards line opposite where infringement took place."* In other words, remembering there was no penalty spot at this time, the ball had to be placed for a penalty on the 12-yard line in line with the place where the infringement took place. This was always defeated, presumably for the sensible reason that savvy players would simply deck their opponents right on the corner of the pitch, where the chances of scoring from the resultant penalty were negligible, but would be more cautious in the centre of the field.

Repeated failure to get this adopted led to a new attempt, in 1901, to make things fairer for the attacking side, viz, *"The place of the penalty kick is changed from the penalty line to a penalty half circle with a radius of 12 yd."* Yes, that means there would have been an arc around the goal and the penalty taker could have taken the kick from any position on that semi-circle. Unsurprisingly, this was defeated as well.

The Scottish football authorities seem to have had a thing about semi-circles, because in 1948 they proposed a *"Change of the penalty area to a semicircle of 22 yd. Removal of the semicircle of 10 yd."* That 10-yard semi-circle was the one at the top of the penalty area, but why the Scottish authorities thought it was a good idea to create a hockey-style 'penalty area' arc around the goal is not recorded. It was defeated anyway…

The SFA made constant attempts to change the offside law, principally to get it altered so that only two players were required to keep an opponent onside, not three as was the case for most of the early decades of the game. Although previously discussed in the publication "The Scottish Referee" in 1893, the first proposal put forward by the SFA to IFAB was in 1902. Subsequently, various similar attempts followed, including the idea of having lines across the pitch at either 25 yards (1920) or 40 yards (every year from 1921 to 1924), outside which the attackers could not be offside. All these were either withdrawn or defeated, but…

In 1925, the SFA's proposal that Law 11 (offside) should change to a *"Reduction to two opponents nearer their own goal line,"* was accepted. That is still Law 11 today, albeit it has been totally muddied by the new change to 'second phase offside,' where the Assistant referee waits until the attacking team have almost scored or a player has been seriously injured - and the fans are consequently in a state of high excitement/anger - before pouring cold water on their respective parades by raising his flag.

A year before this, an SFA proposal made a significant change which is still with us today, but whose wording caused a bit of controversy as players realised that it allowed them more leeway than was intended when the changes to the laws were published (of which more below). In 1924, the SFA proposed that Law 13 (Free Kicks) be amended thus, *"In addition, a corner kick can be used to score a goal directly"* and this was accepted by IFAB.

Another area where Scotland's football administrators tried to introduce new thinking was in the use of substitutes. Substitutions had taken place in the nineteenth century. Eton College used them in the 1850s, although they were called 'emergency' players rather than substitutes. The first recorded use of the world 'substitute' was in 1863, when a match report in Bell's Life in London and Sporting Chronicle stated, *"The Charterhouse eleven played a match in cloisters against some old Carthusians but in consequence of the non-appearance of some of those who were expected it was necessary to provide three substitutes."*

In 1889, the Wales goalkeeper didn't turn up for a game against Scotland. A local amateur called Alf Pugh volunteered to play in goal, which he did for around twenty minutes until Sam Gillam, a goalkeeper who had played for various clubs around England and Wales replaced him. Gillam therefore became the first person to be used as a substitute (in the modern meaning of the word) in international football.

The first substitution in the Scottish League was a war-time measure and took place on 20th January 1917, when Morgan came on for the injured Morrison in a Partick Thistle vs Rangers match at Firhill. A substitution was then made in the Scotland Under-23 trial match against Clyde in 1955, and in the Scotland vs Scottish League international trial in 1964. However, the Scottish League did not allow substitutes until 1966. Archie Gemmill, then of St Mirren, was the first substitute in Scotland after the practice was officially sanctioned, coming on in a League Cup tie on 13th August 1966. Soon after, Queen's Park's Paul Conn became the first substitute in a league game, against Albion Rovers on 24th August.

In 1923, IFAB allowed substitutions in non-competitive matches, but only for a serious injury and provided both sides agreed. In the 1930s, some countries began to allow substitutions in non-competitive matches for reasons other than injuries. This was officially frowned upon by the various British Associations, although they seemingly also turned a blind-eye to it. In 1938, there were occasions when substitutions were allowed in matches against foreign countries, but only if both sides and both national Football Associations agreed. Scotland did not make use of this provision until a war-time international in the spring of 1945, when Leslie Johnston replaced Tommy Bogan, and scored, against England. There is an excellent description of the history of substitutions on nachspielzeiten.de which you should be able to find if you *Google "Football substitution – the real story based on documents."*

Substitutes were not used again in international football until they were introduced in the 1954 World Cup. However, the SFA, showing a far-sightedness that many of its current critics in the media would find surprising, made a proposal to IFAB in 1949 that *"In international matches played by FIFA members, the goalkeeper may be substituted due to injury during the whole game. The substitute must not take the position of the goalkeeper."*

Intriguingly, in Peter Craigmyle's autobiography, the famous Aberdonian referee records a trip he made to Malta at Christmas, 1948. He was there to referee the match between a Maltese select and S.K Austria and before the game he recounted that a local football official, *"told me privately (before the match) that the Maltese would have several substitutes standing by. I then determined to put a stop to this – it seemed to me a farcical situation. Indeed, I'd never before known anything like their system of substitutes."*

However, despite Peter's reluctance, he reckoned without the local fans. Watching a friendly match the day before his game, he was astonished when the Maltese goalkeeper fluffed a simple save and the fans roared for him to be replaced and didn't stop shouting until this happened, mid-match. Several other substitutes then took the field during the game. Before his 'international' match, Mr Craigmyle took the teams aside and said he wouldn't allow any substitutes.

Whether the SFA were aware of this when they put forward their proposal is unknown, but the sequence of events suggests they may have been. Quite why they should want a sub for an injured goalie to be only an outfield player is a mystery, but the proposal was defeated anyway and the idea didn't make it to the footballing statute book.

After the 1966 World Cup Finals in England, when the winner of the two previous competitions, Brazil, had to play with ten men after Pele was carried off injured in a group match and Brazil failed to qualify from the group, it was realised that increasing the number of substitutes was a good idea. In 1967, IFAB increased the number allowed from one to two, then in 1994 this increased to three (but with the third being a goalkeeper) and then in 1995 three outfield substitutes were allowed. In 2018 a fourth sub was allowed if a match went to extra time and in May 2020, as a result of the Covid pandemic, five substitutes were allowed to help prevent player fatigue due to the congested match schedule as a result of the temporary suspension of the game while the virus was spreading throughout the world. Similarly, the number of players listed as potential substitutes increased, from just two named individuals in 1967 to three in 1994 and then seven in 1996. In friendly matches, since 2004, up to six substitutes are allowed, although sometimes it seems like a dozen are made.

* * * * *

The Laws of the Game

As described above, before 1886 it's fairly easy to find many different descriptions of the (often violent) ways in which football was played across the United Kingdom. However, even after that date, it was still a pretty bloody business at times, as this satirical article from 1889 makes clear (note that the paragraphs used in the preface and introduction to this book are also part of this piece - and some of the language may not be regarded as 'politically correct' in the 21st century).

"Football is a nice friendly game, where each player does his best to cripple his neighbour. The player who cripples the most receives a badge, which he hangs round his neck, and cherishes in the same manner as a red Indian nurses the scalp he has won in battle. Those who are mutilated get a benefit. Benefits are sometimes the best: but their success chiefly depends on the chance of one's recovery, and the number of tickets sold.

"As there are two ways of killing a man, there are two ways of playing football. Neither of them is up to much, and both are rougher than dominoes. One is called Rugby; the other Association. Rugby is named after a large asylum in England, where the inmates becoming too numerous, the directors invented the game as a speedy plan for getting rid of the superfluous patients. Association derives its name from the numerous societies it provides with material, such as – funeral societies, and sick nursing associations. Since football

155

became so popular in Perth, two ambulance wagons have sprung into existence; and this itself says a good deal for the progress of the game in this place.

"The chief object of the game is to kick a ball through between two sticks, and when this is done it is called a 'goal.' A person stands between the posts, his duty being to prevent the ball going through. Sometimes, he comes to grief, and he is kicked through along with the ball. This martyr is called the goalkeeper and is the only player who is allowed to touch the ball with his hands. When 'fisting' out a shot, he sometimes manages to miss the ball and hit one of his opponents in the eye. This is a privilege granted only to goalkeepers, and is the only chance they have of retaliating for being pitched through the goal thirty-seven times during a match. Goalkeepers have the worst job, and ought to be armed. Were they armed with a two-pronged fork or a broadsword, more people would go to witness the games."

Perthshire Advertiser, Monday 4 March 1889.

Despite this cynicism, the game prospered. One of the main reasons for this was the simplicity of the early rule-book. Although in essence still a simple sport with simple rules, the laws of the game have been diluted by numerous additions, amendments, modifications and guidelines. Anyone Googling this subject today will find that they can download the official IFAB document that is the 2020-21 laws, running to a mere 225 pages, of which over 100 are on the actual 17 Laws. For those who wish the full and unabridged version, you'll find the laws of the game at this web address:

https://www.fifplay.com/downloads/documents/laws-of-the-game-2021-2022.pdf

With that in mind, let's have a random look at some of the more interesting early amendments and the subsequent modifications that have brought the game to where it is today, starting with the most important people…

The Players
(LAW 3)

Why do football teams have 11 players? Why not 10, or 12? Well, we don't really know, but as the game began to develop in the second half of the nineteenth century, varying numbers of players took part. The Surrey Rules of 1849 state, *"That the sides shall consist of not more than twenty-two each; but if that number of members shall not be in attendance, then of any smaller number, shall be arranged by those present."*

Petra Tabarelli notes that prior to 1870 there were games involving teams of eight players and others with different numbers, usually up to but not exceeding 11. Neither the original Sheffield Rules nor the FA's rules specify the number of players. It does seem that no-one really knows why eleven players were settled on. I have read some accounts that suggest that it was because having 11 players allowed teams to cover every area of the pitch, but given the nature of early football, where teams had only a handful of defenders and about seven or eight forwards and ran together, this seems unlikely. Another suggestion is that it was simply copying cricket, which was by far the most popular sport in the country (in Scotland as well as England). As we have seen, several football clubs were spin-offs from existing cricket clubs, so this theory is plausible.

Although the convention of teams having eleven players was settled fairly quickly, it wasn't until 1897 that IFAB actually wrote this into the laws of the game. It also transpires (i.e. I didn't know), that since 1997 a game can start if one side has fewer than eleven players, but not if it has fewer than seven. The minimum number required for a match to continue at that time was left to the discretion of national Football Associations, but since 2016 IFAB has mandated that a game may not continue if one side has fewer than seven players.

Corners
(LAW 17)

In the 1870s and 1880s, the rules were getting more like the ones we know today. The corner kick was introduced in 1871, but at that stage it was not possible to score a goal directly from a corner. The people who were responsible for that were the Scots, or, to be more precise, the Scottish Football Association. As noted above, this wasn't permitted until 1924, when it was proposed to IFAB by the SFA, and the first recorded instance of this happening was in a match between old rivals Uruguay and Argentina. Uruguay were the reigning Olympic champions at this time and as a result, when Argentina's Cesáreo Onzari netted directly from the corner, it became known as the *"Gol Olimpico,"* a term still used in Hispanic football across the world today.

Intriguingly, when I interviewed former referee Willie Young, he told me that in fact it was Cumnock Juniors who scored the first goal direct from a corner kick, at least according to a man he met who said he was a relative of the player who did it. True or false, the idea of a *"Gol Cumnocko"* doesn't have quite the same ring to it… and, given the intense rivalry that permeates Ayrshire Junior football, I suspect that rival claims would soon be made from the relatives of players in Beith, Auchinleck, etc.

More interesting from a Scottish point of view, this 1924 change to the corner kick law also brought about a huge controversy that, for a few days, took up many column inches in the press. It's the kind of story the press love and, as the cuttings on the next page show, essentially what happened was an administrative cock-up.

As the third cutting, on the right, reveals, when IFAB *"altered the Rules to permit a player to score from a corner kick, they inadvertently put the reading of the amended Rule in such a way that it is now possible for a player to dribble the ball."*

157

Footballers being footballers, they will always take any opportunity to gain an advantage, especially when it's sanctioned by officialdom. The referees were not impressed, with Andrew Allan (cutting on far left) making it clear *that he was going to have none of this corner-kick dribbling nonsense.*

The players were, understandably, happy to use their new found freedom to benefit their team, so it was hurriedly decided by the SFA Council that a corner kick would come under the law which covers free kicks. As the cuttings indicate, in doing so the SFA were falling in line with the English FA who had already come to this decision, but officially there was no change in the rules until the next time IFAB met and the laws were then amended to make it clear that the player taking the corner could not touch it until another player had done so.

You would have thought that put an end to the matter, but in fact a further change to the rules meant that dribbling from corners was back on referees' radar in the twenty-first century. Once again, another amendment to the laws was to blame. In 1997, the law that every schoolboy of my vintage knew, namely that the ball had to travel its circumference before it was in play, was changed so that it merely had to be kicked and have moved to be in play.

In 2009, in a game between Manchester United and Chelsea, Wayne Rooney went over as if to take a corner and gently rolled the ball just outside the quadrant, before strolling away as if he was leaving it for someone else to take. Ryan Giggs walked over and then started dribbling with the ball before crossing it for Ronaldo to score with a header (this is available on YouTube). The referee, Howard Webb, made them retake it. In this instance, Webb was wrong, but it didn't make any difference as United scored from the retaken corner.

Then in 2015, in a match between New York Red Bulls and Chicago Fire, a player rolled his studs over the ball, moving it a matter of inches inside the corner quadrant. In what seemed like an off-the-cuff decision, he moved away and another player ran across as if to take the corner. The second player then dribbled with the ball, crossed it and Red Bulls scored. You can also find this on YouTube and it's obvious that the second player is talking to the linesman to check that he agrees the ball is in play. This time, the goal was allowed. Subsequently, the rule was changed in 2016 to say that the ball must *"clearly"* move.

Before we leave the corner kick, I must make mention of the habit modern players have of placing the ball outside the quadrant before taking the corner kick. This is a matter of contention, usually from the point of view of the opposing fans. However, from what I can glean from various refereeing websites, it is understood that so long as the ball is *"within"* the quadrant - including touching/overhanging the outside of the line of the quadrant – then everything is fine and the game proceeds. And if you are one of those fans who get so upset (I know, I know, I do too), it's worth bearing in mind that there is no specific reference at all to this in the Laws of the game. To prove the point, here is the relevant bit of Law 17…

The Corner Kick

A corner kick is awarded when the whole of the ball passes over the goal line, on the ground or in the air, having last touched a player of the defending team, and a goal is not scored. A goal may be scored directly from a corner kick, but only against the opposing team; if the ball directly enters the kicker's goal, a corner kick is awarded to the opponents.

1. Procedure

• The ball must be placed in the corner area nearest to the point where the ball passed over the goal line.
• The ball must be stationary and is kicked by a player of the attacking team
• The ball is in play when it is kicked and clearly moves; it does not need to leave the corner area.
• The corner flagpost must not be moved.
• Opponents must remain at least 9.15 m (10 yds) from the corner arc until the ball is in play.

All clear now? As you can see, there is nothing whatsoever in the 'procedure' about where the ball is *specifically* placed on the quadrant – it just has to be *"in the corner area"* – whatever that means. In reality this means that you can continue to give the opposition player dogs' abuse if he puts it mere millimetres outside the line, but it won't make a blind bit of difference.

Kick-off
LAW 8

Some old fans (okay, me) miss the old-style kick-off, with two players standing at the centre spot and then one kicking the ball forwards and the other (in theory) having to wait until it had travelled its circumference (23–24 inches, 58–62 cm) before it was in play and he could pass it back (or very occasionally forward) to a team-mate. Today, only one player stands at the centre spot and he almost always kicks it backwards to a team-mate: the end result is the same. In other words, the introduction of this change (in 2016) has made no material difference to the game. That said, it's worth noting that prior to this being introduced, the ball had to go forwards to begin every match. Psychologically, philosophically even, this is what fans want to see. Now, although it can, in theory, go in any direction, the ball invariably goes directly backwards … sometimes setting the tone for the entire match. Still, life is too short to get massively upset about this and, to be honest, in the old days I can't actually remember the ball travelling any more than about a few inches (as opposed to the two feet it was supposed to go) before it was kicked back by the second player.

However, before the old-fashioned approach to kick-off that I grew up with was adopted there were a number of other methods of starting the game, most of which hark back to its handling version. The Surrey Rules of 1849 refer to the ball being *"tossed up in the centre of the ground,"* something that still happens, in a slightly different form, in two of the games that diverged from the core rugby and football codes of the nineteenth century. In Gaelic football, four men compete for the ball after it's tossed upwards, while in Aussie Rules the ball is bounced down first, unless the ground is not amenable to the ball bouncing well, in which case it is thrown up and two players jostle for possession.

Most of the nineteenth century rules have some form of a kick-off from the centre of the playing field. The 1863 FA laws specified that a coin was tossed at the start of a game and the team losing the toss then had to kick off. This was changed in 1873 when the team winning the toss was allowed to choose whether to defend one particular end or, alternatively, they could take the kick-off. It is, of course, easy to Google this sort of stuff and find out all the various changes that have happened over the years, but I was still surprised by what I learned as I dug deeper into the evolution of the laws. For a start, I discovered that in the 1860s there were no instructions as to where the players positioned themselves on the park at the start of the game. The only prohibitions were that they could not be in an offside position and they had to be 10 yards from the ball at kick-off. It wasn't until 1874 that all players had to be in their own half at kick-off – something that I thought was still the case today, but further digging revealed that in fact this had to be changed when the kick-off law was changed so that the one person taking the kick-off could stand in the opposition half (another indication as to why the change to the kick-off law was completely unnecessary).

There will, no doubt, be those who wonder why in a book about Scottish refereeing there are so many references to the English FA and its laws. This is simply because it is those first FA rules that, by and large, have formed the cornerstone of the laws of the game ever since. However, as we have seen, Scotland, principally through the SFA, did have an influence in some key areas. Another of these was in the establishment of a break for half-time. Initially, there was no provision for half-time in the 1863 FA laws. Various clubs lobbied for a change of ends - but only provided no goals had been scored in the first half. The kick-off for the second half was then taken by the side that had taken the original kick-off. However, in 1875 Queen's Park proposed that there should always be a break at half time and the teams should change ends, with the kick-off at the start of the second half being taken by the team that didn't kick-off at the start of the match. This offered the chance for teams to recharge their batteries, although sometimes they found time to entertain both themselves and the crowd. On 24th January 1891, Leith Athletic entertained 'the Invincibles,' Preston North End, to a friendly match. As described by Dave Twydell in *"Rejected FC of Scotland,"* the massive crowd watched on as, *"The Preston North-End players had their own little picnic on the pitch. Drummond, the Leith captain, entertained the crowd with turnbar balancing feats, whilst the other players amused themselves by having shies at a bottle."*

When I started watching football (1960s), the half-time break was only ten minutes. In 1995, IFAB increased the break to 15 minutes. This was three times longer than when half-time intervals were first specified by IFAB in 1897, when the players only enjoyed a break of five minutes. At that same IFAB meeting in 1897, the duration of the match was fixed at 90 minutes: previously, there was no law that specified the duration of a match and the length of the game differed from area to area. In the early 1860s some games only lasted an hour and others much longer, although 90 minutes became the norm during this decade.

As regards what happens after the referee has tossed a coin before the start of a match…that was (yet) another area where I had much to learn. The original FA laws said that the team losing the toss should kick-off, but in 1873, the captain winning the toss was allowed either to choose ends or take the kick-off. That was the situation when I played football and I thought it was always thus, but in 1997 the law was changed back and the captain who won the toss only had the choice of which end to defend/attack. The team that had lost the toss then kicked-off the match. However, this was changed again in 2019, to allow the winning captain to elect either to kick-off or to choose which end to defend/attack.

On a similar subject, namely the re-start of a game, the drop-ball was introduced in 1888. Many of us today can remember when a dropped ball was contested by a player from each side and after a stramash the game would resume. Sadly, this wonderful spectacle has now been banished and the ball is effectively handed to the team who were in possession when the game was stopped. The original law stated that, *"If the referee stops the game even though the ball has not crossed the goal line or touch line and there is no offence, the game is restarted with a dropped ball. Procedure: throwing the ball up at the place where play was suspended. The ball is in play when it touches the field of play."* What's interesting (if you are an anorak like me) is that the ball was thrown up, not simply dropped. However, this was changed in 1905, when the instruction to referees was that the ball be *"thrown down."*

Penalties
LAW 14

The penalty was yet another subject where I discovered I had a lot to learn.

Imagine that a penalty is given for your side. As the penalty taker runs up, the goalkeeper charges out of this goal to within six yards of the penalty spot and saves the kick. The place would go mad, the players would mob the keeper, the fans would jeer and shout, the goalie would be booked and the penalty re-taken. Unless, of course, this happened in the late nineteenth century, when it would have been perfectly allowable…

The penalty kick was first introduced in 1891. Prior to this, what we would consider an indirect free kick was awarded for any infringement. The introduction of the penalty kick was too much for celebrated London amateurs, Corinthian FC (whose white colours were adopted by Real Madrid and whose name was adopted by the major Brazilian club SP Corinthians Paulista). In the true Corinthian spirit, their players believed that no gentleman would deliberately foul an opponent, so if awarded a penalty they would deliberately miss, while if they had one awarded against them their goalkeeper would stand to one side and let the ball enter the net. Contrary to what some fans might believe, there is no truth in the rumour that this philosophy is still prevalent at some clubs today...

I suspect most people, like me, believed that the penalty kick was always taken from a "spot" (in fact, the rules refer to *"the penalty mark"*), directly 12 yards from the centre of the goal. However, given that pitches were not marked with a penalty area, (which, as noted above, was introduced in 1902), the referee only gave a penalty if he judged that a relevant rule had been broken within 12 yards of the goal-line. The player taking the penalty kick could then place the ball anywhere he chose along a line 12 yards from the goal. The other players had to stand "at least six yards behind the ball, that is, at the 18-yard line, when the kick was taken. Amazingly, at least to our current way of thinking, the goalkeeper was allowed to *"approach the ball up to six yards until the penalty kick is taken."* In 1902, when the penalty area and penalty 'spot' were introduced, all players, apart from the kicker and the goalie, were obliged to stand outside the penalty area. At this time, there was no arc at the top of the penalty box: this was introduced in 1923 so that all players, apart from the two most important participants, were 10 yards from the ball.

Of course, most penalties are given for a foul or some other sanctionable misdemeanour on the part of a player. Which brings us nicely to...

Fouls and Misconduct
LAW 12

Keeping order has been a problem for referees since the earliest days of the game. Any sport which involves fit, strong young men running about and kicking and heading a ball has obvious potential for misdemeanours, both deliberate and accidental. Although the public schools may have had a gentlemanly ethos, much of it was underpinned by Victorian muscular Christianity and as a result the earliest players were expected to give and take kicks without complaint. However, those who wished to continue the practice of 'hacking' were consigned to the outer darkness (rugby) but despite that there were still many instances of what the authorities call 'fouls and misconduct.'

In November 1886, the SFA held a meeting to discuss a new draft for bye-laws to deal with the issue of 'rough play.' The Minute of this meeting tells us that *"after a full & exhaustive discussion"* it was agreed to submit the proposed new bye-law to the General Committee of the SFA for their approval. This bye-law contained the following:

1. *That the definition of "rough play," as specified in Rule 10 [Laws of the game], is tripping, ducking, hacking, jumping at a player, pushing and charging from behind.*

2. *The referee shall have the power during the game to deal with players guilty of violent charging, or using threatening and abusive language, without consulting the umpires.*

3. *The referee shall further take note of anyone infringing these bye-laws, and shall forward his name to the secretary of the Association within three days thereafter, along with a statement specifying the nature of the offence.*

4. *Players found guilty of violating these bye-laws shall be suspended from taking part in cup-ties and friendly matches for such time as the Committee may deem expedient.*

The ground club shall, on all occasions, secure the services of a neutral referee, and take all precautionary measures for the safety of officials and visiting team.

6 CARLTON PLACE, GLASGOW,

1st November, 1907.

DEAR SIR,

Rough Play and Misconduct

My Committee desire to direct your attention to the regrettable prevalence of Rough Play and Misconduct, and wish to impress on Referees that the powers given them by Law 13 and the Rough Play By-Laws should be fully exercised.

Yours truly,

John K. McDowall, Sec.

Copy of letter to referees, SFA Referees' Committee

This new bye-law was obviously designed to deal with an existing problem. However, it doesn't seem to have had a lot of success in changing players' behaviour, for 21 years later the SFA's Referees Committee met again, in November 1907, and after their meeting they wrote to the clubs and referees separately to make their wishes known. The letter to the referees (shown here), asks them to apply fully the powers available to them in order to try to suppress *"the regrettable prevalence of Rough Play and Misconduct."*

Meanwhile, a similar letter sent to the clubs, while couched in the same Edwardian language, was perhaps a bit too pleading and, at the same time, overly optimistic:

That this was indeed a little bit optimistic is borne out by the fact that after another two decades or thereby, the SFA Referees' Committee listed some of the recent 'misconduct.'

"Players Reported for Misconduct
Fined £5 Stg., and Severely Censured – D. McLean (Forfar Athletic F.C) – previous infringement – for striking; reported by J. Mackay. R. Elder (Brechin City F. C.), for interfering with referee; reported by J.C. Holland.
Severely Censured – J. Murdoch (Stenhousemuir F.C.) for attempted striking; reported by J. Mackay.

Censured – A. Bain (Fraserburgh F.C.) – for ungentlemanly conduct: reported by J. Graham.
Deferred – Report from R. Innes re T. Gilroy (Falkirk F.C.) and T. Morgan (Heart of Midlothian F.C.).

Official Reported
W.C. Low (Secretary, Fraserburgh F.C.), censured for refusing to give the name of a player to referee; reported by J. Graham.

Stonethrowing
J.C.Holland reported he was struck with a stone during Brechin City v. Queen of the South Scottish League match at Brechin, on 5th October, 1929. Brechin City ordered to post warning bills.
Fraserburgh F.C. censured regarding reported stonethrowing at match v Forres Mechanics F.C. on 28th September, 1929.

Complaint regarding Referee
Complaint re M. Quinn, noted.

Circular – Following to be issued to clubs and referees:-
'I am instructed to draw the attention of your club to the increasing prevalence of questioning referees' decisions by players.
'A player is entitled to enquire from a referee as to his decision, *but he is not entitled by word or action to show dissent from any such decision.*
'Clubs and players are warned that this undesirable practice of players surrounding the referee and making frantic appeals must cease forthwith, and referees are instructed to strictly administer the Law dealing with this matter.
'This notice must be prominently displayed in the players' dressing room.'"

Leaving on one side that Angus and the North-East of Scotland seem to have been the epicentres of football crime in those days (and that there are a couple of referees mentioned more than once, which makes one wonder if they were the unpopular ones with the players and fans), anyone who has watched any football match, at almost any level, in Scotland in the last few years will struggle to see much change in players' behaviour between 1929 and 2022.

In fact, nothing even changed in the short term. The SFA Referees' Committee meeting on 19th December, 1934 recorded that...

"*Players Reported for Misconduct*
Suspended until 19th March 1935 – J. McMeekin (Edinburgh City F.C.) for filthy language to referee and threatening to strike him: reported by W. Baxter.
Suspended until 2nd January, W. Simpson (Blairgowrie F.C.) for remarks to referee; reported by J. Grieve.
Severely Censured -and fined £5 – W. Bruce (Albion Rovers F.C.) for remarks to referee; reported by M.C. Hutton

Severely Censured and fined £1– A. Becci (Arbroath F.C.) for kicking and getting into grips; and R. Kemp (East Stirlingshire F.C.) for striking; reported by J. Welsh. J. Wylie (Partick Thistle F.C.) for getting into grips and unsatisfactory evidence; reported by W. Gilchrist. Severely Censured – J. Russell (Dundee F.C.) – for kicking: reported by H. McLachlan. A. Mason (Beith F.C.) for getting into grips; reported by W. Gilchrist. A. Love (Aberdeen F.C.) for attempted striking; reported by D.G. Rees.

Spectators
Ross County F.C. was censured and ordered to post warning bills on report by D.G. Fraser regarding misconduct by spectators at conclusion of Highland League match v Inverness Caledonian at Dingwall on 24th November, 1934."

What's interesting about these reports is the levels of punishment meted out for specific offences. Clearly *"threatening to strike the referee"* is not good and J. McMeekin deserved his £5 fine (£366 today) and his lengthy suspension. However, if the use of *"filthy language"* was punished in a similar way today then virtually every footballer (and a few referees) would be seriously out-of-pocket. Also, *"getting into grips"* seems to have been a fairly regular occurrence (possibly equivalent to what we would now call *'handbags'*?) but those indulging in this, or *"threatening to strike,"* seem to have received less severe punishments than those who made *"remarks to the referee."*

Players' fitness and injuries

As noted above, players had to do something spectacularly bad before they were punished by the football authorities. If you compare the tiny number of players mentioned in these reports of the Referees' Committee with the number who are yellow or red-carded every week in the modern game, it's clear that we are far harsher on miscreants in the twenty-first century than we have ever been. However, as many of the referees I interviewed for Section I of this book noted, there didn't seem to be any more serious injuries back in their day than there are now. In order to investigate this, I got in touch with Alistair McCracken, the former club doctor for St Johnstone. This is what he told me…

"During my time at Saints, I did a couple of injury audits over a five-year time span and you are correct in your assumption that actual fractures were fortunately a comparatively rare phenomenon.

What has to be remembered though, is that diagnostic techniques have greatly improved the care and rehabilitation of injured players. In addition, the advent of the highly skilled physiotherapist replacing the sponge man, who was probably an ex-player with a diploma in massage, has improved on-the-field assessment of players.

"I would suggest that many of the injuries which players were actively encouraged to 'play on' with during the 1960s and 1970s would be stoutly resisted by the modern-day player: (Paul) *Pogba and* (St Johnstone's) *Buck McCarry come to mind as a comparison.*

"In summary therefore, my suggestion is that the number of unrecognised injuries in earlier times was probably much greater than realised and that this probably led to greater long-term disability among retired footballers of that era than might be seen today."

For the record, when it comes to serious foul play, the current Law 12 states:

A direct free kick is awarded if a player commits any of the following offences against an opponent in a manner considered by the referee to be careless, reckless or using excessive force:

- *charges*
- *jumps at*
- *kicks or attempts to kick*
- *pushes*
- *strikes or attempts to strike (including head-butt)*
- *tackles or challenges*
- *trips or attempts to trip*
- *If an offence involves contact it is penalised by a direct free kick or penalty kick.*

Careless is when a player shows a lack of attention or consideration when making a challenge or acts without precaution. No disciplinary sanction is needed.
Reckless is when a player acts with disregard to the danger to, or consequences for, an opponent and must be cautioned.
Using excessive force is when a player exceeds the necessary use of force and endangers the safety of an opponent and must be sent off.

A direct free kick is awarded if a player commits any of the following offences:

- *a handball offence (except for the goalkeeper within their penalty area)*
- *holds an opponent*
- *impedes an opponent with contact*
- *bites or spits at someone on the team lists or a match official*
- *throws an object at the ball, opponent or match official, or makes contact with the ball with a held object*

There is a whole lot more in this Law about *"Playing in a dangerous manner"* and *"Impeding the progress of an opponent without contact,"* as well as information on what goalkeepers can and can't do (including the widely-ignored 'six second rule'). Interestingly, under the section on the list of offences that result in an indirect free-kick, I discovered that a ref can award one if a player *"is guilty of dissent, using offensive, insulting or abusive language and/or action(s) or other verbal offences."* In other words, abusing the ref should, in theory, lead to an indirect free kick: something that would cause mayhem every couple of minutes during the average match and every thirty seconds in most local derbies.

Law 12 also covers handball offences. It includes a small graphic (my version of which is shown here), which purports to explain the area of the arm that, following contact with the ball, will result in a free kick and the (tiny) bit that won't. As you can see, for any ball striking the upper portion of the arm, it is well-nigh impossible for any referee to decide whether a free-kick or penalty should be given. Which is why, as referees will tell you, the most important Law of the Game is the unwritten Rule 18 – use your common sense.

Before we leave Law 12, there is one area it covers which is a source of extreme annoyance for fans of all clubs.

"Simulation"

I suspect that most fans would agree that the three things which get them most angry are players spitting on each other, cheating, and one of their side seemingly not trying and/or shirking out of a challenge.

Cheating, or *"simulation"* as the football authorities prefer to call it, is rife in football. It happens in almost every game. The media positively encourage it by their endless analyses, conducted in slow motion, and their discussions about whether a player has *"felt contact"* and *"gone down."* Most pundits are former players and, like referees, they tend to circle the wagons and shy away from having a consistent view on this. Yet for fans, the feeling that your side has been cheated out of a goal or a point is one of the worst in football. Most fans can accept if they have been beaten by a better side, or even if they have been beaten by a fluke goal but if they think a winning goal, usually from a dead-ball situation of one kind or another, has resulted from one of the opposition conning the referee, they leave the ground in a very bad mood indeed.

Of course, as with managers not adopting a consistent position about penalties for or against their team, the problem is that fans usually supress their annoyance about cheating when one of their own players has taken a dive and secured a match-winning penalty. While I'm not naïve enough to think that the Corinthian days will ever return, the use of the word *"simulation"* to describe what is blatant cheating is pure sophistry. The counter-argument will be that you can't accuse a player of cheating if he hasn't actually done so, but the moment a referee books a forward for diving in the box that is, in fact, exactly what he is doing – not just accusing but, by passing sentence, being the judge and the jury as well. If the footballing authorities, from IFAB down (and especially the media), called cheating what it is, rather than indulging the cheats with the far less pejorative *"simulation,"* there would be, I suggest, a degree of peer pressure on clubs and players to stop doing it. Meanwhile, hell resolutely will refuse to freeze over and cheating will continue.

Cheating is the wrong way to win a game, whether it's because a player has taken a bung from a bookie or has thrown himself down in the last minute to win a free kick or penalty. There are no degrees of wrongness here: it's simply wrong. I don't think there is any chance players will ever change unless there is a concerted effort to make them do so, but whenever even a tentative attempt is made to enforce some of the laws it hits the buffers.

For example, in the 2000-01 League Cup (then the CIS Insurance Cup), an experiment was held whereby referees could advance a free-kick ten yards forward if they received any abusive comments about the initial decision. In addition to this, the player(s) who complained about the original decision were also booked. This experiment was also carried out in England in some of their less important competitions and contemporary media reports suggest that referees and the football authorities generally welcomed it, but the clubs wouldn't wear it and it was dropped.

Another attempt to enforce the laws more vigorously occurred in season 2016-17, when it was agreed more rigorously to enforce penalties for shirt-holding in the box. St Johnstone were awarded three spot-kicks in a match against Falkirk by referee Bobby Madden. Two of these were for shirt-pulling. Self-important, ex-footballers, all queued up to condemn Madden, while the media didn't exactly help the refs, with The Scotsman's report containing the following:

"...while fair is to be celebrated, consistent would be even better and would help mend the tarnished relationships between po-faced, finger-wagging officialdom and the people who play, coach and watch the game and who have little of any positivity to say about the men and women in black."

Ironically, the article was actually broadly supportive of referees. However, although The Scotsman was right in seeking consistency (which, it should be stressed, Bobby Madden actually applied in this match), the language used in this quote about officials does nothing to help foster a better understanding of their job. The chances of the person who wrote the article actually knowing the laws properly will almost certainly have been less than zero. With clubs, former players and the media slating the referees about this attempt to enforce the rules, the latter backed down and players to this day regularly grab opponents' shirts with seeming impunity in the box (although, mysteriously, they tend to get pulled up for doing so outside it).

Law 12 creates much of the controversy in the game, for obvious reasons. It is probably the one that, more than any other, I'd suggest you read up before you next head to your team's ground and start to give the referee and/or opposition grief for their foul play and misconduct.

Throw-ins
LAW 15.

As noted, originally throw-ins were taken with one hand and the ball had to be propelled at a right angle to the touchline. Some football historians suggest that the one-armed throw-in wasn't used in Scotland, but the photo from St Johnstone's 1887 match with Arbroath shown above illustrates that this did happen. Moreover, in the mid-late nineteenth century (and in the first official international match), the team taking the throw-in was the one whose player first laid hands on the ball after it had crossed the line. Given the occasional contretemps we see nowadays when players believe they should have been given the throw, it's not hard to see how this would have erupted into an unseemly squabble over the ball.

In 1994-95, the English Isthmian League (then called after its sponsors, the Diadora League) tried a new FIFA initiative that the world's governing body hoped would add a new, exciting attacking dimension to the game: the kick-in. It had previously been trialled at the 1993 World Youth Cup and the experiment was extended to leagues in England, Belgium and Hungary the following season. Under this new 'rule,' the player putting the ball back into play from the touchline could kick it instead of throwing it, so long as they raised their arms first to indicate what they were about to do. To say this was unpopular is an understatement, with some club's managers refusing to participate, and one, St Albans City, telling their players their contracts would be cancelled if they tried it. For those who did embrace this change, throw-ins became just like free-kicks (presumably this hadn't occurred to FIFA/IFAB) and the idea was kicked into touch at the end of the season, never to be seen again. As we have seen, and shall see again later, this wasn't the only slightly barking idea that officialdom has tried to foist on the game over the years and, to prove the point, the concept of kick-ins is currently being resurrected – of which more later...

Extra time and determining the outcome of a match
LAW 10.

Before the standardisation of the rules there wasn't an agreed regulation concerning extra time. Early matches certainly went to extra time, but it was up to the teams to agree this beforehand. In the 1883 FA Cup final at the Oval Cricket Ground in London, Blackburn Olympic beat Old Etonians but some of the Etonian players blamed their captain for being *"too sporting,"* by agreeing to extra time on the grounds that the Lancashire side might struggle to find the funds to pay for another trip to the capital.

Games in a knock-out tournament that were level after 90 minutes could be continued with extra time or they could go to a replay. In Brian Doyle's immense archive of statistics on St Johnstone, there were many early Cup matches that went to one or more replays and this, rather than extra time, seems to have been the norm. In those days, in the Scottish Cup there were as many replays as it took to reach a final result, although an extra 30 minutes was added to the first replay as early as 1919-20 (and may have been introduced during the First World War years).

There seems to have been no agreed method of deciding extra time and it could even proceed as it did in our – and, I'm sure, every other - school playground, with 'next goal's the winner,' or, if you were playing in the local park it might go on until darkness forced the game's end. Sometimes, both these things happened, as for example in the 1922 German Championship final between Hamburg and Nuremburg. The sides were tied after 90 minutes, so they opted for the 'next goal's the winner' method. Unfortunately, after 99 more minutes, no-one had scored and it was so dark that the game had to be abandoned. It is fair to assume that the players must have been exhausted.

During the Second World War and its immediate aftermath, a popular tie-breaker for deadlocked cup matches was counting corners. This was also used for several years to decide drawn matches in the end-of-season Glasgow Charity Cup. Also in the Second World War, and in the next few difficult years of austerity (and bad winters, 1947 being one of the worst of the century), some competitions in the UK (notably the FA Cup) played matches to a finish rather than going to the traditional replay. This method was also used at one time in the Scottish League Cup, which began in 1946-47, as was the provision of a second period of extra time, consisting of two halves of seven and a half minutes. This 'extra' extra-time remained in place in some Junior competitions (such as the end-of-season Erskine Hospital Cup in Glasgow) until the late 1960s.

For much of the twentieth century, where there was no prospect (or there was a real difficulty in arranging) a replay in a Cup tie, games were decided on the toss of a coin or the drawing of lots. Some of the arrangements were bizarre, to say the least. The first major instance of drawing lots came in 1928, when FIFA organised a post-Olympics tournament. The final was played in Holland, between the Dutch and Chile. On drawing lots, the Netherlands won, but, possibly due to embarrassment at the 'home' side being declared victorious in such a random manner, the Dutch awarded the Cup to Chile.

Another example of the convoluted process involved in drawing lots came in the 1990 European Championship group games, when, with Italy and Ireland level on three points, two goals scored and two conceded, Sepp Blatter (who was then No. 2 at FIFA) got involved. According to the report in the New York Times, he arranged for *"a slip of paper bearing each team's name* (to be put) *into each of two orange plastic balls, which he placed in a goldfish bowl. Another two yellow balls were marked 2 and 3 and placed in another goldfish bowl. He then asked one of the blue-uniformed World Cup hostesses to pull a ball from each bowl."* Ireland won by this method and progressed to beat Romania in the first of the knock-out rounds. Italy was less fortunate, being drawn against – and subsequently losing to – West Germany.

In the semi-final of the 1968 European Championships, the Soviet Union and Italy were scoreless after extra time. After some debate over the actual coin to be used (a peseta and a rouble were apparently rejected), a Dutch guilder was used, the Soviet skipper called incorrectly and Italy went through to the final.

Two years later, in 1970, an appendix to the laws allowed penalty shoot-outs, the idea having been dreamt up by Israeli Yosef Dagan after he had watched his country lose the 1968 Olympic quarter final to Bulgaria on the drawing of lots. Yet again there is a Scottish connection, with the actual decision by IFAB to proceed with penalty shoot-outs (except they called it 'kicks from the penalty mark'), being taken at their annual meeting on 27th June 1970, in the Caledonian Hotel in Inverness.

In England, in the Watney Cup in 1970, Manchester United took part in the first penalty shoot-out, with George Best being the first to score in this way - and Denis Law becoming the first to miss. As far as Scottish teams are concerned, the first club to take part in a penalty shoot-out is often thought to be Aberdeen, who went out 5-4 on spot-kicks to Honved of Hungary in 1970. However, just a few days before Aberdeen met Honved, Airdrie were actually the first Scottish side to take part in a shoot-out, beating Nottingham Forest 5-2 on penalties in a Texaco Cup first round tie. More predictably, the introduction of penalty shoot-outs has led to depressingly defensive tactics as the second half of extra time peters out, followed frequently by intensive, nerve-shredding excitement until someone balloons the ball over the bar and your team or country is declared the winner (or not).

In more recent decades, we've seen a number of experiments about how best to decide a match during extra time. One of the more interesting ones was introduced in the North American Soccer League in the late 1970s to settle drawn (League) matches. Instead of penalties, this 'shoot-out' involved a player dribbling the ball from the edge of the centre circle and shooting at will or trying to take it past the goalkeeper, who could advance to the edge of his penalty area.

Then there was the 'Golden Goal,' introduced by FIFA in the 1990s, whereby it was hoped that teams would go all out to score and thus create more excitement (and bring the game to a conclusion more quickly). The authorities reckoned without the timidity of football managers, who, rather than getting their teams to flood forward and try to score, instead shut up shop, hoping to go to a penalty shoot-out. Nevertheless, a Golden Goal decided a number of major tournaments, notably the 1996 European Championship, when a goal by Germany's Oliver Beirhoff beat the Czech Republic in extra time in the final, and also four years later, when David Trezeguet's Golden Goal against Italy decided the same competition.

More Golden Goals followed in some of the rounds of the 2002 World Cup, but it clearly wasn't having the impact that FIFA wanted, so they lowered their sights and in 2003 declared that a 'Silver Goal' would now decide extra time. Under this rule, the team that was in front at half-time in extra time was declared the winner. This was even less popular than the Golden Goal and after Euro 2004 it too was consigned to the dustbin of history.

Hutchison and Mitchell, in their research for their book on the Edinburgh Foot-Ball Club, tried to find out what clothing the Edinburgh Foot-Ball players might have worn, but other than a letter from one member to another, asking him to bring his *"football coat,"* they concluded that it is not possible to know what, if any, special kit players of this era wore. It seems that, for the most part, they simply wore outdoor clothes and shoes or boots. Given that the games of football described in their book were often played on a field which was grazed by sheep, whoever had to clean the players' clothes and boots would not much have enjoyed doing so…?

As we have seen, nineteenth century teams would often wear the same-coloured cap to distinguish them from their opponents. Bearing in mind that many people simply couldn't afford to buy distinctive football kits or boots, it's easy to understand why the early teams kept things simple. St Johnstone, for example, in their early days wore white shirts – the same shirts they would have worn to play cricket (the photo of the first St Johnstone team to win a local cup – shown here, courtesy of the club – actually has the players in their cricket colours, complete with pads).

Given the prevalence of "hacking" it would have seemed sensible for the nineteenth century footballer to wear some form of protective equipment. Indeed, some photos of players from this era do show legs encased in early shin-guards, which first made an appearance in 1874.

These first shin-guards were simply cut-down cricket pads. Sam Weller Widdowson played both cricket and football and is acknowledged to be the man who first did this, in 1874. He apparently got a bit of stick from his team-mates, but his idea caught on and after Nottingham Forest became the first team to wear them on a regular basis, others followed suit. Not every player liked them though. Those of you who are old (and lucky) enough to remember Paul Sturrock playing for Dundee United, will recall that 'Luggy' didn't wear shin-pads and also kept his socks rolled down. Many other players did this as it was believed to help prevent cramp, but the powers-that-be decided that it was too dangerous and today all players, even the goalkeepers, have to wear shin-guards which, as Law No. 4 points out, must be completely covered by their socks.

In England, according to Dave Moor of Historical Football Kits, who is reportedly the expert on the subject, once games began to be arranged between clubs, schools and universities, teams began to wear the same colours, often those associated with their public school or university. On the (English) National Football Museum website, he describes the earliest strips thus… *"...what glorious colours they were! Cerise and French grey, chocolate and pink, white and magenta, brown and green, maroon and pink, violet and orange, crimson and black are just a few of the more exotic jerseys that could be seen at the time. Various types of headgear were de rigueur including caps, snoods, hoods, turbans, fezzes and tartan Tam O'Shanters."*

In the same way that we saw that some of the most famous names in football manufacture go back centuries, the same applies to football jerseys and related kit. Bukta began life in 1879, while in 1920 the company Humphrey Brothers Clothing was founded. Four years later, Humphrey Brothers recast themselves as Umbro and started to compete with Bukta in what was to become in time, a seriously large market.

The registered colours of Scottish clubs are included in the respective annual handbooks of the SFA and SFL, going back to these organisations' earliest days. Some early clubs wore what were called (and still are today, for leisure purposes) 'guernseys' – thick, woollen jerseys; but for most of football history the jerseys and shorts worn by the players were made of cotton and, the colours apart, pretty much the same design, with a collar, a short, open neck with a few buttons to fasten it, and long shorts with a pyjama-style cord to secure them. Socks were woollen and the boots, of which more below, were designed as much to protect the feet as to allow the ball to be played. Put a rugby player and a football player beside each other and, based on their playing kit, it was pretty much impossible to tell them apart. Training tops were all made of wool and, as almost any photograph of a players at training during the 1930s will reveal, looked decidedly uncomfortable.

Interestingly, in the very earliest days of the game, when a team played in 'stripes' it meant they wore what we would now call 'hoops.' According to the Historical Football Kits website (historicalkits.co.uk), this was because the looms that produced the cotton could only do stripes horizontally. To create a vertical stripe required the material to be cut up and re-sown. However, once the technological issue was resolved, vertical stripes became very popular.

In the late 1920s, for some bizarre reason, the Scottish League tried to force away clubs to wear black shorts and home clubs white shorts. In the Daily Record of Thursday, 29th September 1927, Waverley (the pen name of Willie Gallagher, the most famous sports reporter of the day) wrote that at the previous day's League Management Committee meeting it was decided that *"in future, white knickers must be the nether garments for home wear; away – black is the order."*

Fans and players were none too enamoured of this, with a report in the (Daily) Record of 29th March 1928 pointing out one of the flaws in this new approach, viz, *"Rangers turned out with white pants at Tynecastle yesterday, instead of in black which, under the new regulations, should be worn by visiting clubs. And it was a good job, for ere the finish had they been in black the players would hardly have been visible – the shades of night were falling quickly."*

In 1928, Arsenal wore numbers on the back of their shirts for a game against Sheffield Wednesday - the first time this has been done. Then, in the 1933 FA Cup, the finalists, Manchester City and Everton, wore numbers on the backs of their shirts for the first time. Everton's players were numbered 1-11, but Man City's wore 12-22. Arsenal experimented again with players' numbers later in 1933 and then in 1939 they were made mandatory in England. In Scotland, we were slightly later with this rather sensible innovation. Although Scottish clubs started to wear numbered shirts after the Second World War, this wasn't made compulsory until 1960. Celtic, as I remember from my young days, sported their numbers on their shorts, not their backs, until forced to follow the rest in 1995. In the 1950s, as artificial fibres became more commonly used in everyday clothing, some clubs turned out in very shiny tops which looked quite snazzy compared to the traditional jerseys. The first time such jerseys appeared was in the 1953 FA Cup final (the famous Stanley 'Matthews final'), when Bolton wore both shirts and shorts in this new material.

Picture courtesy of St Johnstone

The photo here shows St Johnstone in 1956 in what the Dundee Courier described as, *"a loose-fitting, deep-blue garment like a jockey's silk."* I imagine these shirts must have been uncomfortable to wear. Those who remember the (mystifying) popularity of nylon bedsheets in the 1960s and 70s will know what I mean! Unsurprisingly, these new fabrics didn't really take off and clubs returned to cotton tops, but with artificial fibres increasingly used for socks and then shorts. Note the T-panel ball in the photo.

Sometimes, there were practical issues with the kit, such as the time in 1962-63 season when some of the St Johnstone players complained to manager Bobby Brown that their shorts were uncomfortable. Upon investigation, it was discovered that the sports goods firm Lillywhites had only sent 34-inch waist shorts, but Saints had also ordered sizes 38 and 40. This reflects how much the build and athleticism of the players has changed. I suspect it's unlikely there would be many present-day footballers requiring such a large waistband.

Round and V-shaped necks also became popular in the 1950s as a result of the increase in the number of friendly matches against European opposition, some of whose teams sported clean-cut V-necks rather than the old-fashioned collars that were normally worn. This 'continental kit' also featured shorter jerseys made of a much lighter weight of cotton and was the progenitor in some ways of the modern shirts and shorts we see today.

The first St Johnstone jersey I had (which, sad git that I am, I still have), was the classic 1970s design, made of cotton in royal blue with a white V-insert at the neck and white collar and cuffs. The shorts were white, again made of cotton and the socks were white, with two blue bands on the turnover and were made of nylon or some other artificial fibre(s) – and, of course, there was no advertising and the only indication of the maker (Umbro) was a tiny tab inside the collar.

Since then, as we know, football kit has changed out of all recognition. Today, cotton has been replaced by 'highly-engineered' polyester mesh which, its makers claim, does not trap body heat and sweat to the same extent as natural fibres. Naturally, given the commercial imperative that, more than ever, drives professional sport, advertising covers increasingly wide areas of the shirt and its sleeves.

The man largely responsible for the move to shirt sponsorship was the Wolves' legend Derek Dougan who, as Chief Executive at non-league Kettering Town, introduced a local tyre company to the club's jerseys for a match in January 1976. The FA were not pleased, but the genie was out of the bottle and in season 1977-78, Hibernian became the first top-flight team in the UK to have a shirt sponsor. This advert was actually for the makers of the shirt – Bukta – and although shirt advertising caused a huge fuss, with TV companies refusing to show teams which had ads on their shirts, it soon became the norm. Advertising on football kit has proliferated since then, with the size of the logo/name-style on the shirt front gradually increasing and with ads subsequently appearing on the back of shirts and sleeve advertising logos spreading like a rash. The kit manufacturers have also got into the act by adding their logos to the shirt. In the olden days, the only way you knew who made your jersey was because there was a tab on the inside of the neck that had the maker's name. Now, the manufacturer's logo is an intrinsic part of the design. While I'm more or less relaxed about this, I would point out the increasing frequency with which shirts designs are changed (to say nothing of the rising cost of the shirts, shorts and socks) means that fans are being asked to shell-out a lot of money for something that often is current for only one season. The necessity to commercialise football means that we are likely to see more advertising in the years ahead. Ten years ago, I remember watching football on the TV in Argentina and being taken aback by adverts that flashed onto the screen for a few seconds while the ball was in play. Personally, I don't want to see this, but if someone offers enough money and/or Scottish football is even more desperate for cash than it is now, it will probably happen.

It's not just adverts. If you Google *"when did names start on football shirts UK,"* you'll discover that the 'answer' is 1992, when the Premier League started in England. However, this is another area where Scotland was the pioneer. In 1979, when the Scottish international side took the field for a friendly with Peru, the fans were surprised to see the players' names on the backs of their shirts. SFA Secretary Ernie Walker came up with the idea after seeing players names on shirts in the USA and he presciently noted in the programme that *"they will be commonplace in the future"* and that in 20 years' time, *"as likely as not, club sides will probably have followed suit."* Scotland thus became the first international side to have the players' names on their shirts. Perhaps they were too far ahead of the curve, for, although well received, after 13 more games the shirt-names were dropped. They were resurrected in 1992, when Scotland played at the European Championship finals in Sweden and they are now, as we all know, universally used throughout the senior game.

Squad numbers were introduced for the Scottish international team in the 1980 and 1981 British Championships and were introduced for club sides in England in 1993-94 but it wasn't until 1998 – with the formation of the Scottish Premier League - that Scotland's top-flight players were allocated squad numbers.

Goalkeepers

Yet another thing I didn't realise (but, given the number of old photos of St Johnstone I've seen, I should have) is that when you look at most photos from the late nineteenth century of any Scottish club, you'll not see anyone in goalkeeper's kit. In those early days, goalkeepers didn't wear distinctive jerseys and in fact different people sometimes played in goal in the same match. The report of the first official international match in the North British Daily Mail tells us that both England and Scotland rotated their goalkeepers at half-time, with an outfield player swopping places with the keeper in each case. It wasn't until 1909 that goalkeepers in Scotland had to wear a different coloured shirt from the rest of the team. Green was the favourite colour for goalies, mainly because with only a small number of clubs favouring that colour there were few opportunities for a clash. In England, 'keepers were restricted to green, blue, scarlet and white tops, with yellow strictly forbidden, except for international matches where, following a ruling by the IFAB in 1921, yellow or black were the colours allowed.

In Scotland, most people of my generation or older recall that goalkeepers tended to wear yellow, usually the woollen polo-neck jersey that is associated with famous keepers like Bobby Brown. In fact, for several decades it was a Scottish Cup rule that goalkeepers had to wear yellow or deep yellow-coloured jerseys, and that in the event of a clash of outfield colours, *both* teams had to wear change strips. Those rules had sensibly been changed by the early 1980s.

In the 1970s, the general rules governing keepers' jerseys were relaxed and they could wear a much wider range of colours, but even up to the mid-90s they generally wore the same-coloured socks and shorts as their outfield colleagues. Since then, as we know, goalkeepers' kit has, at times, resembled the proverbial explosion in a paint factory. However, yet again the laws of the game throw up all sorts of new discoveries (at least for the average fan like me) and one thing I have discovered is that there is a specific provision for what should happen if both teams' keepers have the same-coloured jersey and neither has an additional, alternatively coloured, top. In these circumstances, Law 4 states, *"the referee allows the game to be played."* This is, for once, Law 18 in action...

Goalkeepers, of course, are physically closer to the fans than the other players. For those brave enough, this offers exciting opportunities to wind up the opposition, with Ayr United's Hugh Sproat famously wearing green when playing Rangers and blue when playing Celtic in the 1970s.

Not only were the earliest goalkeepers not required to wear any distinguishing colours, the FA's first stab at the Laws of the game in 1863 didn't actually require one specific member of the team to act as a goalkeeper. Instead, any player was allowed to catch the ball. It wasn't until 1870 that all players were forbidden from handling the ball. They must have quickly realised that this didn't work and the following year (1871) the laws were changed to allow teams to field a goalkeeper who, alone amongst his team, was able to handle the ball *"for the protection of his goal."* In 1873, Queen's Park proposed (to the FA - of which they were then members) that *"the goalkeeper must not carry the ball."* In effect, this was the 'two step' rule, whereby the keeper had to release the ball very quickly. Just quite how they released the ball to a team-mate seems to have been a matter of contention, because in 1875, Vale of Leven (again via the FA) proposed *"the goalkeeper may throw and hit the ball."*

Subsequently, several revisions involved the length of time a keeper could carry the ball (or not) and where on the field of play he could actually handle the ball. Up to 1887, it was still possible for the keeper to handle the ball anywhere on the pitch, but after that date he was restricted to only handling it in his own half. Then, in 1912, came a major change, which persists to this day, with the goalkeeper only able to handle the ball in the penalty area.

On the same subject, all those who played football as boys in the 1960s and 70s will recollect shouting *"four steps!"* every time the goalkeeper took more than four paces with the ball in his hands. This rule was introduced in 1931 because the previous 'two-step' rule was clearly impractical. The intention behind this rule was to stop goalkeepers wasting time: in theory there was nothing to prevent them just standing with the ball in their hands. However, goalkeepers being a cunning lot, they simply devised ways in which the ball wasn't actually in their hands. Old TV footage from the early 1960s shows goalkeepers bouncing the ball as they ran to the edge of their box (Hibs and Celtic goalie Ronnie Simpson was a great exponent), so in 1967 the laws were changed again and 'keepers were not allowed to take another four steps after they had bounced the ball or thrown it up in the air.

The four-step rule didn't make much difference, either on the school playing field or at Muirton Park, but in theory it was the law. It was clearly better than when keepers were restricted to only taking two steps while holding the ball, but it was apparent that this regulation was being honoured more in the breach than in the observance and in 2000 the law requiring the keeper to take his hands off the ball after six seconds was brought in instead. This is similarly ignored by referees and goalies alike, but it's still, in theory, punishable by an indirect free kick.

In 1995, the law that permitted players to charge each other *("tackling without contact with the ball")* was written out of the rulebook. It had, for many years before that date, been consigned to the bin by referees applying Law 18 and using their common sense to forbid it.

The oldest fans alive today may have seen forwards charge a goalkeeper when the latter was (more or less) in possession of the ball, knocking him into the net and, as a result, claiming a goal, but for those of the younger generation who find this hard to believe, I suggest you Google *"Nat Lofthouse, 1958 Cup final goals against Manchester United."* In the video, Lofthouse, the famously strong and powerful England centre-forward, slams into Harry Gregg, the United keeper, who, having parried a shot up into the air was then trying to regain possession of the ball almost on his goal-line. Lofthouse charges him into the net and the goal is given. Today, not only would it not stand, but there is a very good chance the Bolton striker would be sent off.

The other major change in my lifetime that really has affected goalkeepers was the introduction of the 'pass-back' rule in 1992. The wording in the current laws, says that an indirect free kick is awarded if the goalkeeper *"touches the ball with the hand/arm, unless the goalkeeper has clearly kicked or attempted to kick the ball to release it into play, after:*

- *it has been deliberately kicked to the goalkeeper by a team-mate.*
- *receiving it directly from a throw-in taken by a team-mate."*

At a stroke, a major weapon in a team's defensive armoury was removed. The thinking was, obviously, to prevent a team that is leading from running down the clock by simply passing back to the goalkeeper at every available opportunity. It certainly did this, but there was a cohort of goalkeepers whose inability to kick a moving ball any distance with any accuracy meant that their careers became shorter than they might previously have been. I recall one in particular who wasn't very popular with his team-mates, who would deliberately pass the ball back to his weaker foot in order to embarrass him.

Away kit

Today, when clubs change both their home and away kits every season – and frequently have a third strip to add to try to make even more money – we are all accustomed to the away team changing when there is a colour clash. Even with the plethora of different colours available, sometimes colour clashes still happen. On 11th January 1995, Dundee turned out at McDiarmid Park against St Johnstone wearing the latter's away jerseys because the referee adjudged the Dee's change kit to be too similar to St Johnstone's home strip (their home strip also being too similar). It's fair to say that this didn't go down too well with the home fans – and the fact that Saints' keeper, Alan Main, made a terrible blunder to allow Dundee to snatch a last-minute draw didn't help either. However, it wasn't always the case that the away team were the ones who changed strips.

As I was writing this book, I received an email with a picture of St Johnstone playing at Ibrox. It was from the late 1960s and featured Derek Robertson, one of Saints' two very good goalkeepers from this time (the other was Jim Donaldson if you're interested). In the background was a Rangers' player, wearing a striped jersey. The person who sent it wanted to know if I knew the identity of the Rangers' player (it was Willie Henderson), but what seemed strange was why Rangers, as the home side, were wearing their change kit. Then I remembered that in those days it was the *home* team that changed when there was a colour clash, not the away team.

This, I believe, stems from a much earlier injunction which we know applied in England and therefore almost certainly would have been adopted north of the border either before or after the English ruling. In 1891, all English Football League sides had to register their colours and no two teams were allowed to register the same strip. However, a year later, when the Second Division was established, the English League required all teams to have a set of white jerseys to be used if there was a clash of colours. And to make things easier for the away team, who would otherwise have to carry extra kit to the match (not so easy in the nineteenth century), it was the home team that changed. This then carried on until, I believe, the early 1980s, when, as we are accustomed to today, the away team changed.

Referees' kit

I am indebted to John Litster for much of what follows. John attended his first match (Raith Rovers vs Alloa) in October 1963 and since then he has watched thousands of games, in the process amassing an enormous volume of data, facts and figures (and also some entertaining trivia) about the Scottish game.

Most of us who have watched football over the last six or more decades tend to think of the referee as the man in black (or frequently, as noted in the introduction, 'the bastard in the black'). That's because, for the baby boomer generation in particular, both referees and football boots came in one colour only – black. Black had become the preferred colour after the First World War. This made sense, given that no team wore black and only a handful wore navy blue or maroon which might have clashed with it. For those occasions (Dundee, Raith Rovers, Hearts, Arbroath, Stenhousemuir, etc.) where there might have been considered to be a clash between the referee's kit and the players' jerseys, referees tended to wear khaki. John Litster recalls that his mother, whose football spectating was entirely done at Stark's Park, *"was astonished to discover several decades later that all referees did not wear khaki, as that was all she had ever seen them in."*

However, at first there were no hard and fast rules and colour clashes still occurred. At the same Scottish League Management Committee meeting (September 1927) that decided that away teams must wear black shorts and home teams white ones, it was also recorded that *"The question of referees wearing a distinctive sweater is to be considered further."*

A few months later, the need for distinctive clothing for referees was publicly made by Waverley in the Daily Record of 12th January 1928, when he wrote, *"The need for a distinctive rig-out for the referee was made very evident in the Alliance game at Paisley. The man in charge, dressed in shorts and a blue jacket, with white collar overlapping, was so like a Raith Rovers player that mistakes were frequently made by the Fife players. Ultimately the game was stopped, and the whistler got a cheer all to himself when he re-appeared sporting a red jersey."*

For the start of the following season (1929-30), the League told the referees that they should wear khaki. However, many were reluctant to do so, with the Record reporting on 5th August 1929, *"What will happen if our referees refuse to obey the League sartorial mandate as they threaten? The order to turn out in khaki jackets has not gone down well."* In that day's paper, an advert appeared, stating that *"The Scottish Football Referees' Association had decided not to comply with the Scottish Football League's mandate to wear Khaki Blazers. MEMBERS PLEASE NOTE.*
W. Cuthbertson, Secy. Pro. tem." There had been a unanimous decision by the referees the previous Saturday evening, although arguably the most famous (and flamboyant) referee

of the time, Peter Craigmyle, announced that he would wear khaki to referee the forthcoming Hibs vs Airdrie match on 10th August. In what was presumably a show of solidarity, one of his linesmen, Mr P Kilbride of Polmont, also wore khaki. That same weekend, Mr W Whiteside, Paisley, who officiated at the Second Division game at the Gymnasium (the Edinburgh home of St Bernards FC), went one better than the official regulation by wearing not only a khaki jacket, but khaki shorts as well.

The other referees were not prepared to play ball though, but the SFL were not prepared to give up and even in 1939 they were issuing instructions that referees should wear khaki jackets, as shown by this note to officials (image courtesy of Stevie Walker) sent from the League's headquarters on St Vincent Street in Glasgow.

Sometimes, the referee dispensed with a jacket and just wore a plain shirt. This could cause problems though, as happened in the annual Glasgow vs Sheffield Inter-City match at Hampden Park, on 22nd September 1930, when the away side turned out in white shirts and black shorts. The referee, Mr J Thomson of Burnbank, was wearing a white shirt without a jacket. The captain of the Sheffield team was Jimmy Seed (later a famous manager of Charlton Athletic between 1933 and 1956) and on a number of occasions he passed the ball to the referee. Consequently, he asked Mr Thomson to stop the game, go off the pitch and put on a jacket, which he did.

Jackets, as worn by referees for the middle decades of the twentieth century, were, as noted, either black or khaki, but Peter Craigmyle, as shown here, occasionally favoured a dark-striped number, but mostly wore what he described as his "*usual green* (khaki) *blazer, black knickers* (shorts) *and special rubber boots.*" One of the most famous referees of the 50s, 60s and 70s, Tom (Tiny) Wharton, was one of the last to persist with a blazer/jacket - and also one of the last to apply Brylcreem to his hair. However, despite Mr Wharton's elegant dress sense, jackets became less popular with referees in the 1950s as the black, pull-over tunic took over. This, in turn, remained the favoured garment for all referees until the 1970s.

As described previously, a member of each club frequently ran the line for League and Cup matches. Conventionally, they wore a suit (or jacket and trousers), collar and tie, with the trousers tucked into football socks and some of the better-heeled wore plus-fours. John Litster tells of Robert Adamson, a Kirkcaldy chemist and Raith Rovers director, who was on the SFA Council and acted as Scotland's linesman in international matches up until the mid 1920s. For these duties, Adamson wore a tweed jacket, plus-fours and a collar and tie. We know this because he was included in the official team pictures taken before international matches – and very smart he looked too.

John suspects that in the mid-War era, khaki was chosen for eminently practical reasons; namely that at a time with a far higher percentage of men in uniform, military kit was relatively easily obtained. Even in my own early days of watching football, I can recall that light khaki shirts were worn as a change top for referees. The earliest John Litster can recall a referee not wearing khaki as a change top was when Tommy Muirhead of Stenhousemuir appeared in a red football strip (with white collar and neck insert) in the mid 1970s. However, as we found out in Part I above, it may well have been the famous Scottish referee Brian McGinlay who was responsible for the move to using non-traditional colours for the officials. Brian certainly did this on one occasion when Tommy was running the line for him and it's probable that was one of the first times (since the match in 1928 referred to above) that a Scottish ref had worn a red top. One thing that they did all have though, was the SFA badge. I have struggled to find out when it became compulsory for referees to have the governing body's badge on their strips. With the re-organisation by the SFA of the regional Referees' Associations after the war, it seems likely that an SFA badge was required from the late 1940s onwards. Prior to that time, the more independent Scottish Football Referees Association (of whom more below) were less likely to have succumbed to SFA pressure to use the badge. However, one thing I do know is that until comparatively recently, all officials bought their kit privately and as a result they all had to sow the badge on themselves (or, more likely, ask their wives to do so).

Messrs McGinlay and Muirhead were still the exceptions though, and referees' clothing at that time was largely conservative and drab. John Litster offered a good example of how this continued to be the case, recalling that in the late 1970s and 80s he was a member of the Glasgow SFA Referees Association and attended the monthly meetings on a Friday evening in the City Halls in Glasgow. Contrary to what you might think, these meetings were well attended, possibly because perfect attendance in those days guaranteed a ticket for the Scotland v England match, home or away. However, as is often the case with committee men, an obsession with seemingly trivial matters was never far away and John recounted how, *"A good example of the influence of this Association is that there was an 'any other business' discussion on refereeing kit, when the chairman (Ronnie Marshall) recalled that at a recent League game, his kit bag had black socks with a white top, one of his linesmen had black socks with two white stripes, and the other one had black socks with three white stripes on the turnover. The recommendation of the Glasgow Association was that its members should pack all three types, and a decision could be made pre-match as to which was worn as a uniform."* To be fair to the referees concerned, given that all officials bought their own kit at this time, all they were doing was trying to settle on a means of all three officials looking the same – as all teams do on the park.

In the late 1980s and early 1990s, there was a radical change in the way in which football kit, especially jerseys, was designed. The 1988 Dutch World Cup strip was probably the first to make a major impact. Rather than a solid colour, this Dutch shirt was made up of various shades of orange, based on a design of small, recurring triangles/chevrons with the vignette of colour in each going from dark orange to white. Club sides aped the Dutch approach and some referees too wanted to move on from the somewhat boring uniformity that had, for good reasons, coloured their approach to their clothing (referees don't usually want to stand out from the crowd).

Consequently, referees began to wear a wider range of colours, always taking care, naturally, not to clash with the two teams. In 2002, Specsavers agreed a sponsorship deal with Scottish referees which has continued to this day. When Specsavers renewed their contract in 2014, there was, as usual, a photo-opportunity for the media, with three current referees posing in the various new jersey designs, complete with the company's logo on each arm. In a sign of how far times had changed, not one of the jerseys was black: instead, they were navy, yellow and red.

The irony of the Specsavers deal was not lost on John Litster. When he was General Manager at St Johnstone in the 1990s, the company had approached the club, wanting to buy trackside advertising. However, their proposed advert poked gentle fun at referees and, as John told us, *"Conscious of the complete absence of a sense of humour at Park Gardens (the then SFA HQ), I asked Mr. Farry if there would be any objection, to which the answer was 'of course.' You can imagine my thoughts when Specsavers became the official sponsors of the SFA referees..."*

The first use of modern technology to enable referee and assistants to communicate came in the mid-1990s, with the introduction of linesmen's flags with a buzzer which, when pressed,

182

would alert the referee to whatever the linesman wanted to bring to his attention, thus reducing the number of occasions on which a referee missed a linesman's signal. A decade later the officials were also connected by mike and headphones, thus presumably increasing the number of times they were able to hear the players swearing. Today, the referee takes the field not just in a natty shirt, shorts and socks, but also with his mandatory (as laid down in the laws) whistle, watch, red and yellow cards and a note book (presumably a pen or pencil too). In addition, at first-class level, he will be miked up and able to speak to all his assistants and he also carries a can of spray foam for use in marking the exact place for a free-kick and for delineating the nearest point/line where defenders and/or a defensive wall can stand.

Boots

"*Scottish Football Reminiscences and Sketches,*' published in 1890 and referred to above, includes a chapter titled, "*The Conquerer's Football Boots.*" It starts…

"*My football boots are getting what might be called shabby genteel now, and no wonder. If they could speak they would tell you many a strange episode in the life of an Association football player, and how he kept his place in a leading club for nearly a dozen years. They have become old and dear friends, those well-worn boots, and although now somewhat curled up at the toes, have kicked many a good goal out of a hot and exciting scrummage in front of an opponent's upright posts, and even an International tussle; but now that they, like myself, have retired from active duty…*"

A more recent, and quite brilliant, book, called, "*Elegance, borne of brutality: an eclectic history of the football boot*" takes the reader through the development of this most essential piece of kit, starting with the earliest boots of the nineteenth century, memorably described by authors Dave Kemp and Ian McArthur as, "*clumsy, armoured clodhoppers that reached above the ankle and weighed a ton.*" Today's younger fans, used to immaculately-tended pitches that are green almost all-season round, might wonder why such footwear was necessary, but it should be remembered that, until comparatively recently, football pitches were not manicured lawns, but rather frequently muddied, rutted expanses of earth and grass. Here are some descriptions of the state of the pitches that St Johnstone were used to playing on in their early decades.

The first is taken from Peter Baxter's "*Football in Perthshire,*" and describes of one of the earliest games involving St Johnstone, in the spring of 1885. This was for a match between Fair City Athletic and Saints, played on 2nd May, on Fair City's pitch at Hillyland in Perth. Baxter wrote, "*Rain for a day or two had made the puddled pond in a fearful state, but Mr Henderson allowed the clubs to play on an adjoining field. Soon the players were frightful objects, but each manfully did his best for his side, and heeded not the ankle-deep clay, or a ball six times its ordinary weight. Football reputations were unknown, and it was the winning of the match each player earnestly strove for.*"

St Johnstone's first park was the Recreation Grounds, opposite Perth Prison. The first game actually played by Saints on their new pitch took place on the 12th of September 1885. The match report in 'The Scottish Umpire' began by describing the meteorological conditions, thus: *"The weather at Perth on Saturday was of that description usually credited with being the most beneficial for that interesting biped, the duck."*

In the 1908-09 season, Saints were drawn against Glasgow Rangers in the Scottish Cup. The tie was scheduled for 23rd of January 1909, but there was a major problem - the pitch was unplayable. The Fire Brigade were called to action and from Thursday morning to Friday at noon they continued to pump water from the playing surface. A squad of men then scraped the pitch, deposited tons of cinders on it and rolled them in. Further rain on Friday and Saturday morning threatened to nullify their efforts, but when the game started the conditions were reportedly as ideal as could be expected.

It was no different anywhere else in the country. Andy Mitchell records how Arthur Kinnaird and his fellow Old-Etonians often struggled, *"in dreadful conditions, such as the pitch at Charterhouse which was 'utterly unfit for play, the centre of the ground being occupied by a circular patch of soft mud of no mean width, through which it was almost impossible to wade'; against Brixton, the match kicked off in a fog 'so intense that the goals were entirely invisible.'"* In the circumstances, it was hardly surprising that the contemporary soccer boots were as suited for hiking and mountaineering as they were for football. Difficult though it was, it may also have been these match conditions that led players to try passing the ball, as opposed to trying to dribble it through the glaur.

In the very early days of Scottish football, Queen's Park FC was all-conquering. On the 30th December 1876, Vale of Leven won 2-1 at Hampden, the first time Queen's had lost a home match. Afterwards, the Queen's officials noticed, to their horror, that there were jagged tears in the turf, which they ascribed to Vale having taken to the field in spiked boots. A real stooshie followed, with accusatory letters and ripostes flying back and forth, including the somewhat fanciful suggestion from Vale supporters that crows' feet might be responsible. There was no backing down from either side and the matter remained unresolved, albeit it did bring to the fore the subject of the studs, cleats or bars that players were attaching to the sole of their boots.

The studs (or bars) used to provide grip in those days were made of leather and individually nailed into the sole. I recall as a smallish boy in the 1960s reading up the rules of football and wondering why they referred to the use of 'bars' as well as studs on a boot as I had never seen a bar on the sole of a boot. However, they were clearly a key component of the early boot and in 1888 IFAB specified that, *"Bars measure at least one and a half inches in length and a half inch in width. Studs are round with a diameter of at least half an inch and never are conceal or pointed. Bars or studs in the soles of the shoes must not project more than 0.5 inch. Their fastenings must be driven in flush with the leather."* Although surpassed by studs, bars were used by some manufacturers to help players cope with the mud, blood and thunder of the early game.

In 1904, a Northampton footwear manufacturer called Manfield came up with a design that became the pre-eminent football boot of the first half of the twentieth century – the famous

Manfield Hotspur. This boot sold on the basis of its quality and value for money and by 1920 it was estimated that 80% of footballers in Britain were playing in Hotspur boots. Given that pitches were not that much better than they had been in the nineteenth century, the design of the Manfield Hotspur was not radically different from its predecessors, but that didn't mean that others manufacturers didn't try to come up with some unique selling point that would help them capture what was a substantial market. Wm Abbot and Sons of Ludgate in London produced the "Abbo" boot, which promised that its *"non-skid toe"* would prevent the ball from slicing when wet. It apparently did this by the simple expedient of several rows of stitching across the toe-cap.

The place where the first glimmerings of the modern football boot were seen was probably Argentina, where players were wearing low-cut boots as far back as the 1920s. Other Latin American countries followed but for the UK the big step on the way to the modern football boot came when England went to Brazil to play in the World Cup of 1950. Stanley Matthews, arguably the most famous player in the world at that time (think Messi or Ronaldo today), went to watch Brazil's opening match and was amazed at the Brazilians' ability to move more quickly over the ground and to kick the ball with more swerve and accuracy than their opponents. He realised that it was their lightweight footwear that made much of the difference and consequently he took a pair of Brazilian boots back to England. There, he approached the manager of the Co-op's shoe factory, who subsequently created the first modern, low-cut football boot in Britain. The Co-op's first attempt produced a pair of boots that weighed only 1lb 9oz (710gms in today's money), far less than the conventional boot of the day (a pair of which weighed c. 1kg). Further revisions to the design and cut of these Matthews' boots reduced the weight to a (then) staggering 10oz (280gms) but today, the lightest boots you can buy are only 3.5oz (99gms). The Co-op's boots were advertised by Matthews (thus guaranteeing sales) as *"so soft, without toe-caps, you could fold them up and put them in your pocket."* It transformed the way the game was played and over half a million pairs were sold between 1950 and 1958.

Finally in this section, it's worth noting that Law 4 only requires the following compulsory equipment, namely:

• a shirt with sleeves
• shorts
• socks – tape or any material applied or worn externally must be the same colour as that part of the sock it is applied to or covers
• shinguards – these must be made of a suitable material to provide reasonable protection and covered by the socks
• footwear

Goals and goal nets
LAW 1

Goal nets are a fundamental part of the game. Without them, several journalistic cliches would not exist, to wit, *"the onion bag," "hit the back of the net," "almost burst the net," "just the side-netting,"* etc. The celebrated Liverpudlian engineer and Everton football fan John Alexander Brodie is recognised as being the inventor of the goal-net in the late 1880s (he submitted a patent in 1889, which was accepted the following year), although the original idea may have come from Birmingham. Their use in Scotland was sanctioned in 1891. Despite their obvious advantages, they were not used in every game straight away and there are photos of games several years later without any nets in the goals. The issue of goal nets came to the fore in the 1893 Scottish Cup final, where Queen's Park defeated Celtic 2-1. The Scotsman's report tells us that, *"Doyle had inadvertently to concede a corner to Sellar, and, amidst the greatest excitement the referee allowed a goal, although many believed that the ball had gone past and the Celts protests were in vain."*

Celtic claimed the ball had actually passed outside the post and subsequently petitioned the SFA to make goal-nets mandatory for all Scottish Cup semi-final and final matches, which was agreed, although even goal-nets don't guarantee errors won't be made.

My fellow St Johnstone historian Brian Doyle discovered that Saints first played in a game with nets on the 5th of April 1895, for a match against Forfar Athletic at the Recreation Grounds in Perth. Bearing in mind that St Johnstone were at that time an amateur team, playing mainly in friendly matches and local cup competitions, it is interesting that it took such a relatively short time for this new technology to spread across Scotland at all levels of the game.

Famously, in January 1993, referee Les Mottram didn't allow a goal for Dundee United in a match at Firhill when a shot from the Tangerines' Paddy Connolly hit the stanchion at the back of the goal, bounced out, was then caught (in his hands) by a Thistle defender and thrown back to the Jags' keeper. Mottram waved play on…

There must be something about Firhill that affects referees, because 25 years later a shot from Thistle's Kris Doolan hit the underside of the bar, rippled the back of the net and fell, clearly over the line, before bouncing back out and being cleared out of play on the stand-side touchline. On this occasion, the unfortunate whistler was Barry Cook, who consulted with his linesman and then awarded a throw-in.

As with the Celtic incident in 1893, the Les Mottram "ghost goal" one hundred years later led to a change in the physical structure of the goal; this time with stanchions being replaced, initially by elliptical metalwork at the back of the top of the goalposts from which the net was then pegged back to the turf - and nowadays by the complete lack of any additional element to the posts, with the net being stretched back by fine ropes that are secured to posts behind the goal. This, in theory, means there is no danger of the ball rebounding out from behind the goal-line, as it did so unfortunately for Paddy Connolly, Dundee United and, of course, Les Mottram.

The goal frame itself has also undergone modifications over the years. Initially, most goal posts and crossbars had flat surfaces, which led to the ball invariably crashing straight back into play if it hit them, unless it caught the inner-side of the post or the underside of the bar.

Although wood was the most commonly-used material for goals, in 1920, the elliptical post was developed in Nottingham by the Standard Goals company. Unsurprisingly, Nottingham Forest is believed to have been the first team to use them. The elliptical shape made the posts more stable when assembled, while the use of aluminium rather than wood made them more durable, easier to maintain and lighter, as well as making them safer for the players.

Many Scottish clubs stuck with the wooden, square-faced posts. Hampden Park had square posts and bars and it was these that led to the eventual banning of their use by FIFA. The movement to get rid of them began in earnest after the European Cup final between Bayern Munich and Saint Etienne played at Hampden in 1976. Bayern won the game 1-0, but St Etienne twice hit the crossbar and were convinced that at least one of these strikes would have rebounded into the goal if the bar had not been square-faced. In 1987, FIFA agreed to outlaw the use of square posts and bars and today goals are round or elliptical. Technology continues to evolve and now many crossbars have a slight upward curve in the middle to counter the effects of gravity which would otherwise pull them downwards over time.

Offside
LAW 11

Many years ago, I was at McDiarmid Park watching St Johnstone play Raith Rovers in the League Cup. The Rovers scored a goal that was so blatantly offside that, forgetting the fact that my children were present, I launched into a diatribe at the linesman in front of the East Stand. I wasn't the only one and the poor man was on the receiving end of what can only be described as the foulest of foul abuse.

Later, I saw the highlights of the game (which Saints lost). From the replay of that goal, it was clear that our defender, Paul Cherry, was, for reasons best known to him, on the far side of the pitch picking daisies (or at least not paying attention to proceedings) and playing the Raith players well onside. Since then, I've always been wary about shouting at linesmen for seemingly duff offside decisions.

On another occasion, chatting informally with a friend who was at that time a director of Motherwell, he told me of a game he'd gone to see at Cliftonhill between Albion Rovers and another team that shall remain nameless. For those of you who have not experienced the joys of that seminal lower Division ground in Coatbridge, there is about six feet between the advertising hoardings and the playing surface. The linesmen have no hiding place and my friend recalled how two visiting fans spent the entire game pursuing the unfortunate linesman on their side of the ground, mainly in order to cast aspersions on various aspects of his character and alleged sexuality. With only a few minutes remaining, their team broke away and scored what looked like the winner. As the fans scampered around in glee, they slowly came to realise that the linesman had his flag up. The referee came across, consulted his assistant and then disallowed the goal. As play resumed, the linesman cast a glance over his shoulder at his tormentors that seemed to say, *"up yours."* It was, my friend, avers, never offside in a million years…

The source of the most contentious disagreements in the game (until the introduction of VAR), offside was originally adopted from the rugby/handling form of the game. This meant that in the 1860s, a player was offside if, upon receiving the ball from a forward pass, three opponents were between him and the goal-line. This wasn't changed to the current two players until 1925, following a proposal by the SFA (as described in the pages above), but there had been some important changes in the interim. In 1907, it was agreed that a player could not be offside in his own half of the pitch and in 1920 it was no longer the case that you could be offside from a throw-in.

That change in 1907, whereby a player could no longer be offside in his own half, came about as a result of influence from Scotland, or to be precise from Clyde FC, who first suggested it in May 1905. Their proposal to the SFA was rejected but when the Scottish forwards were persistently caught offside in the international game against England in 1906 Clyde took their suggestion to the SFA once more, this time with success. The English FA followed suit and the new rule was passed by IFAB the following year.

Of course, the idea behind the offside law is to prevent players hanging around near the opponents' goal and thus stretching the game out. A few minutes thought and it ought to be obvious that without some form of offside law much of the subtlety and strategy of the game would disappear. More specifically, a match would end up being just a long-ball game with defenders holding back in a defensive mass to mark forwards who were 'goal-hanging' in the hope of gaining an advantage. Despite this, there have been a number of attempts to introduce changes that drastically modified or did away with offside. Over the years, IFAB and FIFA have authorised a number of trials, often involving an arbitrary distance from the goal, outwith which it was not possible for a player to be offside. These included (amongst others) the following:

As noted above, in 1920, there was a Scottish proposal to IFAB that offside should only apply within 25 yards of the goal. This was rejected, as was a much later request from Scotland in 1974 to try this as an experiment. Similar proposals from Scotland and England that offside should apply from 40 yards out were rejected in 1920, 1921, 1922 and 1929.

Offside within a line 18 yards from goal was trialled in Scotland in 1972. This was also tested in Italy at the 1991 Under-17 World Cup and in Sweden and Finland in 1992.

An experiment with offside only inside the penalty area was tried alternately in England, Northern Ireland and Scotland from 1971-1974. Older readers will recall that this trial involved the Scottish League Cup and the Drybrough Cup in 1973-74 and 1974-75.

The fact is that not much changed as a result of these trials, presumably because the experiments did not result in more goals or exciting play. There is, however, some evidence from a match in 1956 between Belgrade city rivals Partizan and Crvena Zvezda where this did happen. Not only was there no offside in this game, but throw-ins were replaced by a kick-in and corner kicks were taken from the spot where the ball had crossed the goal line, (unless that was in the penalty area). To help, there was not one but two referees, plus two linesmen and a separate time-keeper. The final score was 7-4 and according to a match report, *"The fans went home most contented."*

The fans may have been content, but no-one else seems to have been impressed, because the experiment wasn't repeated for many years. The next seemingly serious attempt to introduce change came in 2010, when former FIFA president, Sepp Blatter, met with officials from hockey, a sport that had dispensed with offside 12 years previously. Nothing came of this, but in 2016 there was an experiment in Germany between two fifth-tier sides from Berlin where a game was played for 60 minutes without any offsides. The hope of the organisers was that it would lead to more goalmouth action, but it wasn't a success. One of the teams, Tennis Borussia, devised a strategy which consisted of not bothering to play the ball through the midfield, pushing the full-backs high up the field (as happens in hockey), keeping one player constantly in attack and forming a supposedly impenetrable circle of defenders.

The organisers may have expected more goals but what they got was one goal, scored after five minutes by a player who would normally have been offside. Judging by the reports, the game became stretched and the midfield largely redundant, although there was more wing play. Unfortunately, there were also far too many long balls over the top to forwards in what would normally be offside positions. Most damningly, as the two sides settled into the new system, as soon as one side lost possession it packed its defence: one report described the entire game as *"end-to-end defence."*

Since then, of course, there has been a number of changes in the way offside is interpreted. It is hard to keep up and the current situation (2021-22) whereby linesmen don't raise their flag until a move has broken down or otherwise come to an end is a nonsense, frustrating for fans and players alike. Similarly, players can now return to play from an offside position and gain an advantage from their previous position on the field. The famous Bill Shankly quote about offside comes to mind here, viz, *"If a player is not interfering with play or seeking to gain an advantage, then he should be."* On a referees' online forum, I came across detailed discussions of the minutiae of the offside law, including a comment about one of the problems with offside as it was previously interpreted: *"I remember and have seen on old clips some of what now seem to us, ludicrous, offside decisions. One in particular I remember at QPR was when the goalkeeper punted the ball straight into the oppo goal, only for it to be disallowed because an attacker was watching the ball sail over his head, about 40 yards from goal but standing in an 'offside' position!"*

The first part of Law 11 is short and to the point and, on paper at least, relatively easy to understand, viz,

1. *Offside Position*

It is not an offence to be in an offside position.

A player is in an offside position if:
• *any part of the head, body or feet is in the opponents' half (excluding the halfway line) and*

• any part of the head, body or feet is nearer to the opponents' goal line than both the ball and the second-last opponent

The hands and arms of all players, including the goalkeepers, are not considered. For the purposes of determining offside, the upper boundary of the arm is in line with the bottom of the armpit.

A player is not in an offside position if level with the:
• second-last opponent or
• last two opponents

Admittedly, it gets more complex later on…

2. Offside offence
A player in an offside position at the moment the ball is played or touched* by a team-mate is only penalised on becoming involved in active play by:
• interfering with play by playing or touching a ball passed or touched by a team-mate or
• interfering with an opponent by:
• preventing an opponent from playing or being able to play the ball by clearly obstructing the opponent's line of vision or
• challenging an opponent for the ball or
• clearly attempting to play a ball which is close when this action impacts on an opponent or
• making an obvious action which clearly impacts on the ability of an or opponent to play the ball
• gaining an advantage by playing the ball or interfering with an opponent when it has:
• rebounded or been deflected off the goalpost, crossbar, match official or an opponent
• been deliberately saved by any opponent

A player in an offside position receiving the ball from an opponent who deliberately plays the ball, including by deliberate handball, is not considered to have gained an advantage, unless it was a deliberate save by any opponent.

A 'save' is when a player stops, or attempts to stop, a ball which is going into or very close to the goal with any part of the body except the hands/arms (unless the goalkeeper within the penalty area).

In situations where:
• a player moving from, or standing in, an offside position is in the way of an opponent and interferes with the movement of the opponent towards the ball this is an offside offence if it impacts on the ability of the opponent to play or challenge for the ball; if the player moves into the way of an opponent and impedes the opponent's progress (e.g. blocks the opponent), the offence should be penalised under Law 12
• a player in an offside position is moving towards the ball with the intention of playing the ball and is fouled before playing or attempting to play the ball, or challenging an opponent for the ball, the foul is penalised as it has occurred before the offside offence

• an offence is committed against a player in an offside position who is already playing or attempting to play the ball, or challenging an opponent for the ball, the offside offence is penalised as it has occurred before the foul challenge

*The first point of contact of the 'play' or 'touch' of the ball should be used

3. No offence
There is no offside offence if a player receives the ball directly from:
• a goal kick
• a throw-in
• a corner kick
If an offside offence occurs, the referee awards an indirect free kick where the offence occurred, including if it is in the player's own half of the field of play.

All clear? Well, if it's not, just remember that offside is a necessary part of the game. Without it, football would be very different, but even with all the well-meaning attempts to "improve" the offside law, it always has been and will continue to be a source of lively debate and discussion. For that reason alone (underpinned by the fact that sports journalists – and fans - thrive on fomenting argument), it will always be with us. In an attempt to try to remove any debate, in the last few years we have seen the introduction of VAR and the reduction of offside to a series of computerised lines placed across the pitch to see if an attacking player's nostril hairs might conceivably be a nano-metre in front of any part of a defender. I do understand the thinking behind VAR, but, as I shall argue in Part III, its impact is detrimental to the fans' enjoyment of the game and, in many respects, it does not achieve what it sets out to do. It's something the first arbiters of the national game would have been amazed to see, but that's not to say they didn't have their own problems…

The referee
LAW 5

Although the first reference we have to a 'referee' comes from a match involving Rochdale in 1842, the men who were responsible for controlling the game were not originally called referees. Instead, as described earlier, there were two umpires (or sometimes just the opposing captains) who were expected to keep order and adjudicate when there were disputes. When they couldn't agree, they referred to a third party – the referee – who stood at the side of the pitch. Over time, the referee's role expanded; first in 1889 when he began to keep time and also was able to give free kicks without being asked (but only if he believed the player's action was dangerous) and also to send a player off for persistent infringements of the rules. It was increasingly clear that there were advantages to having an independent, unbiased arbiter to control matches but it wasn't until 1891 that IFAB revised the rules so that, rather than standing on the touchline and being consulted by the umpires, referees began to take to the field with two linesmen, one on each touchline, to assist them. According to the York City & District Referees' Association's account of the history of Referees Associations, *"This 'neutral' referee was disliked from the outset. Clubs did not like his absolute authority, preferring a mutual agreement between their umpires. Spectators disputed decisions and referees were even assaulted."*

By way of example of clubs' continuing preference for their own officials rather than an independent referee, the Perthshire Advertiser's report of a Northern League match between St Johnstone and Lochgelly United in October 1907, describes how both fans and the opposing clubs conspired to remove one hapless individual – in the middle of a match.

"In the first half, the decisions of the referee (Mr Reid, Dundee) were unpopular and a section of the spectators broke in at half-time…the committees of both clubs met and decided to dispense with Mr Reid's services, Mr W Hood of St Johnstone having charge of the remaining portion of the game."

Referees, of course, are as prone to human foibles as anyone else. Allegedly, this was the case with Aberdeen's Doug Gerrard, a long-standing referee of good repute, who had charge of the 1958 Ne-er Day match between St Johnstone and Dundee United. A Sunday newspaper alleged that Mr Gerrard might have over-enjoyed the previous night's celebrations, claiming that he dropped his whistle several times and controlled play for several minutes from a kneeling position. Mr Gerrard was quoted as saying *"I deny that at any time I did not have proper control of the game."* Whether or not drink had been taken we'll never know, but it seems unlikely that no referee or linesman has taken to the field suffering from the after-effects of the night before. Players most certainly have…

Linesmen, Assistant Referees, Fourth (and Fifth) Officials

The re-structuring of the Laws of the game in 1891, so that referees began to take centre stage and the umpires were turned into linesmen who assisted from the side, started to alter the way in which all matches were officiated and it was such a fundamental and indeed sensible change that it is still the way games are controlled today. It obviously made sense for someone to 'run the line' and indicate when the ball was out of play, but prior to this it was done by a surplus member of each of the opposing clubs. They were expected to favour their own side and it wasn't until the 1898-99 season that neutral linesmen were introduced in England. In Scotland, as Bob Crampsey describes in his centenary history of the Scottish Football League, in the 1897-98 season a League Management Committee debated this subject and, in particular, *"whether linesmen should be allowed to go on to the pitch and coach in the course of a game."* The committee decided they should not.

Several decades later, linesmen were still causing debate. In the Daily Record of 29th September 1927, 'Waverley' wrote, *"For some time I have been hearing complaints against the conduct of certain linesmen at Second Division matches. From now on no player will be allowed to wave the flag, the right way or the wrong way. The job must be done by a club official."*

Although independent linesmen did come into the game at the top level, at Second Division level (and below), someone from each club generally ran the line for League and Cup matches until the Second World War. Despite Waverley's entreaties, some of these, I suspect, will have been players rather than officials. In either case, their loyalties will, naturally, have lain with their club rather than the referee, although their proximity to the fans may have also had an influence on where and when they raised their flags.

The linesman's flag is another of those vital adjuncts to the game that is taken for granted. An incredibly simple aid to the man in the middle, the flag was used for the obvious reason that it is a clear, visual signal and doesn't make any noise that would distract from the referee's whistle.

One of the other advantages of the linesman's flag is that in an emergency it can be bodged together from the kind of things that tend to lie around football grounds. John Litster recalls that Rutherglen Glencairn used to cut-up old strips for their corner and linesmen's flags, and remembers at one midweek match watching someone trying to hack off a piece of a broom handle so that a square of old football strip could be nailed to it. And it wasn't just old football strips that could be used to make flags. John recalls his mother being first amused when a linesman used his hanky as a flag at Nairn Thistle's Junior ground in Kirkcaldy and then appalled when he used the flag as a hanky.

One thing I didn't know about linesmen's flags, or to be more accurate, yet another in the long list of things I didn't know about the game in general, was that the different ways in which the flag is waved send specific signals to the referee. While I was vaguely aware that, in general, the flag tends to be pointed in the direction of whichever

THROW-IN   SUBSTITUTION   OFFSIDE   OFFSIDE

team will have possession of the ball for a free kick or throw-in, I didn't realise that the linesman also indicates a range of other things, including where, approximately, on the pitch a player is offside. As shown (far right on the diagram here), the angle at which he holds his flag tells the referee and the fans if the player is (flag down) on the near-side, (flag up) far-side or (flag straight out) the centre of the pitch. This is quite handy for fans as it enables them to identify – and then, of course, berate - the right player who has strayed offside during a promising move.

In more recent years, the number of officials at a match has proliferated. The fourth official has been in place for some time now (officially introduced in the Laws in 1991, deemed part of the officiating team in 1995 and given increasing powers since then), but experiments with even more assistant referees behind the goal seem to have been largely abandoned, mainly because they have been superseded by goal-line technology. The latter was introduced in 2012, at the World Cup in Brazil - and, as many Scots will tell you, some 46 years too late for a certain Russian linesman. The great thing about goal-line technology is that the referee knows virtually instantaneously if the ball has crossed the goal-line and the game is not held up, as it frequently is with VAR.

Female Officials

One significant change that did come about in the twentieth century was the introduction of women referees and lineswomen to the senior game. The 1995 Women's World Cup, held in Sweden, saw the first all-female team of officials at a World Cup, for a match between Sweden and Brazil. They also produced a special badge, for a "Lineswoman.'

Then, in 1996 IFAB considered an amendment, *"to replace the words 'linesman' and 'linesmen' in the Law by the words 'Assistant Referee' and 'Assistant Referees,' where applicable"* on the grounds that *"the word 'linesmen' does not accurately reflect the tasks of the linesmen who are, in actual fact, assistants to the referee."* It was passed and came into operation the following year.

Although, on the face of it, this was simply an exercise in semantics, there was actually another good reason for changing the words used to describe the person who beetles up and down the touchline waving his or her flag. That was, as per the 1995 Women's World Cup, that there were increasingly more female lines(wo)men and, rather than having to refer to 'lineswomen' and 'linesmen' it would be better to have an all-encompassing word (or rather words) to describe the two people who work with the referee to control a match. However, for older people and angry football managers, the word 'linesman' or 'lino' does still spring easily to one's lips. I remember Tommy Wright, when he was manager at St Johnstone, bellowing, *"Hey, lino, do your job!"* with fairly monotonous regularity (and, in my, completely unbiased, view, Tommy may well have been correct more often than not).

Although women had been involved in running the line since the (very) late 20th century, it wasn't until the early years of the current century that a woman refereed a senior football match in Scotland. In world terms, women were quite late to the party. Petra Tabarelli believes that the first woman to referee football matches involving men was Edith Klinger from Austria, who officiated from 1935 – 1938. FIFA, however, recognises another woman, Drahşan Arda of Turkey, as the world's first female referee. She refereed her first semi-professional match on 26th June 1968 and continued officiating for another thirty years in Turkey and Germany.

In Scotland, the changes necessary to allow women to officiate football matches began in the late 1960s. The Minutes of the Edinburgh Referees' Association for their Council meeting in September 1969 record, *"The Council raised no objection to women taking this course... (the Entrance Course for referees)."* The SFA, unsurprisingly, were not expected to be quite so progressive in their thinking and the Minutes continued, *"...provided they understood that the SFA would possibly not allow them to sit the official exam."* Although 30 people then signed up for the course between 1969 and 1970, none of them was female.

This, however, was only the beginning of the movement to allow women to become referees. In September 1974, the first women applied to sit the Edinburgh Referees' Association entrance exam.

There was some discussion on whether they should be allowed to do so and the Minute for the Association's Council meeting at that time recorded that: *"Mr McCartney informed the Association that two women had applied to sit the trainee classes for referees. Mr Tait agreed to seek guidance from the SFA on this question."*

The SFA obviously didn't like to rush things because they didn't reply until February 1975, telling the Edinburgh Association that while they were happy to approve of refereeing classes for women, they did not approve of mixed classes. It took them nearly a year to change their minds but in February 1977 they announced they would allow mixed classes and in May 1977 Mary Falconer passed the exam and became the Edinburgh Association's first female referee. There may have been other women similarly constrained elsewhere in the country by the SFA's approach, but the dam had now been breached and women started to become involved in refereeing in increasing, albeit still small, numbers over the next few decades.

That said, it wasn't until the twenty-first century that a woman referee took charge of a high-profile match. The lady in question was Morag Pirie, who refereed a Highland League match between Huntly and Wick Academy on 2nd August 2003; the first time a woman had controlled a semi-pro game in Scotland. Like all the women who took up the challenge of officiating in what has been, at least until very recently, a male-dominated sport, Pirie suffered misogynist abuse. A few months after making her debut as a senior referee, she ran the line in a match between Albion Rovers and Montrose. Albion Rovers' manager, Peter Hetherston, was sent to the stand for his comments to her, but doubled down on them afterwards, making it clear that, in his view, there should be no place for women in football. Perhaps it was the natural reaction of a manager whose side have just lost (Montrose won 1-0), but the fact that he added that, *"She should be at home making the tea or the dinner for her man who comes in after he has been to the football,"* didn't help his cause, even though he claimed this statement was merely a joke. The SFA didn't see it as such and Hetherston faced a disrepute charge, but he resigned before the hearing took place.

Morag Pirie subsequently became the first woman to officiate at a national Cup final when, in November 2007, she was an Assistant referee at the Scottish Challenge Cup final between St Johnstone and Dunfermline. I was at that game and in what may be an indication of how uncontroversial her presence was, I couldn't recall her running the line when I spoke to her, some 14 years later, about her career. As she said to me (see Section I above), that's how it should be. She's right: an official's sex is nobody's business but their own.

Another woman who made football history in Scotland was Kylie McMullan, who became the first female Assistant referee in an SPFL Scottish Premiership match when she ran the line on 10th May 2014 for St Mirren's home fixture against Hearts.

There is no reason why women should not play an increasing role in refereeing, although it must be said that those ladies brave enough to be in the advance guard had to experience not just the usual array of abuse that officials are subject to but this, not infrequently, was also imbued with a degree of sexism that, fortunately, is not quite as prevalent today as it was in the past.

The guidance from the football authorities states that the referee, whether male or female, along with the rest of his or her team (Assistant Referees and Fourth Official) is responsible for controlling the game as efficiently, effectively, and unobtrusively as possible. It notes that each official will have his or her own personality - and this plays an important part in the makeup of the team. Officials develop their own style of conduct; it is the referee's task to lead the team and to harness the qualities of all its members within a common boundary of standard practices. The guidance goes on to say that an individual's style should not interfere with their control of the flow of the game - and that it is important that the entire refereeing team establishes clear communication between each other and the players (and the team managers) without causing undue attention to be drawn towards themselves and away from the match itself. In many games, that is a forlorn hope. Even though spectators want to see a game of football and not witness officials who attract attention to themselves for one thing or another, it's all too easy for the referee to stand out, no matter how much they may want to be part of the background. That said, some officials do stand out for both the right and the wrong reasons and a few have gone down in football history. Three of the most famous are Peter Craigmyle, Charles Faultless and Tom (Tiny) Wharton.

Peter Craigmyle published his 'autobiography' in 1949 and although it is little more than a booklet, it is fascinating. An Aberdonian, Craigmyle began refereeing in 1919 and did his first Scottish League game in 1920, between Hearts and Albion Rovers. His early career set his style: a showman but a sincere and honest individual who was prepared to admit his gaffes. The latter included the fact that he didn't know the rules when he first refereed a match (something that modern refs are frequently, and erroneously, accused of) and then when he was drafted in at short notice to referee a game at Pittodrie between Aberdeen and Morton, he awarded a goal because he was convinced that a shot from the Dons' Jacky Connon was destined for the top corner of the net. Racing to point to the centre spot, he turned to discover that the keeper had, in fact, got a finger to the ball and turned it aside. It wasn't a goal and he reversed his decision. Then, as it would be today, it was the main story on the sports pages, but they were more forgiving in the inter-war period and it didn't stop Peter from going on to have an amazing career.

One of the things that staggered me, although it should not have given the number of match reports from this period I have read, was that in his entire, 31-year career, Peter Craigmyle only sent off two players. In those days, you just about had to commit first-degree murder to get dismissed, which is almost what Celtic's Joe Cassidy did, hitting Falkirk's Tommy Scott with a punch which split his jaw. To make Peter's decision easier, Cassidy walked off before he was ordered to do so. Peter was due to referee the Old Firm match ten days later but after the game against Falkirk the Celtic officials suggested to the SFA that it would be better if he did not. To his credit, he refused; however, he was staying in Glasgow as he had a game between Rangers and Dundee to referee on the Monday and he was advised to stay in his hotel room, with the receptionist instructed to tell anyone inquiring for him that he hadn't been seen since the Falkirk game. In the event, the Old Firm game finished in a scoreless draw without incident.

Of course, in those days, everyone travelled long distances by train, which caused problems for a referee based in Aberdeen. Craigmyle described how he cultivated friendships with Station Masters throughout Scotland, who would arrange for express trains to slow down to a crawl at the appropriate station so that he could jump off with his bag and then be picked up by a pre-arranged car and taken to the ground.

Photo courtesy of the Glasgow Referees' Association

Charles Faultless had a brilliant name for a referee, but he is probably less well known nowadays than Peter Craigmyle or Tiny Wharton, although he certainly should be.

Born in Bridgeton, Glasgow in 1908, Faultless was a natural sportsman, playing golf, tennis and water polo. He played in goal at football and had separate stints as an amateur with Morton and Motherwell. Like many other referees, he took up the whistle when an injury – in his case a broken leg – brought his playing career to an end. During the Second World War, he was a physical training instructor in the RAF and at one point was in charge of the Bomber Command football team, which had 10 internationalists in it.

After the war, Charles returned to refereeing and became the most celebrated official of his era. His career reached its zenith when he refereed several matches in the 1954 World Cup. These included the game which is likely to remain the highest scoring match in a World Cup for some time, if not ever – the quarter-final tie between Austria and the host country, Switzerland, which the Austrians won 7-5.

Indeed, his fame was such that there is a Charles Faultless trophy, a magnificent Cup (pictured here), which he presented to Glasgow Referees Association on his retirement from refereeing in 1954-55. The Glasgow Association still has this trophy and it is awarded each season to the Glasgow member who receives the highest national cup final appointment (i.e. Scottish Cup Final, Scottish Junior Cup Final, Scottish Amateur Cup Final, Scottish Welfare Cup Final, Scottish Schools U18s National Final).

Tiny (he was six foot four inches tall) Wharton was the equivalent of Peter Craigmyle in the later post-war period. His humorous advice to younger referees is remembered to this day: *"if you are having difficulty refereeing 22 players, try 20."* Former Hearts boss Jim Jeffries recalls that in his time as a young player, *"we all respected Tiny Wharton, who was not just a big man but was also a really big presence on the pitch. It was generally accepted that if he said something you didn't dare question it."*

It's fair to say that some referees were not quite as fit in those days. At least that was probably the reason for several of the stories told about Wharton. On one occasion, he pointed out, *"If you can't see a foul from 20 yards, you can't see it from two yards!"* Another time, having awarded a corner, seemingly incorrectly (at least according to the defenders), he allegedly said, *"I've just sprinted 50 yards to follow play,"* he told them. *"If you think I'm now going to sprint back another 50 yards to take up position for a goal-kick you're off your head."*

A more serious controversy occurred when Tiny was photographed shaking hands with the Rangers' captain John Greig before an Old Firm game. It looks very much like a masonic handshake and as a result spawned conspiracy theories galore. Interestingly, in the official history of St Johnstone, we published a photo from the 1930s of a testimonial match between Saints and Manchester City. In it, Harry Ferguson, whose benefit it was, is clearly giving a (reciprocated?) masonic handshake to Matt Busby, the City captain, under the watchful eye of the referee, Peter Craigmyle. However, to extrapolate from these instances to then say that all referees are somehow crooked or biased is both unfair and incorrect.

For Tiny Wharton, the facts are simple: he refereed many Old Firm games, as well as European fixtures and 16 internationals. In the words of the great, late Bob Crampsey, he was *"the Jeeves of the refereeing world – any temporary difficulty and he dealt with it with the minimum of fuss."*

Peter Craigmyle's record of only having sent off two players in his entire career was actually par for the course in those days. There is, as far as I know, no study of all the cautions and dismissals in Scottish Football since the League began in 1890. In researching St Johnstone's history, Brian Doyle and I have read countless match reports but until the more recent decades it was very rare to find any incidents which resulted in a player being sent off. One of the few involved a man who would go on to become Chairman of Celtic, Desmond White. Playing in goal for Queen's Park, at Hampden on 27th February 1937, he was taken by surprise by a pass-back in the 70th minute. St Johnstone's Andy McCall, *"rushed in and White appeared to strike him full in the face. Referee Webb immediately ordered White off the field. Hampden's 6,000 spectators were stunned. White was the first Queen's Park player to be sent off in 20 years."*

It must be said, that while the innocent party in this incident, McCall was clearly, as they say, 'able to look after himself.' In the St Johnstone directors' minutes of 11th March 1937, under *"Correspondence,"* we can read, *"Letter from Scottish Football Association intimating that the following cautions have been given: A. McCall, Aug 22nd, Oct 3rd, 1936, and February*

20th 1937. The secretary (David Rutherford, who was also the manager) *intimated that he had warned A. McCall, and instructed him not to repeat these offences."*

In the last few decades, we've had referees like Hugh Dallas, John Rowbotham, Kenny Clark and Willie Young. All big personalities and all good referees (although they could have stinkers just like any player), but it's arguable that today's referees, having to cope with the sewer of social media and the incessant media attention that has become more and more insistent on creating a story on the most nebulous of grounds, find it harder to command respect in the way that those of earlier years did. Based on the interviews with referees, linesmen and managers in the earlier part of this book, readers can make up their own mind as to whether the spirits of the past are still permeating the game today and, especially, whether the modern referee has the same latitude and opportunity to apply that mythical, yet crucial, Law 18 (use your common sense) as his or her forebears.

Referees' Associations

The first ever referees' society came into being in 1893, in London. The primary purpose of the London society was to ensure that those purporting to be referees actually had some qualifications before they were appointed to officiate a given match.

Another early Referees' Association was The North Staffs Referees' Club, formed in 1896. It was swiftly followed by other regional referees' societies and by 1899 there were 27 referees' societies in England with 773 members. On a local basis, these societies began to get together and teach each other the rules of the game in order to ensure that things went as smoothly as possible, yet in those early days there was no nationally agreed qualifications that a person had to have in order to referee a football match. Consequently, the appointment of people to officiate different games became too complicated and it was at that point, in 1897, that the Football Association assumed responsibility for the organisation of all referees in England.

Then, as now, referees were sworn at, generally abused and occasionally assaulted. In 1906, James Catton, the editor of the 'Athletic News' wrote a series of articles urging referees to get together to strengthen their position. These were enthusiastically received by the regional Referees' Associations in England and in 1908 Charles Sutcliffe, a solicitor, proposed that, *"in consequence of certain unpleasant experiences of referees in many parts of the country,"* a Union for referees should be formed. A meeting was held on 9th May 1908 in Nottingham, attended by over 300 referees. It was reported that when the move to create a Union was put to the meeting *"every hand went up."*

In Scotland, the first referees' body was the Scottish Football Referees' Association (SFRA). The first reference to this organisation appears in the SFA minutes in season 1899-00, but they may have been formed earlier. The SFRA was made up of regional Referees' Associations, all answering to their own committees. The SFA, in effect, used the SFRA as an agency for the supply of referees to games across the country. This changed after the Second World War. In 1945, the SFA, led by Sir George Graham, conducted a review of football with a view to creating a blueprint for the sport in the post-war world and this included ideas on various aspects of refereeing. Subsequently, a small group of former and current referees met to discuss the SFA's suggestions and it was agreed that, for the first time, the national governing body would play a central role in the Referees' Associations. This would involve organised physical training and an annual summer meeting, held in St Andrews. Only eight local Referees' Associations were envisaged initially, although this later became 12. The local bodies would continue to have self-autonomy with regard to local, 'domestic' matters, but Supervisors would be appointed to liaise between the officials and the SFA. The intention was to promote consistent interpretation of the Laws of the game, improve standards and ensure that matches were controlled by the best qualified people available.

Several of the existing Referees' Associations, under the auspices of the long-established SFRA, were, to put it politely, not keen on this and there was significant opposition, with some regions electing not to take part in the new structure. However, all eventually did so and the structure that we have today is still, by and large, as was agreed in this post-war period.

Edinburgh was one of the areas that was not keen on the SFA's involvement and it wasn't until 1951 that they came under the SFA umbrella and formed their own, new regional Association. However, the previous East of Scotland Football Referees' Association (part of the SFRA) wanted nothing to do with this new upstart. As recorded in the Edinburgh Association's golden anniversary history, the Edinburgh Evening News reported (early in May 1951), *"The war between the East of Scotland Football Referees' Association and the breakaway body sponsored by the SFA advances…(and) it is a great pity that the rift was allowed to drift into open conflict, but there you are – the men upon whom we rely for controlling our soccer games cannot agree on a policy of control for their own domestic affairs."*

While the two rival Associations were fighting, those men charged with trying to control local games of football still had to cope with all the usual challenges. In 1951, Referee Supervisor Mr J Calder, *"referred to the case of referee Purves who had allegedly been assaulted while officiating in a Junior game at Thornton."*

Of course, like all such organisations, the Referees' Associations have committee structures, fund-raising raffles, annual dinners and social events. Even after the dispute between the two rival Referees' Associations was resolved, there was all the normal internecine bickering and internal warfare that comes about when men (there were no women involved at this time) come together to organise anything. The Mr J Calder referred to above was soon subjected to *"a series of complaints,"* and at the May 1953 Council meeting, *"a letter was read from the SFA, advising that 'Mr Calder has been relieved of his appointment as Supervisor'."*

Similar shenanigans continued over the years. In 1965, pressure grew to expel a Mr Crossman, a Class 1 referee from 1956 to 1964, for *"reputedly acting outwith the Association in connection with the possibility of the SFA appointing Mr George Gullan as a Supervisor."* After several heated meetings, the Edinburgh Association's Minutes for the 4th of November

1965 recorded, *"in the chaos that ensued, various members prevailed on one and all to rally round and save the Association in this time of crisis…Mr Gow accused the office bearers of being childish, and Mr Tait said that he objected to Mr Gow's remarks on a personal basis…"*

It wasn't just in Edinburgh that there were problems. Disagreement, if not outright conflict between regional Referees' Associations was not uncommon, but in August 1957 the Glasgow Association wrote to all the others suggesting they form a National Council. The driving force behind this was the SFA's refusal to provide referees with sufficient tickets for the Scotland vs England match. Despite this appalling situation, there was not enough support for a National Council at this time.

However, over the next few years the SFA managed to continue to upset the referees, not only in relation to the lack of international tickets but also by paying what the referees deemed insufficient fees per match and by a perceived lack of support in the media. Consequently, the idea of a National Council was revisited in 1959 and representatives from across Scotland went to a meeting in Glasgow, chaired by Tom Wharton of that city's Association. The Council was formed, but some regional Associations did not join in and, although it kept going, in 1968 the SFA refused to recognise it and in 1970 it was eventually wound up.

Three years after the National Council was disbanded, another attempt was made to create a national body for Scottish referees. Once again, the reason for this was the referees' unhappiness with the SFA. An attempt by the Ayrshire referees to get a new national body going went nowhere, but in 1974, after three Class 1 referees were not listed on the ballot for league matches, the officials were once more roused to anger and all the regional Associations met in Dunblane in September. The result of this meeting was the formation of the Scottish Referees' Liaison Committee, whose remit was to act as an intermediary between the officials, the SFA and the Scottish Football League. From 1975, the SFA did agree to meet regularly with the Secretaries from the regional Referees' Associations, with the first such meeting taking place at the refs' annual summer jaunt to St Andrews, but only a few months later, in September 1975, the SFA refused to deal with several issues put to it by the Liaison Committee. Further pressure was put on the Committee in January 1976, when the SFA threatened to stop their regular meetings with the Referees' Associations' Secretaries if the Liaison Committee was not disbanded. It was, and the meetings with the Secretaries continued, but it was clear that the SFA were the ones calling the shots.

While all this was happening, the old guard of the SFRA, who had jousted with some of the new, SFA approved regional Referees' Association, notably Edinburgh, as they were set up after the war, carried on as best they could. The SFRA had remained in regular contact with the SFA up to the Second World War and after it continued with its district branch network. However, the problem for the SFRA members was that a referee could not progress to the Official SFA List unless he was a member of an SFA regional Association. Consequently, the SFRA, having previously been a powerful, national body, diminished in importance after the war and its role changed to providing referees mostly to non-league and other 'non-authorised,' minor league games, including Boys Brigade (BB) matches. This led to some claims of hypocrisy on the part of SFA-recognised officials. John Litster, who passed the refereeing exams in Glasgow in his youth, recalls a senior referee, a member of the Glasgow Referees' Association, who reminded his colleagues at one meeting that BB football was unauthorised, and therefore out of bounds for SFA-qualified referees. This same referee annually refereed the local BB football final played on the Queen's Park Victorian XI's ash pitch within the forecourt of Hampden Park!

As the SFRA's importance withered, it was supplanted by the 12 Regional Referees' Associations, acting in concert with the SFA. Attempts were made to merge some of the SFRA's regional bodies with the SFA's regional Referees' Associations, but they foundered, largely on the SFA's continuing insistence that the SFRA's members would have to sit the SFA exam before they could join.

Subsequently, in 1989, the SFRA agreed to their members sitting the SFA exam and to sending delegates to the recognised, regional Referees' Association meetings, but they refused to change their name, despite the SFA's 'encouragement.' Many SFRA members held out, but their days as an independent organisation were numbered and in 1991 the SFA increased the pressure on them by issuing an open invitation to SFRA members to join their local Referees' Association. By October 1992, the SFA had decided on a course of action and announced that from the start of the 1993-94 season they would no longer recognise the SFRA, on the, not unreasonable, grounds that FIFA was insisting on only one official referees' body in each country. Within a few months, the SFRA was gone.

One constant (and often reasonable) gripe of the referees is the way they are treated by the media. For most of the history of the game this was the press, both national and local. As noted a few paragraphs above, referees in the 1950s felt that the SFA did not support them sufficiently in tackling what they believed were unfair comments in the press. As someone who has looked at a lot of newspapers from the late nineteenth century onwards, I need to emphasise that what was regarded as unfair in those days would barely raise a comment today. In those days, society was, in general, politer and better mannered than today, but the press in the 1950s were reckoned, by the referees at least, to be giving too much coverage to remarks made by players in the aftermath of matches. In 1951, the Glasgow Referees' Association sought help from the other regional Associations, complaining that the League's Rule No. 51, which was about players writing for and/or making comments to the press *"is being broken too many times and often to the detriment of referees."*

Then, in 1962, the Edinburgh referees complained to STV about commentary by Bob Crampsey on the Queen's Park vs. Clyde match on 17th January, in which he allegedly made *'scathing remarks about (referee) Mr George Mitchell of Falkirk."* Leaving on one side the fact that the referee, being from Falkirk, was not an Edinburgh Association member (and also the extreme unlikelihood of Queen's Park vs Clyde being on prime-time television today), whatever he said was, by the standards of those days, deemed to be unacceptable. The Sports' Editor (the late Arthur Montford), instead of circling the journalistic wagons and going into bat for his colleague, as would probably happen today, wrote back to the

Edinburgh Association to say that *"the incident had now become something of an embarrassment and that he hoped there would be no recurrence."* Mr Crampsey, a man of the utmost integrity, did not let the sun go down on his wrath. In his Centenary History of Queen's Park, he refers to this incident thus: *"In a match where the refereeing provoked much discussion, Clyde led at half-time by a soft penalty. Queen's had been refused one where the circumstances had seemed identical."*

In days gone by, referees did speak to the press after games. Today, that's not allowed. That is a pity, but, as I'll argue below, completely understandable. In the past, referees did not do themselves any favours. Asked why he had not given St Johnstone a penalty in a match against Celtic in the Drybrough Cup in 1971, when the ball was punched off the line by a Celtic hand, namely that of David Hay, the referee admitted he had seen the handball, but *"he used the advantage rule as the ball was still bobbing about dangerously in the goalmouth."*

Today, adding vastly to the pressure on our officials, anyone with a smart phone can upload video clips to the internet of a referee's performance in any game at any level. Social media make matters worse. 'Pile-ons,' where fans comment, like and share posts and get them trending, are frequently stoked by the 'official' media, especially broadcasters, who use them to create or add to a 'story.' The huge decline of newspaper circulations and the need for the remaining sports hacks to make a living in a 24x7 news environment doesn't help either.

As a result, I can fully understand the reluctance of the referees to speak after games. It is often said by journalists that they would only be expected to confirm what their view was of a particular incident, say a disputed penalty, but no-one who knows how the media works should believe that for a second. On the day I wrote this, TalkSport was focusing on the beleaguered manager of Tottenham Hotspur, Nuno Espirito Santo. He was named 'Manager of the Month' for September 2021, but, after a run of poor results, TalkSport's editors thought it fit to play Frank Sinatra's *"My Way"* as an introduction to various discussions about his likely sacking. In particular, they opened with the words, *"and now, the end is near,"* thus indicating the direction of travel they expected. Espirito Santo was, at that time, still in a job (he was fired later that day). If referees were to agree to be subject to inquisitorial questions by the media's attack dogs – all seeking a 'gotcha' moment - can anyone say with confidence that something similar might not happen to them, and why, therefore, should they agree to it? It goes without saying that journalists would almost never subject one of their own to such behaviour, despite the fact that, as I know from countless hours reading their match reports and summaries, they frequently make egregious errors themselves. Although many are good at their jobs, today's media tend, in my view, to be somewhat thin-skinned, rarely admitting to a mistake and generally sticking up for their colleagues, come hell or high water. If I was a referee, I wouldn't trust them to be fair in post-match interviews or in the way they would milk contentious decisions (even once VAR is introduced) for days and weeks after the event. None of this is to say that referees should be immune from criticism and sanction, as I'll discuss in more depth in Part III of this book.

Today, the 12 Referees' Associations in Scotland, all of which work together with the SFA, not only provide officials for matches at every level across the length and breadth of the country, but also work to develop refereeing and encourage young men and women to take it up. Of course, almost every youngster with an interest in football follows a team, but this is not an issue because none of them will be refereeing in the Senior game for quite a few years at least. There is no official line from the SFA on referees not being allowed to support one team or another, for the eminently practical reason that if there was then there would be very few referees. As we saw in the first section of this book, some referees are completely open about which teams they support, while others are reticent about declaring any allegiance. Of course, a quick perusal of many online fans' forums reveals that paranoia certainly exists about certain referees' alleged bias in favour of one or other of the Old Firm teams or, more generally, about a 'west-coast bias' that is said to permeate Scottish football. While it's certainly true that referees are human and make (sometimes horrendous) mistakes, I can find no evidence that the bias that some fans believe lies behind every blow of a referee's whistle actually exists today. That's not to say that it may not have done so in the past (I certainly heard anecdotal evidence that it did) or might in the future, but in general, and unlike the hard evidence of corruption in a small group of football players that led to a major match-fixing cartel in the 1960s, there is no substantive evidence of referees being involved in anything remotely like that scandal. One thing that has become plain to me in writing this book is that today's referees are a very tight-knit community and are protective not just of each other but also of their trade's reputation. The impression I get is that if anyone did exhibit signs of favouring 'their' team, they would be quickly rooted out - and then booted out.

However, while referees have always been expected to be neutral, as described above, the club officials and spare players who often ran the line for them at lower levels of the game in its first half-century or so were not. In Scotland, there is, of course, the additional problem of the Old Firm, with their historical baggage of religious bigotry and the alleged bias of officials who supposedly favour one side or other of the great sectarian divide. At times, this has required some quick, creative thinking on the part of the football authorities.

For example, in 1905, with Celtic and Rangers both tied on 42 points at the end of the season (goal difference/goal average not being used in those days), it was agreed there should be a one-off game to decide the league. Earlier that season, Celtic fans had rioted when their goalscoring talisman Jimmy Quinn was sent off in the Scottish Cup semi-final against Rangers.

Consequently, it was decided to invite a neutral referee from another country to take charge of the league decider rather than risk further allegations of impartiality being raised against their own referees. The honour/short-straw fell to Fred Kirkham, an English referee who was reputedly strict enough to deal with the febrile atmosphere expected. In the event, the match was reportedly a bit of a damp squib, with Celtic running out winners by two goals to one, presumably much to the relief of Mr Kirkham.

The Referees' Strike

Over 100 years later, the Old Firm were still causing problems for referees, although on this occasion the problem was reciprocated and led to strike action on the part of the officials.

On 25th November 2010, a statement was released by the SFA, saying:

"The Scottish FA yesterday stood shoulder-to-shoulder with both the Scottish Premier League and the Scottish Football League in offering representatives of the Category 1 Referees unequivocal and tangible support in an attempt to avert the planned withdrawal of labour scheduled for this coming weekend.

"These measures received the full backing of the Scottish FA President and the Chief Executive.

"Regrettably, at midnight last night, the Scottish FA were informed that following a further meeting of Category 1 referees there would be no change of heart in relation to the strike and no suspension of action while the Scottish FA implements the measures proposed."

Some of the bureaucrats at the SFA preferred to refer to the strike as *"the weekend of unavailability,"* but none of the referees I spoke to referred to it as anything other than a strike. A scour of the web reveals the basic facts of the matter…

Essentially, as with many industrial disputes, the cause was one incident that, on its own, could, perhaps should, have been avoided. It was said that a referee – Dougie McDonald - had lied both to his supervisor and to the Celtic manager Neil Lennon after a game against Dundee United on 17th October 2010, in which he had changed his mind about giving Celtic a penalty. Celtic had won the game 2-1 and normally that is sufficient to quieten even the most vociferous of managers, but not in this case. Even though the subsequent SFA enquiry agreed that McDonald was right to have disallowed the penalty, the fact of his having told the clubs that he only changed his mind on the spot-kick after being advised by his linesman, when in fact he had changed it before speaking to his Assistant, meant he received an official warning. In other words, he got the decision right, but got the timings of when he changed his mind wrong. If this was done deliberately, one can only wonder why, but even if done inadvertently it was clearly wrong. Well, yes, but not a hanging offence.

The key question of why it was done is worth exploring. In the course of researching this book, I discovered that it's widely believed amongst refereeing circles that Dougie McDonald, on hearing his Assistant was concerned that he would be marked down for his part in what had been a botched but ultimately correct penalty decision, (and knowing that he – McDonald – was going to be marked down anyway) was happy for the linesman to take the credit for providing the correct advice. In effect, McDonald *"took one for the team,"* but, unfortunately, he did not think that the repercussions of doing so would be as severe as they turned out to be.

In the aftermath of the game there was continued disagreement over what was actually said, when it was said and to whom, and McDonald subsequently faced calls to resign. In amongst all this, the key facts – that the decision was right and that, from Celtic's point of view it didn't affect the outcome of the match - seemed to have been lost. Whilst in no way condoning officials lying, does anyone truly believe that football clubs and managers (and the media) are not similarly economical with the truth when it suits them?

The issue did not go away and over the next few weeks further comments made by players and officials led the referees, believing their integrity was being questioned, to vote to withdraw their labour. They had already threatened to do this in 2008, in relation to pay, but this was a dispute of a different magnitude. While all referees will admit to making mistakes, the one thing they cannot abide is the suggestion they are in any way biased. They (sadly) expect it from the fans, but when it comes from anyone at a club, even when said in the heat of the match or its immediate aftermath, it is unacceptable. Referees at this time were getting not just the usual dogs' abuse at games but also an increasing number of unpleasant threats away from the game, including death threats to some senior figures. Just writing that last sentence is quite chilling. This is football we are talking about, not The Godfather.

The strike went ahead, with officials being brought in from overseas to allow games to take place over the weekend of 27th November. This was the first time that a foreign referee had officiated at a Scottish league match since the league decider between the Old Firm in 1905. The day after the strike, Dougie McDonald retired.

Unfortunately, what you find on the internet only scratches the surface of what was actually happening and why referees were so angry. One referee who was intimately involved in the talks with SFA Chief Executive Stewart Regan (who had only just been appointed in October 2010), told me that it was a misconception that the strike was all to do with that one game six weeks previously. It may have been the catalyst, but he explained that one of the reasons why it was quite a few weeks before the strike actually took place was because there were lots of other contributing factors that weighed heavily with referees at that time. As well as players and managers making insinuations (it was alleged that a Rangers' player had said all referees were turning into Celtic players and a Celtic player claimed that refs actually wanted to give decisions against his side), some senior football club officials were also giving referees a verbal kicking in their interviews with the media (Vladimir Romanov of Hearts prominent amongst them). So-called fans were searching out referees' workplace email addresses and also those of their bosses, then sending messages along the lines of *"do you know you have a bigot working for you."* One referee's mother received a death threat, by text, that included her home address. After the death threats were made, the clubs, obviously, condemned them, but also denied having done anything to stoke up the tensions. The media, naturally, were all over what was, for them, a great story. The idea that the continuing sniping and criticism did not affect fans' behaviour was demonstrated to be completely false when a 11 year old boy reached over the tunnel at a match at Forfar on the 6th November 2010 and smacked the referee across the back of the head. The club dealt with the culprit, but also claimed it *"wasn't a major incident."* For the referees, it was the straw that broke the camel's back.

After the strike, the officials returned to their duties, having received an assurance that things would change. There was little chance of that holding and a few years later, in 2013, an incident involving a referee and a Dundee United player resulted in the latter receiving what many believe was too lenient a punishment from the SFA. Threats of strike action were made again, but did not go ahead. Then, in 2019, after referee John Beaton's phone number was made public, a host of appalling threats to him and assaults on other players were brought to the fore, with The Sun newspaper reporting that a leading referee had said, *"a strike won't be far away."* This referee went on, *"In recent weeks we've had clubs such as Rangers and Celtic coming out with comments after games because they didn't get the result they wanted. Craig Levein at Hearts has also been very critical of us. All this is fine but the SFA should be stepping in and dealing with these clubs and individuals. We are made out to be the bad ones and I've had abuse from fans when out doing my shopping with my family."*

In 2013 and 2019 no further action was taken by referees. However, sadly, social media has increasingly provided a multiplicity of poisonous channels for public hectoring and vile abuse, too often from a position of anonymity. The mainstream media will naturally flock around a story involving a possible referees' strike too. No matter what you may think of the performance of any referee, whether on a public park or at Hampden Park, they do not deserve this kind of attention from the lunatic fringe of Scottish football. With referee numbers on the decline in some parts of Scotland the last thing the game needs is for refereeing to become a job that no-one wants to do…

Referees' pay and industrial relations

Partly in response to the continuing issues confronting referees, a trade union has been created in Scotland for our officials. Previously, some senior officials wanted a national body to help with negotiations over wages and conditions. As a result, the SSFRA (Scottish Senior Football Referees' Association) came into being in 2005, with John Underhill as its first president. Referees at this time were getting £190 and linesmen £85 each per game at the top level. Stuart Dougal, who had taken over from Underhill as SSFRA President, went mad about this and by 2007-08 referees were paid £575 a game. That was still felt to be at the lower end of the scale compared to most other referees in Europe and under Dougal's leadership the officials demanded a rise to take their pay to £1,000 a match by 2010. According to the press at the time, they were only offered an increase of 3% and this prompted threats of strike action. However, the authorities backed down and agreed a fee of £800 a match, with Assistant Referees receiving £400 a game and Fourth Officials £200. Reported in the Guardian newspaper, Stuart Dougal said*, "This allows the season to begin as scheduled on Saturday. We are confident that we will not only secure but enhance the £800 figure we initially proposed"*

In the event, they didn't get an enhanced figure, nor did they get the £1,000 a game they wanted by 2010 and, in fact, it wasn't until 2011 that they got a rise – of £40 - taking a top referee's pay for a Premier match in Scotland to £840. Today, I believe it is £850 and while that's still a decent amount of money for a day's work (and yes, I know there is a lot more to it than the day of the match), it is, as we shall see presently, nothing like the fees that some referees earn in other countries.

James Bee took over as President of the SSFRA in 2011 and stayed in the role until 2014. James was coming to the end of his career, so as he told me, *"I hadn't much to lose. The younger guys, understandably, don't want to be seen rocking the boat with the SFA and so they toe the line."* He went on, *"you need to realise that Championship referees back then had only had one increase in the previous 16 years, and that was just a tenner! In 2014, and after their increase, Scottish referees were still amongst the lowest, if not the lowest, paid in Europe. A benchmarking study was done that showed our pay didn't even compete with what our equivalents were paid in countries like Albania, Hungary, Austria and Iceland. During my time as the SSFRA President, Rangers, Hibs and Hearts were in the Championship and I used that fact as part of my argument for a rise for officials in all the lower leagues."*

To give you an idea of what referees receive in other countries, a 2020 survey found that in Spain, the top country for referees' pay, 'el árbitro' gets £5,800 a game and his Assistants £2,750. The next best countries to be a referee are Germany, where the equivalent figures were £3,650 and £1,000, and China with £3,500 and £1,200, and then Italy on £3,000 and £850. There is then a considerable gap to England, where refs got £1,500 and Assistants £850 per game, but this is on top of a salary that reportedly ranges from £38,500 to £42,000. The table below shows rates of pay for referees and their assistants in various countries.

COUNTRY	Referees 1st League		Referees 2nd League		ARs 1st League		ARs 2nd League	
GREECE	£1,661		£441		£570		£212	
NORWAY (***)	£1,413	Note 3	£850		£914		£349	
BELGIUM	£1,336		£324		£462		£162	
DENMARK	£1,216	FIFA	£284		£730	FIFA	£202	
	£923	Non-FIFA			£567	non-FIFA		
PORTUGAL	£1,094		£765		£547		£383	
SWITZERLAND	£1,040	midweek	£510	midweek	£311		£212	midweek
	£709	weekend	£345	weekend			£179	weekend
TURKEY	£892	net of tax	£418	net of tax	£505	net of tax	£224	net of tax
AUSTRIA	£856		£587		£428		£318	
SWEDEN (*)	£652	Note 1	£326		£326		£163	
HUNGARY (**)	£240	Note 2	£160		£160		£120	
SCOTLAND	£840		£195		£420		£98	

Note 1 (*)   5 top Referees receive £3,240 per month *in addition* to match fees. These referees are used for development work throughout the country but are not permitted to visit Federation or Regional FA offices. The remaining top referees receive £810 per month *in addition* to match fees.

Note 2 (**)   12 top Referees receive a monthly salary ranging from £2,430 to £3,240 in addition to match fees.

Note 3 (***)   Top referees are also paid monthly, according to ranking, annual fees ranging from £28,350 down to £12,150. FIFA Assistant referees are paid £810 monthly in addition to match fees.

All figures courtesy of James Bee.

These figures are one of the reasons why James Bee set up the Prospect Scottish Football Referees Union, affiliated to Prospect Union which has 150,000 members across various professions. In England 99% of refs are members of Prospect Union but in Scotland only about half of the senior list referees are members. This figure is on the rise, helped by incidents such as the one that involved a young referee in a rural part of Scotland who was fined £100 for allegedly telling a fan at a Junior match to fuck off, after having endured a lot of abuse himself. Unfortunately, despite his vehement denial of having sworn at the club official, the fan's wife backed up the story and that's why the fine was issued. Given that his fee for running the line in this match was less than £30, it does make me wonder why, at a time when we need more referees, this young man was not given more support by the refereeing authorities and the SFA. Players, coaches, manager and club officials all swear at referees: the latter should not be chastised unduly if they sometimes snap back, as was the case in years gone by. That doesn't mean condoning it, it just means being pragmatic. Law 18 anyone?

While some may question why referees need a trade union, as James sagely notes, *"if ordinary fans knew that conditions and pay were better, they would be more likely to want to become a ref. You'd attract more people and get more officials in each of the regions of Scotland, some of which are struggling to recruit new refs at present. The more referees come through the system, the higher the chance of finding more natural talent and identifying those officials who are good enough to referee at the highest level. And better referees make for better games. So, everyone's a winner."*

* * * * *

After all that, it's time for another wee digression. Of all the fundamental things that people associate with football, the smallest is also one of the most important. In fact, it's so important that the game could not take place without it. It is, of course…

The referee's whistle

Like the name Sam Weller Widdowson, the inventor of the shin guard, that of Joseph Hudson, of Birmingham, also deserves to be far better known than it is today. From a straw poll of my friends, that would not be difficult, because no-one had heard of him (they hadn't heard of Widdowson either). The reason Hudson should, in my opinion, have his name in lights is because he and his brother designed and manufactured the first Acme City whistle in the early 1870s and were later responsible for producing the most iconic of all whistles, the Acme Thunderer.

Whistles have been around for thousands of years, but the first time a whistle was used in a football match by a referee was in 1878, in an FA Cup game at Nottingham Forest. Prior to this, referees used to wave handkerchiefs to get the players' attention (just imagine this in a derby today). We don't know who had the idea of getting the ref to use a whistle, but it is believed that the brass whistle used in the Nottingham game was the "Acme City," which suggests that Hudson, who, after becoming a major supplier to the police, may well have also been responsible for its introduction into the world of sport.

The Acme Thunderer was introduced in 1884 and was the first pea-whistle in the world. The difference between the earlier, pea-less whistles and the Thunderer was profound. The latter was far, far louder than the former, but today technology has caught up and football and other sports use both pea and pea-less whistles. Acme is still the principal supplier of the former and a company called Fox 40 is the leader in the latter. The Fox 40 was invented by a man called Ron Foxcroft, a professional basketball referee, who, along with an industrial designer called Chuck Shepherd, came up with the idea in 1987 because he believed that pea-whistles jammed too often. His whistle is called the Fox 40 because Mr Foxcroft was that age when he invented it.

With no moving parts to jam or freeze, the Fox 40 was quickly very successful. However, as a traditionalist, I'm glad to say that Acme whistles are still very popular as well and I believe that the Thunderer is still the most used sports whistle in the world. Moreover, as I learned from Jim Fleming, the rugby referee, there are different kinds of Thunderer, each with different modulations of pitch, and rugby referees prefer one with a lower pitch rather than one that is shrill. One thing that did surprise me though was the price of these things. The screenshot below (August 2021) has whistles from only a few pounds to nearly £45.

Referee Whistle Fox 40 With CMG...	Molten Valkeen Football Referee...	ACME Tornado 2000 Whistle -...	Acme Thunderer 60.5 Metal Official...	Fox 40 Classic Fingergrip Whistle -	Fox 40 Classic Whistle -
£5.99	£44.76	£3.60	£5.14	£8.00	£6.00
Amazon.co.uk	Newitts.com	The Safety Supply ...	Amazon.co.uk	TheGAAStore	TheGAAStore
				★ ★ ★ ★ ★ (212)	★ ★ ★ ★ ★ (212)

The need for a whistle to be loud, especially when there is a big crowd, is obvious but it's surprising just how much noise they can generate. A referee's blog from Holland in 2012 suggested that the most popular whistles are very noisy indeed. The loudest was the Valkeen (the most expensive in our picture above), at 127.6 dB (decibels), followed by the Fox Blast at 127.3 dB and the Acme T2000 at 126.8 dB. When first tested in London in the nineteenth century, Hudson's Metropolitan Police Whistle could be heard two miles away. The Dutch blog goes on to point out that a loud rock concert is only about 120 dB, which gives you an idea of just how loud these whistles are - although diehard metalheads will retort that this is the mere whispering of a gentle breeze compared to the really heavy bands, with Motorhead, AC/DC and Led Zeppelin all having been clocked at 130 dB.

One person who can vouch for the volume of the referee's whistle is Cross Farm Park Celtic's forward Lee Todd. He was sent off in what I believe may be the world record time of two seconds into a match, when he was surprised by the ref blowing for the game to start. *"Fuck me, that was loud,"* he said, which led to the referee promptly giving him a red card. After the match, Lee protested on the not unreasonable grounds that he wasn't swearing at the referee, claiming that *"he nearly blew my ear off!"* His manager agreed, suggesting that the referee might have applied 'Law 18' and a bit of common sense.

And talking of red cards…

You have to be fairly old to remember football before red and yellow cards. Not only was it difficult to get cautioned or dismissed from the field in the old days, it was sometimes difficult for the fans to know who had been booked (sendings-off were more obvious). Euphemisms such as, *"going for an early bath," "given his marching orders," "sent to the pavilion,"* and (especially before players' strips were numbered) *"had his name taken,"* were used by sports' journalists, but in international games, the inability of foreign referees to understand the players (and vice versa) occasionally led to misunderstandings about what a referee's intentions actually were. It was as a result of this that an English referee, Ken Aston, came up with the idea of the yellow and red cards that we are so used to today.

Mr Aston refereed a couple of matches in the 1962 World Cup, including one between Chile and Italy. This became known as the "Battle of Santiago," with the most notorious incident being the refusal of the Italian Giorgio Ferrini to leave the field after being sent off, allegedly because he didn't understand what he was being told. Four years later, Aston was in charge of the referees for the World Cup in England. The quarter final between England and Argentina was another match full of controversy. Argentina at this time had evolved from the free-flowing Latin exuberance of their early international teams to a system that was described, with good cause, as 'anti-futból.' Antonio Rattin, their powerful, defensive midfielder, was dismissed in this game for a seemingly inexplicable reason and after the match it was reported that Bobby and Jackie Charlton had also been cautioned. During the match, the German referee, Herr Kreitlein, who didn't speak Spanish, seemed to be cautioning many other Argentinians, but when the official match report was submitted to FIFA there were only three cautions recorded.

Aston, who had come to assist the referee in the eight minutes it took for Rattin to leave the field, stopped at a set of traffic lights while driving home and, for some reason, this prompted him to recall his experience in Santiago. Watching the lights change from red to amber was the Eureka moment and he subsequently took his idea for red and yellow cards to FIFA. They were trialled in the World Cup in Mexico in 1970 and their use slowly spread throughout the major football leagues across the world in the next decade. In Scotland, there was quite a debate about their use and we were relatively slow in adopting them. The English FA began to use them in season 1976-77, but it wasn't until a few years later (1979) that we used them north of the border. Then in the 1980s, for some reason, there were a couple of seasons when refs stopped using them. Today, those old cliches about *"an early bath,"* or *"being sent to the stands"* are less often heard and *"given the yellow/red card"* or *"saw red"* (strangely, *"saw yellow"* is less common), are the standard ways in which reporters tell us that a player has fallen foul of the match officials.

How far do referees run?

Today, it is reckoned that footballers run more than seven miles during a match, with a few of the more athletic getting up to nine miles. Goalkeepers, to my surprise, are reckoned to run up to two miles. Referees do much the same mileage as the outfield players, or, quite often, a little bit more.

In the inter-war period, Peter Craigmyle recorded in his autobiography that he was fitted with a pedometer for a match between Orkney and Shetland. It registered ten and a half miles, which he reckoned was a fair average.

Many years later, in 2005, an in-depth, scientific study by the wonderfully named *"Muscle, Ligaments and Tendons Journal"* looked at *"the activity of 68 referees and 170 referee's assistants or linesmen officiating European matches from UEFA and the Champions League together with matches from the English Premiership and the English Championship competitions during the 2005/2006 football season using a computerised video system."*

In total, they studied 328 games and discovered that, on average, referees covered 7.23 miles (11.63 km), and assistants 4.04 miles (6.51 km) per match. What was interesting, and perhaps not surprising, was the difference between referees and linesmen's activity in the two halves of a match. The study found that, *"referees covered significantly greater distances jogging, running and high-speed running in the first half than the second half, and walked more in the second than in the first half. Also, the overall distance covered was less in the second half compared to the first. These variations are consistent with previous studies, and may be accounted for by fatigue as the matches progressed."*

The authors of this study are obviously clever people, but it probably doesn't take a rocket-scientist to work out that all participants in a football match will be more tired in the second half than the first.

The diagonal system of refereeing

Referees' fitness has been a subject of contention over the years and one of the managers interviewed in Part I questioned if they are fit enough. For my part, I have to say that I don't see any indication that this is the case today. Clearly, they, and indeed their linesmen, have to run considerable distances. Also, unlike the players, they have to keep up with play at all times, with far fewer opportunities to stop running. To help them, the diagonal system of refereeing evolved and the local Referees' Associations introduced more regular training nights to keep their members' fitness up to the levels required. Right – hands up – how many of you had heard of the diagonal system of refereeing? A quick straw poll of a dozen friends revealed I was not alone, with the majority, despite all being confirmed football fans, never having heard of it.

The diagonal system of refereeing was introduced by Sir Stanley Rous, President of FIFA from 1961-1974. Sir Stanley was also a qualified referee who first took charge of an international match, between Holland and Belgium, in March 1927 and subsequently refereed the FA Cup final in 1934 before his final international match, once again between Holland and Belgium, a day after that final. That same year, he became Secretary to the FA and embarked on a two-year review of the Laws of the game. Although there had been many amendments since the laws were last redrafted in 1891 (including some major ones initiated by the SFA), the 'Rous Laws' were accepted by IFAB in 1938 and, largely because of the simplicity and clarity introduced by his work, they were not revised again until 1997.

John Lagenus: Public Domain via Wikimedia.

Belgium referee John Langenus (pictured) believed that it was his country's referees who had adopted the first 'scientific' approach to referee and linesmen's positioning in the 1930 World Cup, where he refereed the final. Langenus was an interesting character who taught himself the rules but when he went to sit the exams he failed. Reputedly, one of the questions he was asked by the (English) examiner was, *"What is the correct procedure if the ball strikes a low-flying plane?"* His understandable inability to answer meant he failed the exam. Then, when he began refereeing, he was plagued with self-doubt, partly due to the fact that on one occasion he forgot to wind his watch and thus was unable to keep time in a match. His self-confidence was also dented when he was hit in the stomach by bricks thrown at him by spectators. Clearly, it wasn't just in nineteenth century Perthshire that fans were prone to lobbing bricks at the unfortunate arbiter.

Rous had observed the system used by the Belgian officials during the finals and used it as the basis for his development of the diagonal system. However, this is not to say that referees and linesmen had not previously tried to adopt more formal systems to make it easier to control games.

In 1896 a Referees' Chart was compiled in England which included 'Hints to Referees,' including where to position themselves on the field. By and large, this simply stated the obvious - *"stand near the centre line at kick-off," "keep up with play," "make sure the ball has actually crossed the goal-line before awarding a goal,"* etc. Then, in 1905, an article appeared in Pickford's, *"Association Football"* which mentioned, for the first time, a structured positioning system for all the three officials and it was this that in due course developed into the Diagonal System of Control.

Stanley Rous did, however, create the modern diagonal system that is still in use today. He had experimented with it while refereeing matches in Europe but it was not recognised by the FA until he deployed it while refereeing the 1934 FA Cup final. After that match, he submitted his plans to the FA and they were approved. It wasn't until 1948 that an International Conference of Referees approved its use and it became the global standard for controlling games. In Scotland, the SFA, after some internal debate/confusion, introduced the fixed diagonal system of control at the start of the 1949-50 season, in place of the flexible system previously used.

How the diagonal system of control works

According to all the articles on the diagonal system, the thinking behind it is based on a simple geometric concept. What it means in practice is that there are always (in theory) two pairs of eyes supervising every move across the field in each half of the pitch.

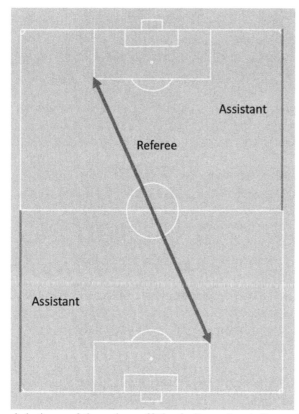

The referee chooses the exact angle to run along based on what's actually happening on the pitch at any time. Crucially, it means that the referee should not have to turn his or her back to the play. Because the Assistant can see what's going on behind the referee's back, the latter doesn't have to make rapid turns or contortions to keep an eye on everything that happens during the match.

When the ball is close to the Assistant towards one end or other of the pitch, the referee can (again in theory) see across the whole penalty box. This allows the ref to conduct the game smoothly without the need to turn his back to the action.

The key to the system is that it allows the referee and other officials to be made aware of everything they need to see during a match, including all possible violations of the rules, off-the-ball confrontations, the ever-present fouls, hand-balls, running battles, offsides etc. If, like me, you weren't aware that this is how our matches are refereed, take a look the next time you're at your local team's ground and see if it increases your respect for the officials. My money is on it not making an ounce of a difference to most fans, but you never know…

One thing that became abundantly clear from my research is that the laws of football are not a sedentary beast. Rather, they are a continuing process; a long chain of adaptation and innovation that continues to this day and will doubtless create fresh controversies in the years to come. However, underpinning the laws, I discovered that there is also something more profound – an actual philosophy of football…

214

The Spirit and Philosophy of the Game

Now, I suspect that you are like me and tend not to think of football as having any sort of philosophical underpinning (although it is [moderately] well known that French, Nobel-prize winning philosopher Albert Camus played in goal for the Racing Universitaire d'Alger).
In my view, based on the vast majority of the games I've watched, there is very little spirit of football, if by that we mean a sense of fair play and respect for the poor men and women who are charged with getting the two teams through to the end of each match without too much blood being shed in the process. Other sports, notably cricket until comparatively recently, certainly had a 'spirit of the game.' My friend, Tony Harding, whom we met previously on the Turn Moss pitches in Manchester watching one referee control two games, recalled that when he played cricket in Lancashire, it was the norm to 'walk' when you knew you had snicked the ball to the wicket-keeper or were lbw. That has changed now and cricketers 'let the umpire make the decision.'

Perhaps the only sport that genuinely has a recognised 'spirit of the game' today is golf.
In contrast, football has never really succumbed to the idea that there is some higher calling – 'the game for the game's sake.' Ask yourself, when was the last time your team deliberately missed a penalty after one of them has taken a blatant dive to win it? It is so rare that any footballer 'does the right thing' that when it does happen it makes headlines for days afterwards. The only major event of this kind I can remember in my lifetime was on December 16th 2000, when Paolo Di Canio, with the goal at his mercy, caught the ball in his hands and refused to score, because he could see the Everton goalkeeper was in agony with a dislocated knee and wanted the game stopped so the keeper could get immediate attention from the physios.

Nevertheless, in the introduction to IFAB's 2021 Laws of the game, under a section headed *"The philosophy and spirit of the Laws,"* we can read, *"Football's Laws are relatively simple compared to most other team sports, but as many situations are subjective and match officials are human, some decisions will inevitably be wrong or cause debate and discussion. For some people, this discussion is part of the game's enjoyment and attraction but, whether decisions are right or wrong, the 'spirit' of the game requires that referees' decisions must always be respected. All those in authority, especially coaches and team captains, have a clear responsibility to the game to respect the match officials and their decisions."*

I will leave the reader to decide whether they regularly witness their team's players, especially the coaches and team captains, showing *"respect (to) the match officials and their decisions."* Based on the preface to this book, this has never been the case and I suspect that it's unlikely to change in the near future. However, it's now time to move on from the evolution of the game and come into the modern era to discover how to become a referee and how technology is increasingly impacting on their role…

Part III

Chapter 1
So, you want to be a referee…

Part I of this book contained a wide range of interviews with former referees. One thing stands out from all of these; namely that for those who have the required personality and are prepared to put in the effort, the rewards are excellent. Although comparatively poorly paid by international standards, for Scotland's top referees there is more to the game than money. The benefits include the opportunity to see some of the world's best players close up, paid-for travel to countries that many would never have imagined visiting and, as a result, the chance to experience new cultures and meet new people. There are a lot of good reasons for becoming a referee. At present, I am reliably informed there are shortages of refs in some areas of Scotland, so if anyone reading this book is inspired to go and take a course and become a referee, I am sure the SFA will be very happy.

That said, there is simply no getting away from the fact that all referees get a veritable mountain of abuse. Acclimatising to this, especially in the early part of their careers, must be hard. It's clearly necessary to have - or develop - a thick skin if you want to be a referee. Moreover, although the lot of a referee has always been difficult, things seem to have got worse since the war. For example, the Edinburgh Referees' Association history cites several examples of serious issues over the 50 years since it was founded in 1951, all of which highlight the potential dangers of life as a football official.

It will not come as a great surprise to members of the Association today to learn (of) a marked increase in cases of verbal and physical assaults against members. Although such instances had occurred since the very first days of the Association, the cases were now more commonplace and more severe. In May 1980, a referee was assaulted whilst officiating at an Edinburgh Amateur match and later that year, in November 1980, another member had his clothes stolen from the Jack Kane Centre ... in November 1983, a member was assaulted in a Border Amateur match and the player concerned was given a 10 year ban. In another case, a player was suspended sine die for assaulting a member in a Midlothian Amateur match."

"Although incidents in Amateur football have been fairly frequent throughout the Association's history, such incidents began to spread to other grades of football. Of particular concern was the spread to the youngest youth leagues. In October 1983, a (referee) abandoned an Under 12 match due to crowd misbehaviour."

"By January 1993, the Council was so appalled that it wrote to Lothian and Borders Police and conveyed its concern about the number of assaults on Association members and the lack of action taken in many cases. Unfortunately, although there is often a prosecution in such cases now, occurrences of serious assault remain too common and is (sic) *one of the greatest drawbacks to the recruitment and retention of referees today.*"

And just to prove that referees are human too, sometimes the disciplinary problems were a result of the referees' own conduct…

"In January 1996, comments made in an article in the Evening News by (referee) resulted in him being censured by Council in March 1996."

"In December 1997, (referee) was suspended until such times as he re-sat the SFA entrance examination, given his total disregard for the Laws of the game whilst refereeing."

"A Special Council meeting was convened … to discuss a complaint by five members of the Association against another member for his 'gross misconduct at a Civic Reception given by the Lord Provost.' A further meeting… resulted in the member being expelled from the Association."

However, my favourite story that shows that referees really are one of us concerns the Edinburgh Association President, Mr Peter Tinley. In 1985, during a football match between the Edinburgh and West Lothian referees, Mr Tinley was ordered off *"for using Foul and Abusive Language towards the referee, and the Social Organiser, J E L MacKinnon, was cautioned for dissent. Council deplored the action of both office bearers and gave Mr Tinley a three match ban and Mr MacKinnon a one match ban, adding that any repeat and all football played by the Association will be stopped."*

It seems that the Edinburgh Association was not alone in having problems when referees played each other at football. I am reliably informed that games of football between referees were notorious and the seven-a-side matches at the annual Referees' Conference were eventually banned. However, while it's good to know that referees are indeed human, it's also the case that some humans are somewhat unhinged in their attitude to referees.

You don't have to search very far online to find examples of this. Consider the following:

Hearts fans' web-page
"How many times have we seen Celtic or Rangers struggling to overcome a lesser team at home, only to get a contentious penalty, or a questionable amount of injury time which leads to a winner?

Hibs fans' web-page
"Cringeworthy but no doubt there is bias by Referees in Scottish Football especially against HIBS."

Celtic fans' website
"An unpopular figure among the Celtic support, shipyard-worker XXXX was a pompous and petty official who was well known for his strong affinity to Rangers."

Rangers fans' website

"Gangsterism and intimidation of refs, both on and off the pitch, has brought us to where we are. The game has been compromised and any chance of competitive element removed by (Celtic). The SFA refusing to back their refs and officials against (Celtic) intimidation inevitably led to an unprecedented and inevitable ref strike in 2010. The socially conditioned myth, however, of Rangers-supporting Masonic refs running Scottish football is still prevalent amongst fans of countless Scottish football clubs."

St Johnstone fan's Facebook post

"Looks like we have fallen to yet another refereeing masterclass of ineptitude. I have not seen it again yet but I am told there was a clear handball in the build up to the goal. This is very disappointing but frankly not unexpected. The standard of officials in Scotland is nothing short of a scandal."

Dundee United fans' web-page

"In all three matches, before the Dunfermline encounter, we lost because of bad refereeing decisions... Celtic lose ONE match and the media make a very big deal about every single refereeing decision that should have gone Celtic's way but didn't!! Yet, the media claim there is no west coast bias? That may be the case, but they definately (sic) have it in for Dundee United!!!"

Aberdeen fans' web-page

"How bad was XXXXX the other night, in what appears to be a par performance for our refs? Although it would have been a softish penalty for McGregor's challenge on Hayes it would most definitely have been given, if the other way round at Parkhead."

Motherwell fans' web-page

"Totally inconsistent and error strewn. Unfortunately their incompetence had a major influence on the outcome of the game. For someone seemingly obsessed with rules, he let off a St Mirren player for booting the ball 40 yards away after play was stopped. If refs aren't going to penalise this indiscretion then its (sic) time rules were changed to allow it."

Mind you, these all pale into insignificance with the following, which is available in a book that you can buy on Amazon...

"In Scotland, it's acceptable to be a Mason and a Referee, despite the obvious connections between the masons and the Orange Order in Scotland .... The relationship is Scotland's NRA/KKK."

I presume the former abbreviation stands for the National Rifle Association (of the USA) and the latter for the Ku Klux Klan. To imply that referees should somehow or other be equivalent to a group as odious as the KKK is for most people, I am sure, not just ludicrous but also might be regarded as potentially libellous. For avoidance of doubt, I am not a mason nor a member of the Orange Order.

It's not just unknown football fans who make their views known. Given their need not to offend potential voters, it is hard to fathom why a politician would also wish to get involved, but following the game between Ross County and Celtic in December 2021, James Dornan MSP tweeted: *"Scottish referees are utterly useless, and if they're not useless then they can only be something much more sinister."*

Of course, it's not hard to start a conspiracy theory. For example, several decades ago it was alleged that supporters of Celtic hired a private detective to trail prominent referees suspected of bias. One of the most famous (some say the best) referees of this era was Jim McCluskey. When it was his 40th birthday, a sales manager of Scottish and Newcastle, whose 'McEwans Lager' motif was adorning Rangers' shirts, called Jim up and asked if he would like a case of lager for his birthday party. Clearly, to some of the more fanatical Celtic fans this might look highly suspicious – possibly even evidence of a Rangers-biased referee accepting a bribe of the principal product of the Ibrox club's main shirt sponsor...

The two men arranged to meet but when the sales manager turned up at the rendezvous and parked his car, he noticed a strange car with a man inside who, it was clear, was keeping tabs on Mr McCluskey. A few days later, on Jim's actual birthday, the sales manager turned up at the McCluskey house and had the door shut in his face by Mrs McCluskey. The fact that he was dressed in a dark-glasses, wore a trilby hat and shabby coat and had a 'press pass' around his neck probably spooked her. If there was a private detective watching he must have been a bit flummoxed.

This, sadly, is how conspiracy theories grow wings. The truth of the matter was that the sales manager was David Gray, a close friend of Jim McCluskey and also a Grade 3 referee in his own right (and a Kilmarnock fan with no interest in either side of the Old Firm). David (who is one of the interviewees in Part I of this book) attended Jim's 40th along with a number of other officials, having first removed his 'press' disguise. The subject of the 'private eye' was a major topic of conversation and was – rightly – dismissed as hilarious by all those present.

On the other side of the great Glaswegian sectarian divide, there is the aforementioned famous photo of Tiny Wharton and Rangers' captain John Greig allegedly giving each other the masonic 'grip' before an Old Firm game. Anyone looking for additional evidence to fuel their conspiracy theories about referees and Freemasonry will be interested to discover that the annual general meetings of the Edinburgh Referees' Association between 1971 and 1975 were held in the city's St Mary's Chapel Masonic Lodge. To increase the paranoia amongst half the city's football supporters, the Association's AGM was held in the city's Hearts' Supporters' Club in 1970 and the same venue was also used regularly for their annual dinner around this time. However, before Hibs fans get too hot under the collar, it should also be recorded that from 1997 to 2000 the Association's annual dinner was held at Easter Road Stadium. It should, of course, be noted that neither membership of an international society nor supporting a football team is illegal or indeed against the rules of football (bear in mind some footballers are masons) and should therefore not be a bar to anyone becoming a referee, but, sadly, as we know, that's not the way some football fans' minds work...

With all that in mind, and bringing things more up to date, the following, taken from the Daily Telegraph of 4th October 2021, should come as no surprise. Under the headline, *"Young football referees leaving game after abuse"* we can read the following:

"Teenage football referees are being forced out of the game by record levels of abuse from coaches and parents at youth games.

"Referees as young as 14 have been left in tears after being sworn at by adults watching from the sidelines.

"One incident included a 15-year-old who was screamed at by the manager of an under-13s team and called 'fucking blind' by a parent."

"James Pearson, chairman of Hampshire FA, said complaints of misconduct had risen by 30 per cent."

Given my comments about the spirit of the game at the end of the preceding chapter, it's clear that any spirit that does exist is spread extremely thinly, if not being non-existent, at the lowest levels of football. Add in the vitriol poured out online and in print and it's not surprising, even if very saddening, to learn of such violence and abuse being meted out to aspiring officials.

Unfortunately, this is not going to change any day soon and it is seen to be part of the rite of passage on the way to becoming a top referee. In the course of interviewing a number of referees for this book, one constant theme from almost all of them was *"if you can stand the abuse for the first six months and you are still enjoying it then being a referee is a great experience."* Also, as one of the young referees I interviewed pointed out, you get fairly well paid for your trouble. So, assuming that you're not put off (and I trust you are not), where do you start your refereeing career?

In Scotland, assuming you don't know any referees, the place to start is the SFA website. Here, on the page https://www.scottishfa.co.uk/scottish-fa/referees/become-a-referee/ you will find the necessary instructions to begin your journey.

When you click through to this page, you'll be told that *"Refereeing can be a highly rewarding challenge, encouraging a healthy and active lifestyle as well as significantly contributing to the development of the game. Referees operate at all levels – from grassroots football right through to the Scottish Professional Football League and international matches."*

You'll also find that Scottish refereeing is organised on a regional basis. There are 12 Associations covering the country. Select the one where you live and get in touch with the Secretary, whose email address is available online at the link to their Association in the SFA website. I'm sure they will be delighted to hear from you and will do their level best to encourage you in your first steps into refereeing.

The other information that matters is also on the SFA website, but the essential requirements are as follows (information correct at time of writing).

Course fee - £35 (includes the first season's membership fee). £15 for concessions (students and unemployed persons).

The course length is generally between eight and 10 weeks for two hours per night. The courses are held twice a year in the January to March and September to December periods. Other courses may be held outside this schedule depending on local circumstances and demand.

There are two parts to the Introductory Course. The first is classroom-based learning on the laws of the game, with an exam in the final week. The exam is conducted on computers at the course venue and involves multiple choice questions, report writing and assessing match incidents on video. The second part involves officiating a match under the guidance of a more experienced referee. Once part two is completed, candidates are able to join the local Referees' Association and become a Scottish Football Association registered referee.

Support is given to new referees by their Referees' Association and a mentor will be arranged to provide guidance in the early stages of their refereeing careers. Direction will also be given on suitable leagues to commence refereeing.

After all this training you may be ready to make your way in the refereeing fraternity. That said, I still don't actually know why people want to become referees, although, as I said above, perhaps the easiest way to find out is to get in touch with your local Referees' Association. You will, I'm sure, be met with open arms and, if you can stick at it, will have the chance to experience top-class football from a unique vantage point available to no-one else, other than the players themselves. Like many of the refs interviewed here, you may, in time, get to officiate at Cup finals and league deciders, or even at the World Cup finals. One thing is certain though: by the time you have completed your training and gained the experience to be considered for a Cup final, the use of technology in football will have accelerated even further. And it's that, increasingly contentious, subject that forms the final two chapters of this book...

Chapter 2
Why change the laws?

As should be abundantly clear by now, it is IFAB who, in their all-consuming oversight of the laws, have the ultimate say on any changes. More to the point, they have the first say too, for it is proposals by individual countries' Football Associations that are then either ratified or rejected by the supreme rule-making body. This, in my view, has both good and bad implications.

On the day I was writing this paragraph, the media were all over the story that IFAB was considering extending the half-time interval from 15 minutes to 25 minutes. The idea seemed to be to offer clubs the opportunity to show some entertainment at half-time, to sell a few more pies and generally cash in. The response, judging by the radio-phone-ins that day, was universally against such a stupid move. And it is that word 'universally' that holds the clue here, because one of IFAB's arguments about their custodianship of the Laws of the game is that they must be *"universally applicable."* Of course, the introduction of a 25-minute half-time break might have allowed big clubs to sell more stuff to the punters, or even introduce a major star to sing their latest hit. But if you are an away fan from Dumfries attending an evening cup tie in Dingwall, the last thing you want is to be home even later. And if you're watching a game at Hazelhead Park, Hamilton Palace or even Hackney Marshes, the opportunities for Adele to come and sing at half time are somewhat limited. It was clearly a dumb idea and was sensibly rejected after only a few days. The question remains as to why it was ever put forward though. It was clearly never going to be *universally* applicable.

Many years ago, I had a conversation with a football administrator in which I suggested that, in the same way we no longer talk about '(life) assurance' but instead use the generic word 'insurance,' we should replace the outdated expression 'the penalty mark' with the commonly accepted 'the penalty spot,' the two expressions now being synonymous. However, the laws say that a penalty kick is taken from 'the penalty mark' and it was explained to me that this is because in places like Africa they might simply scratch a cross or line to indicate the penalty spot. Thus, because the laws must be capable of being universally applied, that's why IFAB continues to use the word 'mark' rather than 'spot.' I have to say I think this is semantical nonsense, or, if you prefer, total bollocks. Leaving aside the idea that anyone marking out a pitch, whether in Africa or Arbroath, would not make a circular 'spot' if that was what the laws said, we all know what the words 'penalty spot' mean in relation to a penalty and it is pure sophistry to pretend otherwise. Why there is an insistence from IFAB that flies in the face of common usage is beyond me. But it does, perhaps unwittingly, reveal something of their mindset…

The argument for 'universality' has already gone out of the window with the introduction of VAR. As is obvious, VAR is not universally applied, nor is it ever likely to be, simply because of the cost involved. Those playing on the aforementioned Hazelhead (or indeed Hamilton or Hackney) playing fields are not going to see five-minute halts to consider an offside decision. *There are now two sets of rules in football: one for the rich and one for the rest.*

That said, the idea of an international body to ensure consistency across the world of a particular sport was eminently sensible in 1886 – and still is today. Creating a set of parameters for the pitch and equipment to make the game universal was a key element in allowing the game to develop internationally. As has been stressed throughout, football's popularity lies in the fact that it is fundamentally a simple game. Moreover, its great strength is that while it has changed considerably in many ways since the late nineteenth century, is still retains the simplicity that makes it loved by millions across the planet.

Most of the changes introduced over the decades have been to the game's benefit. Simple ideas, from substitutes to the spray that shows a player the position from which a free-kick can be taken (and the line behind which the defensive wall must stand) are brilliant. Some though, are of questionable value…

For example, what about the laws about handball and the need for the arms to be in a natural position – or rather, as it says in the laws, for a player not to make their body "unnaturally bigger" - that is generally taken to mean away from the body (something that is frequently checked by VAR)? As Ally McCoist has said on radio, the only unnatural position for any human arm is when it's cut off. What we see today is arguably the antithesis of the word natural: players force their arms behind their backs to avoid them being hit by the ball – a totally unnatural position for a footballer trying to keep his balance. It is never going to be possible to judge handball with total accuracy in a game of football, no matter how you try to legislate for it. Is it intentional? Was the place the ball struck close enough to the shoulder to count as handball or was it in on the few inches from the shoulder where it's not handball? What happens when the ball is fired from two yards away and hits a defender who has his arms in front of his body? Most referees in the latter case would not award a penalty, but some would.

To illustrate how much of a mess the law concerning handball has become, look at the photos here – on the following page - of the official IFAB 2021 Laws of the game. The first shows the old laws, now deleted. The second, immediately below, shows the new text. As you can see, there are some crucial passages that can be interpreted by different referees in different ways in different matches. The phrase, *"A player is considered to have made their body unnaturally bigger when the position of their hand/arm is not a consequence of, or justifiable by, the player's body movement for that specific situation"* reveals the problem.

A player sliding in to make a last-ditch block will, by virtue of their *"body movement for that specific situation,"* have at least one arm in the air for balance. It is, I am pretty sure, very difficult if not impossible for a player to throw his body on the line in this way while forcing his arms behind his back. Yet we have all seen penalties awarded in this situation. Just how does any referee decide what is, or is not, *"justifiable by the player's body movement for that specific situation?"* In the same way that Willie Young told me how goalkeepers were brought in to provide their expertise in the framing of the changes to the law around goal-kicks, I wonder if IFAB spoke to anatomists and physiologists about the handball law….?

Another area where the law has changed and which, in my view, has had a detrimental effect on the game is the move to allow defenders to receive the ball inside the penalty box from a goal-kick. Some like this: I do not. It only works at the very highest level of the game, where the players have the skill to play the ball from the back, and, even then, it's still frequently lumped forward under duress. At the lower levels of the game, including, I'm afraid, virtually all of the Scottish professional leagues, the skill isn't there for this to work the way it is intended. Fans here in Scotland still, I suspect, want to see action, not fancy-dan tomfoolery which results in giving the ball away and conceding a goal.

My main beef with this is that it is changing the actual nature of football. It's instructive that several of the referees interviewed for Part I commented on the more frantic manner in which football is played in Scotland compared with how it was played on the continent during their time. John Rowbotham, for example, noted that when he refereed European matches, he observed the ball being played side to side rather than back to front. That is what we are increasingly seeing at the top level in English and continental football and the change that allows goalkeepers to pass to defenders inside the box from a goal-kick has exacerbated this trend. It is very skilful, but it's not wonderfully exciting to watch. Similarly, the pressing game that is very much in vogue at the moment means that teams pass the ball to-and-fro across the pitch, probing for an opening. Add in the superior fitness of the

---

Law 12 – Fouls and Misconduct (p.98)

1. Direct free kick – Handling the ball

Old text (showing deletions)

(…)

It is an offence if a player:
- deliberately touches the ball with their hand/arm, ~~including~~ moving the hand/arm towards the ball
- scores in the opponents' goal directly from their hand/arm, even if accidental, including by the goalkeeper
- after the ball has touched their ~~or a team-mate's~~ hand/arm, even if accidental, immediately:
  - scores in the opponents' goal
  - ~~creates a goal-scoring opportunity~~
- ~~touches the ball with their hand/arm when:~~
  - ~~the hand/arm has made their body unnaturally bigger~~
  - ~~the hand/arm is above/beyond their shoulder level (unless the player deliberately plays the ball which then touches their hand/arm)~~

~~The above offences apply even if the ball touches a player's hand/arm directly from the head or body (including the foot) of another player who is close.~~

~~Except for the above offences, it is not an offence if the ball touches a player's hand/arm:~~
- ~~directly from the player's own head or body (including the foot)~~
- ~~directly from the head or body (including the foot) of another player who is close~~
- ~~if the hand/arm is close to the body and does not make the body unnaturally bigger~~
- ~~when a player falls and the hand/arm is between the body and the ground to support the body, but not extended laterally or vertically away from the body~~

New text

(…)

Not every touch of a player's hand/arm with the ball is an offence.

It is an offence if a player:
- deliberately touches the ball with their hand/arm, for example moving the hand/arm towards the ball
- touches the ball with their hand/arm when it has made their body unnaturally bigger. A player is considered to have made their body unnaturally bigger when the position of their hand/arm is not a consequence of, or justifiable by, the player's body movement for that specific situation. By having their hand/arm in such a position, the player takes a risk of their hand/arm being hit by the ball and being penalised

Explanation
- Not every contact between the hand/arm and the ball is a handball offence.
- Referees must judge the 'validity' of the hand/arm's position in relation to what the player is doing in that particular situation.
- Accidental handball by a team-mate before a goal is scored and accidental handball creating a goal-scoring opportunity have been removed as offences.

modern player and you have eight or nine men between the ball and the goal at many times in a match. The attackers regroup, passing the ball sideways and back until they find a gap to exploit or a defender makes a mistake. One of the most exciting things you can see in football – the long-range scoring shot - is becoming a bit of a rarity. The game at the top level in England reminds me increasingly of an international rugby union match, which has become a cross between a game of chess and a war of attrition, with a few moments of genuine excitement thrown in if you're lucky. Even then, the excitement is often subject to a final denouement that takes several minutes. Eventually, after watching interminable slow-motion replays, the rugby TMO decides that a square millimetre of the ball has been touched down amidst a heaving mass of a dozen or so intertwined bodies. That is not sport: it's a subjective test of observation wrapped up in a computer game.

I do not kid myself that my concerns will have the slightest impact. For a start, the media, especially the broadcasters, are by and large on-board with VAR (it will give them lots to write and speak about) and their influence will ease its introduction into Scotland. And in the course of writing this book, the decision was taken that VAR would be introduced to the top flight in Scotland in the 2022-23 season – of which more below…

* * * * *

One of the purposes of this book is to encourage people to take up refereeing. I would hope and you would think - the SFA would welcome anything that does make people attend the local courses and become referees. However, it must be said that they do not go out of their way to help themselves. I was always sceptical of much of the media's antipathy towards the Scottish football authorities, but in writing this book I came up against entrenched interests and a lack of willingness to engage with someone who actually wanted to help. I tried hard to get in touch with current referees. I emailed every one of the 12 Refereeing Associations in Scotland, explaining what I was trying to do - and only two replied (with only the Glasgow Association actually helping – as explained below). I found the right people to speak to at the SFA and sent them various emails, trying to arrange interviews with some of today's officials. They said they would help and then stopped replying to subsequent emails. I emailed IFAB twice asking for information and did not even receive the courtesy of a reply. I interviewed one of the country's up-and-coming female referees, whose story is an inspiration to young women and men who want to make their way up the refereeing ranks – and then her local Referees' Association warned her not to let me publish it. At times, today's referees are their own worst enemies. I also spoke to former SFA employees who, it became clear, did not like any kind of criticism and, having initially been interested in this project, subsequently refused to help. The Scottish Football Museum were similarly unhelpful, telling me they would call and arrange a time for me to visit so I could see some of the material I wanted to study, but then never did. Yes, there were others who did help me (as noted, the Glasgow Referees' Association was particularly helpful in providing the photo of the Faultless Cup, for which I am very grateful), but, overall, Scottish football deserves better from those in positions of authority and, I'm sad to say, I am now more cynical about the quality of those running our game than I was before I began to write this book.

Despite this, the SFA can hold its head high in many respects when it comes to the introduction of important law changes. They returned year after year, for several seasons in a row, with their proposal to IFAB to change the offside law from three to two players and eventually were successful and the offside law was changed, to the game's benefit. However, the fact that they are only one of the hundreds of Associations throughout the world, and have, on their own initiative, put forward nearly 200 proposals to IFAB since it was founded in 1886, shows, in my view, the extent of the problem. I don't know how many other Associations have put forward proposals over this time, but it would be reasonable to assume there will have been a lot. By the law of averages, the more proposals are made, the greater the chances of something daft being considered. Like extended breaks at half-time…

Some might think that IFAB, in recent years, has been over-keen to introduce new changes. Some might put it more strongly and say that it seems as if IFAB is prone to meddle continuously with the laws of the game. The 1924 changes to the law about the ball being in play, which led, as described above, to players dribbling the ball from a corner, then led to a further adjustment to stop that happening. Like the changes to the handball law, this is yet another example of IFAB not thinking through the consequences of their actions and having to make constant revisions, to the confusion of players and fans alike. IFAB's argument for change is always that it will improve the game. Well, in my view, the best people to be the judges of this are the fans. Yet we seem to be excluded by the powers-that-be.

The Technical Director of IFAB is, at time of writing, David Elleray, the former English grammar school boy, Oxford graduate (where he was a keen rugby player and rower), referee and public school (Harrow) teacher. He is an immensely experienced referee and neither his background nor his qualifications should be taken to suggest that he has not got the best of intentions. That said, it is arguable that a public-school mindset, whilst probably essential in mid-19th century football, is unlikely to understand what drives the average Scottish (or English) football fan to follow his or her team from week to week. For example, in March 2021, Sky Sports reported that IFAB had decided against allowing referees' VAR decisions to be relayed to the crowd. The report noted that,

"It involved supporters hearing a final decision, and brief explanation, from a referee, but fans would still be unable to listen to match officials during the decision-making process.

"However, after agreeing to a further evaluation, talks over direct communication have been 'paused' ahead of this year's annual general meeting on Friday, Sky Sports News has been told. FIFA says it can see 'benefits' to live communication but further analysis is required before a final decision."

Consider this against the great ecumenical event that is Scotland's Old Firm game. Rival fans feeling angered about a decision are more likely to cause trouble. Even with the correct information they may still cause trouble, but they are probably less likely to do so. This stonewalling by IFAB is, in my opinion, somewhat at odds with the mission statement of IFAB as stated on their website, as shown overleaf…

"The mission of The IFAB is to serve the world of football as the independent guardian of the Laws of the game. As the only body authorised to decide and agree changes to the Laws of the game, we listen to the football community, with the goal to improve and develop the game for players, match officials and fans while protecting and strengthening the spirit and simplicity of football."

This quotation, possibly inadvertently, lays bare what seems to be the order of IFAB's priorities – players first (OK, I get that), match officials next and then the fans. For most of football history, football fans – the industry's customers – were expected to stand and watch games on open terraces with no cover, to have a brick wall for a urinal and no hot water (and sometimes no cold water) to wash their hands. Women's toilets were conspicuous by their absence at some grounds. Fans were corralled, herded and not infrequently treated (it must be said, for some groups, with good cause) as potential hooligans. We had the Burnden Park (Bolton) disaster and the Ibrox disaster - and not much really changed. It took Hillsborough and Bradford to bring an end to the old way of watching matches (although sadly, some young fans today, with no knowledge of the Bradford fire, think it's OK to light flares and smoke bombs in a ground). No sensible industry ignores its customers' views the way football has been prone to do in the past. Any company and/or industry that consistently fails to listen carefully to its customers and instead puts them to the back of its list of priorities should not be surprised if some of those customers eventually leave. With younger people having limited attention spans and far more competition for their evening and Saturday afternoon entertainment, there needs to be more effort made to find out what fans want. My guess is that a moratorium on all changes to the laws for three years would be welcomed by most. Unfortunately, that's not what's going to happen.

We are not quite at the stage of rugby, where the complexity of the laws seems to grown with each passing season, but at times it feels like it. The handball law, as illustrated above, is a perfect example: as successive changes didn't work as well as anticipated, it was felt necessary to introduce others. They in turn were not quite perfect, so further amendments were made. It's not just handball: the change to the kick-off has made no appreciable difference to football, so why was it introduced? Yes, some changes, such as the drop-ball going to the team in possession, are improvements, but second-phase offside is patently a nonsense, so why do we persist with it? Is football really better as a spectacle for the fans if there is patient passing around the penalty box from a goal-kick, until the defenders are closed down and the ball is kicked up the park – as it was before the law changed? Currently, FIFA, at the behest of Arsene Wenger, wants to experiment with 'kick-ins' instead of throw-ins. This is madness and would fundamentally alter the way the game is played. And as we have seen, such an experiment has already taken place and was not adopted. Why won't these people learn?

"If it ain't broke, don't fix it" should be the guiding mantra of IFAB, perhaps, as this is football, with an alliterative Anglo-Saxon adjective preceding the word *"fix"* just to emphasise the point…

Chapter 3
Is technology an evil necessity?

New technologies have been introduced throughout football history. Goal nets, the referee's whistle, the changing nature of football boots, the introduction of floodlighting, hot and cold running water in the loos at football stadia - all these have made a big difference to the nature and enjoyment of the game for players and spectators alike. Nowadays, we tend to forget about these innovations, preferring to focus on the computerised technology that is increasingly dominating the way the game is officiated and results are decided. My concern is that we shall end up with something that is not very different to a computer game. However, there are areas where I believe modern technology can make a huge difference...

HawkEye has been used successfully for many years now for goal-line technology. Its great strength is that it works almost instantly, with the referee being alerted within a second or so that the ball has actually crossed the line (or not), so the game can proceed without interruption. It can't be stressed enough that, from the point of view of the fans, the one thing that annoys us more than anything else about VAR is unnecessary, lengthy interruptions. The media may think this helps create dramatic tension, but they, unlike the fans, who are invested both financially and emotionally in their team, fail to understand just how the wait for a decision annoys the majority of those attending a match. When it interrupts the celebration of a goal, which, let's face it, is the principal reason for going to football as a fan, it is doubly annoying. This also applies to the second-phase offside as practised nowadays, where the Assistant Referee has to wait for a move to play out before raising his flag, even though it is clear from outer space that a player was offside earlier in the move. It will just take one famous player to suffer a serious injury while play is pointlessly continuing in this second-phase for the money men who run the top clubs to step in and demand a change. In addition, while writing this book I watched a match between Chelsea and Manchester United in which Cristiano Ronaldo was clearly offside when receiving the ball: he then ran on and the ball eventually deflected off a Chelsea defender for a corner. If he had scored it would have been disallowed, but because he won a corner the match continued. If Man United had scored from the corner the goal would have been given and all hell would have broken loose – and quite rightly. Just why anyone thinks this makes sense is beyond me. But, as I'll explain, this is what the Premier League has decided should happen.

Technology can, and I believe will, play an increasing role in football in the years to come. Given that nerdy techies are already building the metaverse, where the digital and real worlds will fuse into one, and that this is expected to be working within 10-15 years (if not sooner), who can doubt that these same people could easily apply their intellectual horsepower to something relatively simple, like making an offside decision?

The fact is they are already doing so. It is generally agreed that if a tech story (say driverless cars) makes it to the mainstream media then that technology has already been worked on for many years and is at or close to fruition. In May 2021, the Daily Mail (and others) reported that the English Football League had, in October 2019, explored *"the use of limb-tracking technology to provide instant calls on offsides."* The 2021 article went on to say that *"The* *system has undergone a successful trial at a Premier League club for the last year, and four teams - Liverpool, Chelsea, Manchester City and Manchester United - will have it in place next season (*and moreover*) the system could be fully operational as soon as 2023."*

This 'skeletal player tracking system', has been developed by HawkEye – the same people who provide the goal-line technology that has proved such a success. Moreover, HawkEye has been used for many years in other sports, notably cricket and tennis, and in the latter is the ultimate arbiter of whether a ball is in or out – that is whether it has bounced on or over a line on the court. It's not hard to see how this could be adapted for the ball being in or out of play around the touchlines of a football pitch.

If we get to the point where offsides and the ball in or out of play are controlled by technology, with – crucially - the result being available almost instantly, a large part of the job of the linesman/Assistant Referee will have been dispensed with and their roles will change considerably. It's not hard to see the benefit of this. For a start, all those occasions where the fans at the side of the ground hurl abuse because they think the ball has crossed the line for a throw-in but the linesman believes it hasn't, will by and large disappear.

Of course, it will be said that there is more to offside than simply looking along the line and therefore humans will still be needed to see if a forward is interfering with play or if the ball was last touched by an opponent. However, if one thinks about the way technology has already evolved it's clear that these are not insurmountable obstacles. Billions are being spent developing driverless vehicles that have instantly to take into account potential movement of other cars, changing traffic lights, the idiocy of pedestrians and unfortunate stray dogs, to say nothing of reacting to adverse weather conditions. Offside may be complicated, but it's nothing compared to a driverless car making a safe passage through central Edinburgh as the Scottish weather demonstrates its well-known tendency to give us four seasons in one day. People, especially football officials, may not like the prospect of being made redundant by technology, but it's been happening since the days of the Luddites - and they didn't manage to stop it either. Does anyone *really* think that it will be impossible to produce technological aids which can deal with the vagaries of the offside law?

Of course, just because something is possible doesn't mean it has to happen (of which more presently). There are still many other things Assistant refs do that are necessary (checking nets, checking boots and other equipment, watching for fouls, separating fighting players, etc.), but offsides and the ball in or out of play are two of the more essential ones. A radical re-think is (hopefully) going on right now and if it's not then it should be. Amongst the questions that should be being asked is whether we might eventually see robots run the line. I would be very much against this, but it's perfectly possible that it may happen, with a new role subsequently being introduced for some other form of referee's assistant. The current refereeing hierarchy would, understandably be against this too, but part of their problem might be that the same arguments that would hold for HawkEye and robot linesmen also hold for VAR - namely that it would help reduce errors. Would they be happy to have a reduction in errors and also a reduction in the number of officials controlling a match? I rather suspect not, but what's sauce for the goose…?

To work how I - and I suspect most football fans - want it to work, VAR would have to use technology that can provide *instantaneous* decisions. This issue – the hold-up to the game while we wait for someone to decide what has happened - is where VAR has proved most wanting. There have been numerous problems with VAR in general, but it's the way in which it sucks all the joy out of the most important part of the game that really frustrates the fans. The lines drawn across the pitch to show that a boot or an elbow were offside infuriate everyone, not just because they might mean a goal is disallowed on a micro-technicality but principally because of the delay to the game. The requirement to go back to a previous incident similarly angers supporters, because many of them won't have a clue what it was, having been caught up on the moment of the 'goal.' The infamous Scottish Cup final of 1989 was decided when Roy Aitken of Celtic took a throw-in which should have been awarded to Rangers and then in the move that resulted from Aitken's throw-in, Celtic scored the only goal of the game. I was at that game and like many, possibly most, in the crowd had not realised what had happened, other than the goal being scored. The potential for violence during and, especially, after, an Old Firm match is high enough without creating additional flash-points. However, as I'll explain below, that specific incident would not currently be considered by VAR. That being the case, the potential for trouble would increase exponentially. The only people who would benefit would be the media, because they would be able to milk the controversy for days.

Not only is there that, relatively slight but nonetheless real, danger of crowd trouble, but the problem is that VAR was introduced partly because the amounts of money involved at the highest levels of the game are so humungous that 'getting it right' is seen to be of paramount importance. A wrong decision, we were told, could cost a club £millions, or in Rangers' case in that 1989 final, possibly a major trophy. On that basis, where do we stop with VAR? If a throw-in is (knowingly or otherwise) taken by the wrong side and from it they attack for several minutes, force a corner and then score, is that any more or less legitimate for the time that has elapsed since the shy was taken? This actually happened in a game which I watched live on Sky, between Nottingham Forest and West Bromwich Albion on 18th April 2022. In that instance, the referee over-ruled his linesman, who had correctly given West Brom the throw, and with the Albion players all moving up the pitch in anticipation of their throw-in, Forest capitalised, forced the ball forward, gained a corner and scored from it. Being the second-tier of English football, there was no VAR, but, as I'll explain below, in this instance the goal would have stood, even with VAR.

Then there is the slow-motion replay for potential penalties. No-one in the ground can see any incident in anything other than normal time, so why are we introducing this level of forensic detail into the game?

We are getting to the situation like rugby, where the video is 'rock and rolled' backwards and forwards to see precisely where the 'contact' took place. It's still highly subjective and consequently it's a farce because any additional 'rigour' that might be applied comes down to one human's view of what has happened. We might as well just watch a computer simulation of a match. Painful as it is when your team loses a goal after such 'video analysis' it is, in my view important to remember that this is a game between humans, with all the potential for human error and unpredictability that implies. Mistakes are made, more frequently by players than referees in most matches. Suck it up, go out for a pint and complain about it, then go home and wait till the next time, when you might get the decision and it will be your turn to rejoice.

As noted, the media are, by and large, solidly behind VAR. For journalists, it's a godsend, creating yet more opportunities for them to create stories and stir controversy. The argument that is constantly advanced (I heard it on Radio Scotland the night before I typed these words) is that it enables the right decision to be made and, moreover, that the technology and the speed with which it is interpreted are improving rapidly. Those last points are true, but do not detract from the fact that in too many instances VAR does not actually result in a 'right' decision, being still, as in the pre-VAR days, dependent on a human evaluating a situation subjectively. Two referees are perfectly capable of coming to different decisions on a penalty after being advised by VAR and then watching a replay on the screen. But in the meantime, fans are seething with impatience, deprived of the primary reason for attending a match, to wit, being lost in the joy of celebrating a goal for their team. Make no mistake: VAR has fundamentally changed the way we enjoy football. This, as a friend of mine reflected over an email exchange, is the real tragedy of VAR, namely that we, as fans, feel like we are being robbed of some amazing goals. As an Arsenal fan, he bemoaned two disallowed goals – *against his own team* - in his side's game at Everton in December 2021, noting *"they were criminal - and that's coming from a Gooner!"* He added, *"Those decisions, especially the second one, completely ruined the atmosphere of a really exciting game. I'm fed up seeing, for example, a defender scoring his first goal for three seasons - the pure joy on his face and the fans rejoicing - and then seeing him crestfallen as the ref refers it upstairs."*

The referees themselves are keen. In a rare interview with Radio Scotland. Crawford Allan, the Head of Refereeing at the SFA, said that VAR had increased the number of correct decisions made by officials. Of course, there are no figures for Scotland because we don't have VAR here, but the Premier League in England claims that the number of correct *key* decisions has risen, from 84% to 94% during a match. I do wonder what is the basis for these figures? The statistic just seems to be trotted out, without anyone demanding to see how it has been calculated. It seems to me that there may be an element of the officials checking their own homework here. Almost every weekend as I was writing this section of the book, there were major rows over VAR, culminating in two penalties that were not given to Huddersfield Town in their multi-million pound play off against Nottingham Forest for the right to play in the English Premier League in 2022-23. Given the financial stakes, these were potentially huge errors. There were many people, including former referees, who think that at least one of these penalties should have been awarded. Who decides if they are called 'right' when the VAR balance sheet is finally assessed at the end of last season?

It's worth looking at what the Premier League says on its website about the use of VAR. Its starting position is the advice given by IFAB in the laws of the game. More specifically, as detailed on the following page, the Premier League states precisely that…

- *The VAR will not review incidents outside of the four match-changing situations: goals; penalty decisions; direct red-card incidents; and mistaken identity.*
- *It will not review, for example, fouls or handballs in the middle of the pitch when there is no goal or penalty decision.*
- *It will not review the decision to award a corner instead of a goal-kick, even if the corner produces a goal.*
- *This is because the VAR will only check the attacking possession phase that led to the goal, and the starting point is limited to the immediate phase, in this instance the corner being taken.*

The Roy Aitken 'throw-in,' the 'Ronaldo corner' and the Nottingham Forest goal referred to above all come under the second and third rules above and in each case would not result in a decision being overturned. This, in my view, contradicts the first rule,' where *"only match-changing situations"* are considered. Aitken's taking of a throw that (I am pretty sure) he knew wasn't for his side and Ronaldo's corner (if it had led to a goal), would have certainly been *"match-changing,"* while Forest's goal from the corner against West Brom (albeit due to a refereeing error in giving them a throw-in that they shouldn't have had) put them two in front and helped them go on to win comfortably. In other words, it was match-changing.

More than a few pundits, not infrequently with a (usually well-known) bias towards one team, are all for VAR when it favours their side, or a Scottish side in European competition, but become less enthusiastic when it looks like it is going against their team. Unfortunately, now the genie is out of the bottle, I suspect that VAR will not stop where it is now. Who would bet against European leagues at some future date, with even bigger sums of money available to the participants? If/when this happens, the desire 'to get it right' will lead to complaints that, for example, a corner was mistakenly given and from that the subsequent sequence of play led to a goal being scored. And what will happen in those instances in games where an offence is committed and seen by the TV cameras but not by the referee? Currently, nothing happens. On 28th November 2021, in a match between Brentford and Everton, a Brentford player clearly held an Everton forward by the shirt in the penalty area. The TV pundits were told that it had been noticed by the VAR but, *"The VAR check said there was no clear and obvious error, but if the penalty had been given it was unlikely to have been overturned."* Think about that non-sequitur for a second...

Then, in a match between Tottenham and Liverpool in December 2021, Harry Kane, the Spurs centre-forward was only booked for a challenge that was universally condemned and considered worthy of a red-card. Later in the same game, the referee, having booked Liverpool's Andy Robertson, was asked by the VAR to review his decision, which he subsequently overturned and gave Robertson a red card. The obvious question was why he had not been asked to review the Kane decision. And, of course, the key point in all this is that the Robertson decision will be adjudged to be correct when VAR is being justified by the Premier League and the officials, as will the Kane one, when it is more than arguable that both were wrong. The official stats, naturally, show VAR is working. Lies, damned lies and statistics come to mind…

Where do we go from here?

In the future, who doubts that the world's biggest clubs and Leagues will not demand that 'we' – by which they mean 'they' – get it <u>all</u> correct?" In other words, it won't just be *"clear and obvious errors,"* but any error. That means that a handball outside the current *"four, match-changing situations"* will start to be taken into account. In the race between the technologists, striving instantly to create the cameras and software to makes the correct decisions, and the desire of the biggest clubs' owners, television companies and national FAs to maximise their income, money will win and referees will become ever more integrated into a largely technology-based football officiating system. At present, officials have the get-out-of-jail card of an error having to be *"clear and obvious."* It is not unreasonable to assume that, no matter how much he might try not to, the Video Assistant Referee may well have an understandable desire to support his on-field colleagues. The oft-stated desire to get it right only applies so far. If we take the wish *"to get it right,"* to its logical conclusion, that means overriding officials even if their error is not clear and obvious but has manifestly changed the result of a match. As I said, once the genie is out of the bottle there is no putting it back…

Intriguingly, and worryingly in my view, despite the English Premier League's insistence that VAR will not be used to *"review incidents outside of the four match-changing situations,"* as the interview with former, top-level rugby referee Jim Fleming makes clear, a similar, straightforward focus was the original intention in Rugby Union, but in time the TMO's remit expanded as rugby referees made more use of the technology. As Jim put it, *"once the genie's out of the bottle he tends to want to explore more and more of the possibilities open to him."* And that, of course, is what happened in rugby. The TMO began to be used in the late 1990s, but by 2013 the former Scotland scrum half Mike Blair was writing on the BBC website that, *"the television match official (TMO) has been playing an increasing role recently. They have a bigger remit on what they can adjudicate on and they are being used with more frequency."* In the opening match of the rugby World Cup in 2015, between England and Fiji, some 28% of the stoppage time in the game was due to TMO reviews.

World Rugby, the global governing body for Rugby Union insists in their laws that *"the referee should not be subservient to the system"* and that he is *"the decision-maker and must remain in charge of the game."* In rugby, there are instances of TMOs trying to persuade a referee to change his mind. They do this by saying, *"Would you like to look at it again?"* This suggests they think the ref has made the wrong call and they are trying to influence him to change the decision. In football as in rugby, the referee is supposed to have the final word on every decision, but, as we know from this season's stats (2021-22) for the Premier League in English football, there have been (at time of writing – January 2022), 49 instances where referees have been invited by the VAR to revisit their decision by taking a look at the TV monitor at the side of the pitch. As The Sun newspaper, in its pithy style, put it, *"Scared Premier League refs chicken out of ALL 49 VAR monitor checks this season."* The previous season, the referees went to the monitor 87 times, but only stuck with their original decision five times. It's clear that the referee might, technically-speaking, be making the 'final decision,' but, in reality, it's being made for him or her in the vast majority of these cases.

On Tuesday 19th April 2022, the Scottish football clubs voted to implement VAR, starting from halfway through the 2022-23 season, but only in the Premiership and only once that league resumes in December following the World Cup. Doing so mid-season is, in my opinion, wrong. Whilst unlikely, it is not impossible that a decision taken during the early, non-VAR months of the competition may affect the final outcome of the title. Moreover, the SPFL also intends to use VAR in the semi-finals of the Scottish League Cup in January and February 2023. Suppose one of the teams contesting those semi-finals is only there because of a dreadful refereeing decision that allowed them, erroneously, to win their quarter-final? Surely, it should be used from the start of the following season or for every round in the League Cup so there is fairness for everyone? Unfortunately, as I noted above, there is one rule for the rich and one for the rest: fairness only applies if you can afford it. The fact is that the lower-ranked teams in the top flight (and those outside it) can't easily afford VAR, or at least not at an equal price. That's why the total cost of £1.2m per season is to be met by the 12 clubs on a sliding scale, with the Premiership winners paying around £195,000 and the 12th-place team £67,000. Now that the genie has been released north of the border, expect the football authorities and the media to do everything they can to demonstrate its success. Meanwhile, just don't get too excited every time your Premiership team scores a goal…

Interestingly, in FIFA's 1986 publication, *"Football History, Laws of the Game, Referees,"* Harry Cavan, the Senior Vice President of FIFA, wrote, *"In my view, experiments on change of the Laws are not really worthwhile unless they are conducted over a fairly lengthy period of time, in major competitions. There are also many suggestions to add to the markings of the field, time-keeping devices and light beams from goalpost to goalpost to eliminate 'mistake' goals. The reply of the Board to these kinds of suggestions would appear to be that the Game of Association Football has developed as a major sport because of the simpleness of the Laws of the Game, the unpredictable nature of the Game and the emotions which it produces are the great strengths of football."*

The last sentence of that quotation sums it up for me: it is the simple nature of football and its laws that make it such a great game. Sadly, *"the reply of the Board"* cited in the paragraph immediately above no longer seems to be FIFA policy. Unpredictability is one of football's greatest strengths: it's why almost everyone celebrates every time a minnow beats a Premiership team (especially one of the 'big' clubs) in a cup competition and why we leap to our feet whenever the ball is in within sniffing distance of the opposition goal-line.

Meanwhile, the impossibility of eradicating human error means that we, as fans, will never be satisfied with our match officials. They too are human and therefore occasionally unpredictable. We need to try harder to understand them. For all their faults, their seeming inability to spot the most grievous fouls committed against our team, their apparent ignoring of blatant handball, clear offsides and the ball going yards out of play, we can't have a game without them. And, as the interviews in this book show, there are a lot of plusses to a career as a top-grade football official. The better we, the fans, understand the laws and the challenges faced by referees, the less we are likely to criticise the officials (I can dream) - and the more people may be tempted to join their ranks. Currently, Scottish football needs a few more referees. Why not you?

SELECT BIBLIOGRAPHY

A Load of Old Balls, Simon Inglis, English Heritage, 2005
A history of goalkeeping kit
http://www.goalkeepersaredifferent.com/keepers/getting-shirty.html
Angels with Dirty Faces, The Footballing History of Argentina, Jonathan Wilson, Weidenfeld & Nicolson, 2016
A history of the goal-post
https://www.harrodsport.com/advice-and-guides/a-history-of-the-football-goalpost
Anti-football
http://juanantoniocachola.blogspot.com/2019/02/que-es-el-anti-futbol.html *(in Spanish)*
Arthur Kinnaird, First Lord of Football, Andy Mitchell, Andy Mitchell Media, 2020
Beastly Fury, The Strange Birth of British Football, Richard Sanders, Bantam Press, 2009
Decibel levels of popular referee whistles
https://www.dutchreferee.com/the-decibels-of-popular-referee-whistles/
Edinburgh Referees' Association Golden Jubilee History, 2001, Edinburgh Referees' Association
Elegance borne of brutality, an eclectic history of the football boot, Ian McArthur and Dave Kemp Two Heads Publishing, 1995
Female officials
https://groundhopperguides.com/making-history-female-soccer-referees/ and
https://footballmakeshistory.eu/edith-klinger-muzzled-austrian-referee/
Fifty Years of Football, John Litster, PM Publications, 2013
First yellow card in Scotland?
http://www.scottishleague.net/forum/viewtopic.php?f=3&t=4699
Football History, Laws of the game, Referees, Gunther Furrer, Paulo Godoy and Joseph Blatter, FIFA, 1986
Football in Perthshire, Peter Baxter, Thomas Hunter, Perth, 1898
Football: the first 100 years, the untold story, Adrian Harvey
http://ndl.ethernet.edu.et/bitstream/123456789/24830/1/Adrian_Harvey_2005.pdf
Foreign referees in Scotland
https://www.scotsman.com/sport/1905-last-time-scotland-drafted-foreign-referee-2441861
Games People Played, A Global History of Sport, Vray Vamplew, Reaktion Books, 2021
Head over Heels, Jim Hossack, Mainstream Publishing, 1989.
History of football kit
http://www.historicalkits.co.uk/Articles/History.htm
History of pitch markings
https://gdfra.org.au/history_of_pitch_markings.htm
History of soccer boots
http://fitba2014.blogspot.com/2014/05/history-of-soccer-balls.html
History of the laws of the game
https://gdfra.org.au/laws_history.htm
History of the shin-guard
https://en.wikipedia.org/wiki/Shin_guard
History of the soccer ball
https://soccerballworld.com/history-of-the-soccer-ball/
How far do referees run?
https://www.ncbi.nlm.nih.gov/pmc/articles/PMC3666476/

How Football Began, Tony Collins, Routledge, 2018 (see also **http://howfootballbegan.net**)
How to become a referee
https://www.scottishfa.co.uk/scottish-fa/referees/become-a-referee/
IFAB
https://www.theifab.com/background/
John Langenus (Belgian referee who took charge of first World Cup final)
https://worldreferee.com/referee/john_langenus/
Kick-off
https://www.theguardian.com/football/2016/jan/08/kickoffs-backwards-rule-changes
Laws of the game
https://www.fifplay.com/downloads/documents/laws-of-the-game-2021-2022.pdf and
https://en.wikipedia.org/wiki/Laws_of_the_Game_(association_football)
Manifest Destiny, the Official History of St Johnstone FC, 1885-2015, Alastair Blair and Brian Doyle, St Johnstone FC, 2015
Numbers and names on shirts
https://www.squadnumbers.com/2017/09/20/scotlands-dalliance-names-shirts-1979-81/ and
https://www.nutmegmagazine.co.uk/issue-7/pick-a-number-any-number/ and
https://oldschoolfootball.co.uk/blogs/news/evolution-of-the-football-shirt-number
Offside experiments
https://www.playingpasts.co.uk/articles/football/the-first-football-match-without-offside/ and
https://www.espn.co.uk/football/germany/story/2987104/german-lower-league-clubs-play-football-match-without-offside-rule and
https://www.dailymail.co.uk/sport/football/article-9627259/Premier-League-edge-closer-automatic-offside-calls.html
Original FA Laws
https://sqaf.club/original-rules-of-football/
Penalty shoot-outs
https://www.pressandjournal.co.uk/fp/news/inverness/3489953/penalty-shootouts-have-delivered-joy-and-pain-across-the-globe-and-it-turns-out-the-idea-for-footballs-most-dreaded-decider-was-sanctioned-at-an-inverness-hotel/
Ref Chat: the refereeing forum
https://refchat.co.uk/
Referees' Associations History
http://www.yorkreferee.co.uk/york-ra/national-ra-history/
Rejected FC of Scotland, Dave Twydell, Yore Publications, 1992
Scottish FA Referees' Associations
https://www.scottishfa.co.uk/scottish-fa/referees/referee-associations/
Scottish Football League Centenary History, Bob Crampsey, The Scottish Football League,1990
Scottish football referees' strike
https://en.wikipedia.org/wiki/Scottish_football_referee_strike and
https://www.eurosport.co.uk/all-sports/whistleblower-prompts-dark-days_sto4706870/story.shtml
Scottish Football Reminiscences and Sketches, David Bone, John Menzies & Co, Glasgow, 1890
Scottish Football, a pictorial history, Kevin McCarra, Third Eye Centre, 1984
Scottish Pork Taboo (why sheep bladders were used as well as pig bladders)
http://www.royaldunfermline.com/Resources/SCOTTISH_PORK_TABOO.pdf
Scottish Sport/Football History

https://www.scottishsporthistory.com/football-books.html

Sheffield FC and the birth of modern football

https://www.thefootballhistoryboys.com/2015/08/sheffield-fc-and-birth-of-modern.html?showComment=1462887916908 and https://sheffieldfc.com and https://www.englandsoldestfootballclubs.com/160-years-ago-today-the-1858-sheffield-football-rules-were-published/ and https://en.wikisource.org/wiki/Sheffield_Rules_(1858)_(final_draft)

Sheffield vs Glasgow

https://www.englandsoldestfootballclubs.com/sheffield-v-scotland-the-inter-city-games-1874-1960/

Substitutes

https://www.football-stadiums.co.uk/articles/substitutions-in-football/

Tales from the Touchline: Football Memories from a Referee and Fan, John Dunn, Pitch Publishing, 2021

The Art of Coarse Rugby, Michael Green, Hutchison, 1962

The birth of Partick Football Club

https://www.scottishsporthistory.com/sports-history-news-and-blog/the-birth-of-partick-football-club

and http://ptearlyyears.net/partick-fc-featuring-partick-thistle-cricket-club

The definitive guide to the evolution of the Laws of the game, by Petra Tabarelli. Although a German site and containing articles in German, the guide to the changes in the rules are in English. **https://nachspielzeiten.de** See also Petra Tabarelli interview: https://outsidewrite.co.uk/podcast-the-history-of-football-rule-making/

The diagonal system

https://web.archive.org/web/20070622224933/http://www.footballreferee.org/assistant_referees_diagonal.php

The first football referees

https://www.football-stadiums.co.uk/articles/referees-and-match-officials/

The Foot-ball club of Edinburgh, Andy Mitchell and John Hutchison, Amazon, 2018

The Football Grounds of Great Britain (First Edition), Simon Inglis, Willow Books, 1987

The Illustrated Encyclopedia of British Football, Phil Soar, Marshall Cavendish, 1989

The introduction of goal-nets in Scotland

https://www.thecelticwiki.com/celtic-games/year-by-year/1887-1900/1893-2/1893-03-11-celtic-1-2-queens-park-scottish-cup-final/

The Men who made Scotland: the definitive Who's Who of Scottish football internationalists, 1872-1939, Andy Mitchell, Andy Mitchell Media, 2021

The Only Game, Scots and World Football, Roddy Forsyth, Mainstream, 1990

Thomlinson's football factory

https://www.glasgowlive.co.uk/sport/football/remembering-partick-football-factory-shipped-16321572 and *"The Birth of a Football"*

https://www.youtube.com/watch?v=wy_3X4LuoDM

Trailblazers, the world's first football club

https://blog.nrscotland.gov.uk/2018/04/09/trailblazers-the-worlds-first-football-club-with-john-hutchinson-andy-mitchell/

What's the law regarding the corner quadrant?

https://www.refchat.co.uk/threads/corners-whats-the-law-regarding-ball-in-or-out-of-quadrant.6701/

Appendix: SFA proposals to IFAB, 1887 – 2009. Courtesy of Petra Tabarelli

Note: under the 'Decision' column, 'wit' means 'withdrawn,' 'acc' means 'accepted' and 'def' means 'defeated.'

Year	Law	Association / Federation	Summary	Decision
1887	1	SFA	Touch lines should be rectangular to the goal lines.	wit
1892	14	SFA	Repeated touching of the ball by the player taking the kick is prohibited.	acc
1894	14	SFA	The passage is changed so that the penalty kick is awarded only if the offence prevents a goal from being scored.	def
1896	14	SFA	Change of the place of performance to a place on twelve yards line opposite where infringement took place.	def
1896	14	FA, SFA	Charging an opponent from behind within the penalty area shall be added as an offence punishable by a penalty kick. It is added to the passage that only wilfully played handball in the penalty area is punished with a penalty kick, no longer deliberately handling of the ball. Also changed is that the referee determines whether a penalty kick is awarded. The ball must be kicked forward.	acc
1897	5	SFA	"rule" -> "law". "rule" -> "order". "terminate" -> "suspend". "match" -> "game".	acc
1898	14	SFA	Change of the place of performance to a place on twelve yards line opposite where infringement took place.	def

1899	14	SFA	Change of the place of performance to a place on twelve yards line opposite where infringement took place.	def
1900	14	SFA	Change of the place of performance to a place on twelve yards line opposite where infringement took place.	wit
1901	14	SFA	The place of the penalty kick is changed from the penalty line to a penalty half circle with a radius of 12 yd.	def
1902	11	SFA	Reduction to two opponents nearer their own goal line.	def
1902	14	SFA	Change of the place of performance to a place on twelve yards line opposite where infringement took place.	wit
1902	14	SFA	The place of the penalty kick is changed from the penalty line to a penalty half circle with a radius of 12 yd.	wit
1910	4	SFA	Addition: The referee may also check the shoes during the match and if a player's shoes do not meet the requirements, he may not play.	acc
1910	4	SFA	Studs no longer need to be concealed, but must not be conical.	acc
1913	1	SFA	Enlargement of the playing field (not in international matches).	def
1913	11	SFA	Reduction to two opponents nearer their own goal line.	def
1914	3	SFA	An injured player is to be removed from the field and treated beyond the touch line.	acc

1914	5	SFA	Supplement: The referee shall not stop play for injury. The game is not stopped until the ball is out of play.	def
1914	11	SFA	Reduction to two opponents nearer their own goal line.	def
1920	1	SFA	Two additional lines 25 yd in front of each goal.	def
1920	11	SFA	Addition: Offside is only possible 25 yds in front of both goals.	def
1921	1	SFA	Two additional lines 40 yd in front of each goal.	def
1921	11	SFA	Addition: Offside is only possible 40 yds in front of both goals.	def
1922	1	SFA	Two additional lines 40 yd in front of each goal.	def
1922	11	SFA	Addition: Offside is only possible 40 yds in front of both goals.	def
1922	11	SFA	Reduction to two opponents nearer their own goal line.	def
1923	1	SFA	Two additional lines 40 yd in front of each goal.	wit
1923	11	SFA	Addition: Offside is only possible 40 yds in front of both goals.	wit
1923	11	SFA	Reduction to two opponents nearer their own goal line.	wit
1924	1	SFA	Two additional lines 40 yd in front of each goal.	wit

1924	3	SFA	The clause on removing injured players refers only to seriously injured players. Only then should the referee interrupt the game. If, according to the opinion of the referee, there is a slight injury, he should not interrupt the game.	acc
1924	8	SFA	It is supplemented in the law text to the dropped ball that with offence the opponent a free kick awarded. For this reason, this passage is deleted from the other passage.	acc
1924	11	SFA	Addition: Offside is only possible 40 yds in front of both goals.	wit
1924	11	SFA	Reduction to two opponents nearer their own goal line.	wit
1924	13	SFA	In addition, a corner kick can be used to score a goal directly.	acc
1924	15	SFA	The penalty clause for infringements of the throw-in law is deleted.	acc
1925	1	SFA	Two additional lines 40 yd in front of each goal.	wit
1925	11	SFA	Addition: Offside is only possible 40 yds in front of both goals.	wit
1925	11	SFA	Reduction to two opponents nearer their own goal line.	acc
1930	5	SFA	The referee must ensure during the whole match that he can see the whole match from his position.	wit
1936	16	SFA	The goalkeeper may no longer pick up the ball from a goal kick with his hands.	acc

1948	1	SFA	Change of the penalty area to a semicircle of 22 yd. Removal of the semicircle of 10 yd.	def
1948	3	SFA	Supplement: In international matches played by FIFA members, the goalkeeper may be substituted due to injury during the whole game. The substitute must not take the position of the goalkeeper.	def
1949	1	SFA	Removal of the semicircle of 10 yd.	def
1949	3	SFA	Supplement: In international matches played by FIFA members, the goalkeeper may be substituted due to injury during the whole game. The substitute must not take the position of the goalkeeper.	def
1952	3	SFA	It is specified that a player may only enter the pitch with the referee's permission if his equipment did not meet the requirements and he changed it or if he was injured.	def
1952	12	SFA	No change, just a concrete addition: also playing the ball with the arm is handball.	def
1953	3	SFA	Addition: The law applies not only to newly joining players, but also to rejoining players.	acc
1954	12	SFA	To interpose the body so as to form an obstacle to an opponent will be deleted as ungentlemanly conduct.	wit
1955	12	SFA	To interpose the body so as to form an obstacle to an opponent will be deleted as ungentlemanly conduct.	def
1955	12	SFA	To interpose the body so as to form an obstacle to an opponent will be deleted as ungentlemanly conduct.	def

1956	3	SFA	Supplement: In matches which are not played under the rules of a competition, the goalkeeper may be substituted due to injury during the whole game and another player due to injury during the first half of the game.	def
1956	12	SFA	To interpose the body so as to form an obstacle to an opponent will be deleted as ungentlemanly conduct.	def
1956	12	SFA	To interpose the body so as to form an obstacle to an opponent will be deleted as ungentlemanly conduct.	def
1957	12	SFA	To interpose the body so as to form an obstacle to an opponent will be deleted as ungentlemanly conduct.	def
1957	12	SFA	To interpose the body so as to form an obstacle to an opponent will be deleted as ungentlemanly conduct.	def
1958	12	SFA	To interpose the body so as to form an obstacle to an opponent will be deleted as ungentlemanly conduct.	def
1958	12	SFA	To interpose the body so as to form an obstacle to an opponent will be deleted as ungentlemanly conduct.	def
1960	4	SFA	In International matches, International competitions, and friendly matches between clubs of different national associations, the referee, prior to the start of the game, shall inspect the player's boots and prevent any player whose boots do not conform to the requirements of Law 4 from playing until they comply with the law. Leagues and Competitions may include a similar provision in their rules.	acc

1960	5	SFA	It is the referee's duty, before international matches, International competitions, and friendly matches between clubs of different national associations, to check that the players' shoes meet the requirements of Law 4.	acc
1960	7	SFA	Addition that rules of a league or competition may reserve the right to reduce the playing time of half times.	wit
1962	3	SFA	A player who enters the field without the referee's permission is guilty of ungentlemanly conduct. He shall be dealt with accordingly, unless he has committed a more serious offence, when he shall be penalised in terms of the law infringed.	wit
1962	3	SFA	A player who leaves the field without the referee's permission is guilty of ungentlemanly conduct.	wit
1962	3	SFA	If the field of play is entered without the referee's permission, the match is restarted with an IDFK instead of a dropped ball.	wit
1962	4	SFA	Change that the player is not warned, but has to bear further consequences because of ungentlemanly conduct ("dealt with accordingly").	wit
1962	8	SFA	Removal of the decision.	wit
1962	10	SFA	Addition that the goalkeeper may carry the ball in his own penalty area.	wit
1962	12	SFA	An offence committed outside the field of play while the ball is in play shall be deemed by the referee to have occurred inside the field of play.	wit

1962	12	SFA	Leaving the field during the progress of the game (except through accident) without the permission of the referee is no ungentlemanly conduct.	wit
1962	12	SFA	Removal of the decision.	wit
1962	12	SFA	The term "[…] he persistently infringes the Laws of the Game" is deleted, as it is already included by "[…] he shows by word or action, dissent from any decision given by the Referee".	wit
1963	3	SFA	A player who enters the field without the referee's permission is guilty of ungentlemanly conduct.	wit
1963	3	SFA	A player who enters the field without the referee's permission is guilty of ungentlemanly conduct. He shall be dealt with accordingly, unless he has committed a more serious offence, when he shall be penalised in terms of the law infringed.	wit
1963	3	SFA	If the field of play is entered without the referee's permission, the match is restarted with an IDFK instead of a dropped ball.	def
1963	4	SFA	Change that studs must not project less than half an inch, but not less than a quarter of an inch.	acc
1963	4	SFA	Change that the player is not warned, but has to bear further consequences because of ungentlemanly conduct ("dealt with accordingly").	wit
1963	8	SFA	Removal of the decision.	wit

1963	12	SFA	If the goalkeeper throws the ball vigorously into the face of an attacking opponent inside the penalty area, the referee cautions the goalkeeper and award an indirect free-kicker. If the goalkeeper pushes the opponent with the ball inside the penalty area whilst holding it, intentionally strikes an opponent by throwing the ball vigorously at him, or pushes him with the ball, while holding it, the referee awards a penalty kick.	wit
1963	12	SFA	It is added to the passage that the referee has the choice of awarding a direct or indirect free kick.	wit
1963	12	SFA	Removal of the decision.	wit
1963	12	SFA	The term "[…] he persistently infringes the Laws of the Game" is deleted, as it is already included by "[…] he shows by word or action, dissent from any decision given by the Referee".	def
1963	12	SFA	To interpose the body so as to form an obstacle to an opponent will be deleted as ungentlemanly conduct.	def
1963	12	SFA	To interpose the body so as to form an obstacle to an opponent will be deleted as ungentlemanly conduct.	def
1963	13	SFA	If a player of the opposing side encroaches into the penalty-area, or within ten yards of the ball, as the case may be, before a free-kick is taken, the Referee shall delay the taking if the kick, until the Law is complied with.	CoS

1963	13	SFA	If the free kick is taken outside the penalty area, all opponents must be at least 10 yd from the ball.	CoS
1963	13	SFA	The ball is in play when it has travelled the distance of its own circumference.	CoS
1963	13	SFA	The ball must be stationary when the free kick is taken.	CoS
1963	14	SFA	If one or more players approach the ball at less than 10 yd before the penalty kick is taken, the ball rebounds into play from the goal-post, crossbar or goalkeeper, and the referee has not time to intervene, he should stop the game, caution the player at fault, and restart the game by dropping the ball provided it would not give the advantage to the offending side. Additionally, the referee would apply the advantage clause.	CoS
1964	1	SFA	Removal of the decision.	CoS
1965	1	SFA / CoS	Removal of the decision.	wit
1965	12	SFA	The passage "the goalkeeper throws the ball vigorously into the face of an attacking opponent" is deleted.	acc
1965	13	SFA	If a player of the opposing side encroaches into the penalty-area, or within ten yards of the ball, as the case may be, before a free-kick is taken, the Referee shall delay the taking if the kick, until the Law is complied with.	acc
1965	13	SFA	If the free kick is taken outside the penalty area, all opponents must be at least 10 yd from the ball.	acc
1965	13	SFA	The ball is in play when it has travelled the distance of its own circumference.	acc

1965	13	SFA	The ball must be stationary when the free kick is taken.	acc
1965	14	SFA	If one or more players approach the ball at less than 10 yd before the penalty kick is taken, the ball rebounds into play from the goal-post, crossbar or goalkeeper, and the referee has not time to intervene, he should stop the game, caution the player at fault, and restart the game by dropping the ball provided it would not give the advantage to the offending side. Additionally, the referee would apply the advantage clause.	acc
1966	1	SFA / CoS	Removal of the decision.	acc
1966	10	SFA	Addition that a penalty kick is handled differently.	acc
1966	14	SFA	It is added to the passage that it also applies to penalty kicks for which the playing time is extended.	wit
1966	14	SFA	It is added to the passage that the penalty shot is repeated even if one or more players are within the 10 yards of the penalty-mark encroach before the ball is in play too early.	acc
1966	14	SFA	It's a offence even, if a team-mate of the player taking the penalty-kick encroaches within 10 yards of the penalty-mark before the ball is in play. Again, the kick is only retaken if a goal is scored.	CoS
1966	15	SFA	It is unsporting manner if an opposing player dances or gesticulates in front of the throwing player to distract him when throwing in. He will be cautioned.	acc
1967	4	SFA	A player may not wear spectacles of any description. Contact lenses are permissible.	def

1967	12	SFA	Removal of the decision.	wit
1967	12	SFA	To interpose the body so as to form an obstacle to an opponent will be deleted as ungentlemanly conduct.	wit
1967	12	SFA	To interpose the body so as to form an obstacle to an opponent will be deleted as ungentlemanly conduct.	wit
1968	3	SFA	Reintroduction of the decision, but the power to impose disciplinary sanctions during the half-time now extends to any ungentlemanly conduct.	wit
1968	12	SFA	Removal of the decision.	wit
1968	12	SFA	To interpose the body so as to form an obstacle to an opponent will be deleted as ungentlemanly conduct.	def
1968	12	SFA	To interpose the body so as to form an obstacle to an opponent will be deleted as ungentlemanly conduct.	def
1968	14	SFA	The passage is changed so that for an offence of this law for any infringement by the player taking the penalty-kick always and not only offences after the ball is in play are decisive.	def
1969	3	SFA	Addition: In this case the game is restarted by a dropped ball at the place where the contact or interference occurred.	acc
1969	4	SFA	Addition: This also applies to International Club Competitions.	acc
1969	14	SFA	The passage is changed so that the game is restarted with an IDFK for the opposing team instead of dropping the ball.	acc

1969	17	SFA	It is added to the passage that the game is restarted with a goal kick when the ball passes behind the goal line after the corner kick and touches a player of the attacking team last.	def
1970	12	SFA	The referee has the additional authority of to apply the advantage clause.	acc
1970	12	SFA	To interpose the body so as to form an obstacle to an opponent will be deleted as ungentlemanly conduct.	wit
1970	12	SFA	To interpose the body so as to form an obstacle to an opponent will be deleted as ungentlemanly conduct.	wit
1970	12	SFA	To interpose the body so as to form an obstacle to an opponent will be deleted as ungentlemanly conduct.	wit
1971	3	SFA	Set the minimum number of players to seven. A game is abandoned when a team has less than seven players during the game.	def
1971	10	SFA	Addition that, when a game in a knock-out competition ends as in a draw, the system of the taking of penalty kick may be used to determine the winner.	def
1971	12	SFA	The law is changed so that - if the offence which was the direct cause of the caution - is awarded a DFK instead of an IDFK.	def
1972	3	SFA	In matches which are not played under the rules of a competition, the teams agree on the maximum number of substitutions, which may not exceed 5. The referee must be informed about the agreement otherwise not more than two substitutions are allowed.	mod

1972	3	SFA	Supplement that when a goalkeeper is replaced, the general procedure of replacement must be observed, because in this case the referee's permission is required, not just information to him.	acc
1972	3	SFA	Supplement that when a goalkeeper is replaced, the general procedure of replacement must be observed, because in this case the referee's permission is required, not just information to him.	acc
1972	4	SFA	Addition that a player does not necessarily have to wear shoes in a competition game.	wit
1972	4	SFA	Addition that a player does not necessarily have to wear shoes in a competition game.	wit
1972	12	SFA	If, when a referee is about to caution a player, and before he has done so, the player commits another offence which merits a caution, the player shall be sent off the field of play.	acc
1972	12	SFA	Removal of the passage.	acc
1972	12	SFA	The law is changed so that - if the offence which was the direct cause of the caution - is awarded a DFK instead of an IDFK.	acc
1972	16	SFA	It shall be considered an infringement of this Law, if when it is kicked, the whole of the ball is not within the quarter circle.	def
1973	1	SFA	Additionally another quarter circle of 11 yd.	def
1973	3	SFA	It is added that if the goalkeeper is changed, the referee must first give a signal.	acc

1973	3	SFA	It is added that if the goalkeeper is changed, the referee must first give a signal.	acc
1973	3	SFA	Sanctions in case of an infringement.	acc
1973	4	SFA	Addition that a player does not necessarily have to wear shoes in a competition game.	acc
1973	13	SFA	Change: To distinguish an IDFK from a DFK, in an IDFK the referee raises his arm above his head and does not take it down until the IDFK has been performed.	acc
1973	14	SFA	If the goalkeeper moves from his position before taking the penalty kick on the goal-line, or moves his feet, and a team-mate of the kicker encroaches into the penalty-area or within 10 yards of the penalty-mark, the kick, if taken, will be retaken. The team-mate of the kicker will be cautioned.	acc
1973	14	SFA	It is reintroduced that if an opponent, before taking the penalty kick, falls below the appropriate distance from the ball, the penalty kick is still taken and a goal is given if scored. In addition, it is now added that the player is cautioned.	acc
1973	14	SFA	The addition that this provision also applies to offences for which the playing time is extended is deleted.	acc
1973	14	SFA	The passage is changed so that the referee does not interrupt the game but allows the penalty shot to perform. When a goal is scored, the shot is repeated. The player concerned is cautioned in any case and the game is restarted with an IDFK for the opposing team.	acc

1975	1	SFA	Additionally another quarter circle of 11 yd.	def
1975	4	SFA	"game" -> "match". "boot(s)" -> "footwear"	acc
1975	5	SFA	Clarification: From the field is also sent who persists in misconduct after having received a caution.	wit
1975	12	SFA	It is supplemented as an ungentlemanly conduct to interpose the body so as to form an obstacle to an opponent.	def
1975	12	SFA	Removal of the decision.	def
1975	12	SFA	To interpose the body so as to form an obstacle to an opponent will be deleted as ungentlemanly conduct.	def
1977	1	SFA	Additionally another quarter circle of 11 yd.	def
1977	12	SFA	Charging the goalkeeper when in his own goal area is supplemented as an ungentlemanly conduct. In addition, it is irrelevant whether physical contact is made to opponent at interposing the body to obstacle.	def
1982	6	SFA	Additional duty: to indicate when a substitution is desired. The notice that the referee may dispense the assistant referees from their duties in the event of undue interference shall be deleted.	acc
1982	14	SFA	If necessary, time of play shall be extended to admit of the penalty kick being taken.	acc

1984	8	SFA	It is added that - when infringement occur was stopped and the ball was in the goal area - it is dropped on that part of the goal area line which runs parallel to the goal-line, at the point nearest to where the ball was when play .	acc
1986	3	SFA	In addition, as with any substitution, the substitution shall be deemed completed when the substitute enters the field.	acc
1986	3	SFA	In addition, as with any substitution, the substitution shall be deemed completed when the substitute enters the field.	acc
1986	3	SFA	The substitutes must be chosen from a maximum of 5 announced possible substitutes.	acc
1987	3	SFA	Removal of the decision.	acc
1987	7	SFA	Specification of exactly what is counted as lost time: "treatment on the field of injured players, or the transport from the field of injured players, or substitution, or time-wasting or any other cause".	def
1987	14	SFA	It is added to the passage that after the shot no player may touch the ball before the kick is completed.	acc
1987	14	SFA	It is changed that a goal is not nullified, if, before passing between the posts and under the cross-bar, the ball touches either or both of the goal-posts, or the cross-bar, or the goalkeeper, or any combination of these agencies, providing that no other infringement has occurred.	acc

1987	14	FIFA, SFA	The goalkeeper must not move on the goal line until the ball is in play (and not just until it has been kicked).	wit
1990	11	SFA	Change: An attacking player on the same level as the second-last opponent is not offside.	acc
1993	3	SFA	The law is supplemented so that the yellow card is shown in addition to the caution.	acc
1995	1	SFA	Any kind of publicity is forbidden, also any attachment of cameras, microphones, etc. to the field of play equipment.	mod
1995	3	SFA	Deletion of Supplement: If competition rules require substitute players to be reported to the referee before the start of play, but this does not happen, these players may not be fielded.	mod
1995	3	SFA	In official competitions under the jurisdiction of FIFA, Confederations or National Associations, the rules of the competition state the number of nominated substitutes and allowed substitutes. In other games the number of allowed substitutions is increased from two to three.	mod
1995	7	SFA	Increase the half-time interval to a maximum of 15 minutes. The interval can only be shortened with the referee's agreement.	acc
1995	11	SFA	Supplement that also the attempt to interfere with play is enough to be offside.	acc
1995	12	FA, SFA	It is made clear that tackling without contact to the ball is considered an ungentlemanly conduct. "intentionally obstruction" -> "impeding the progress".	acc

1995	12	FA, SFA	It is made clear that tackling without contact to the ball is considered an ungentlemanly conduct. "intentionally obstruction" -> "impeding the progress". In addition, handball is now forbidden, provided it is deliberately performed, not intentionally. "deliberately": Only handball which is deliberately committed, is forbidden.	acc
1995	14	SFA	"When it is being taken, all players with the exception of the player taking the kick, properly identified, and the opposing goalkeeper shall be within the field of play but outside the penalty area and at least 10 yards from the penalty-mark and must stand behind the penalty-mark.	acc
1996	5	SFA	Change: If the advantage is not accrue almost immediately, the referee punishes the original offence.	wit
1996	6	SFA	Additional duties: to indicated when a player shall be penalised for being in an offside position and when misconduct or other incident has occurred outwit the vision of the referee.	wit
1996	12	SFA	Charging the goalkeeper is forbidden.	wit
1996	12	SFA	It is made clear that tackling without contact to the ball is considered an ungentlemanly conduct. "intentionally obstruction" -> "impeding the progress". In addition, handball is now forbidden, provided it is deliberately performed, not intentionally.	acc
1999	5	SFA	Clarification that the match ball must meet the requirement of Law 2.	mod

2000	3	SFA	In friendly matches, no greater number of substitutions is allowed than in competition games.	acc
2005	3	SFA	Supplement: In other matches a larger number is allowed, but needs mutual agreement before the match. Otherwise only up to six substitutions are allowed.	acc
2005	5	SFA	The referee may also change his decision only until he has finished the match.	acc
2005	15	SFA	Addition: The distance is measured from the point where the ball went out.	acc
2009	3	SFA	Addition: In case of an extra time, the number of replacements can be increased.	def

Printed in Great Britain
by Amazon

82470094R00147